SURFING the MENU

SURFING the MENU

NEXT GENERATION

DAN CHURCHILL & HAYDEN QUINN

SIMON & SCHUSTER
London · New York · Sydney · Toronto · New Delhi
A CBS COMPANY

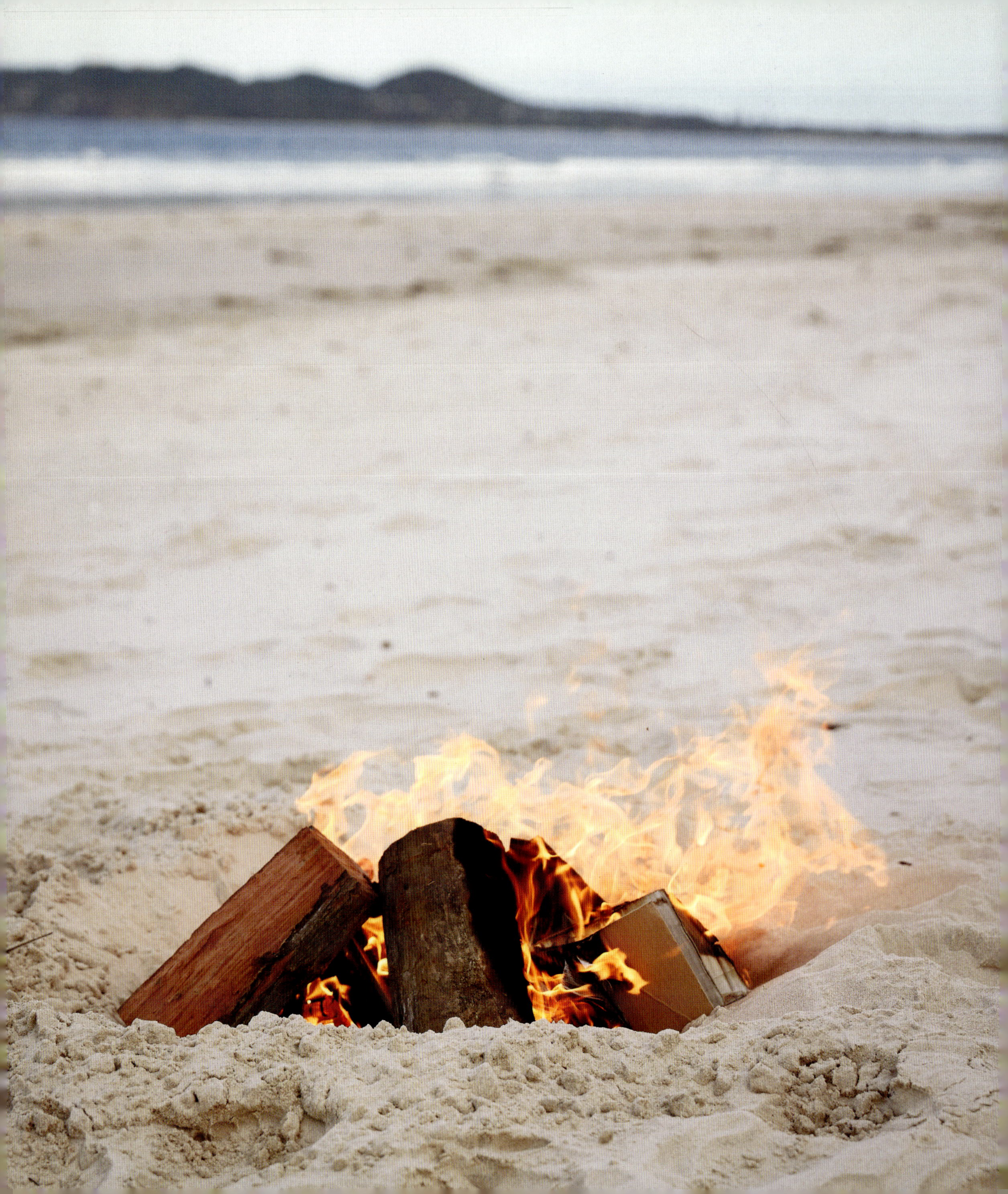

Contents

Meet Dan & Hayden — 10

The FAR WEST
Shark Bay — 18
Wooramel — 36
Carnarvon — 52
Exmouth — 70
Broome — 88

The INLAND NORTH
Kununurra — 106
Katherine — 122

The TROPICAL NORTH
Cairns & Townsville — 140
The Whitsundays — 156
Bundaberg — 172

The FAR EAST
Noosa — 188
Toowoomba — 204
Byron Bay — 218

Thanks! — 234
Index — 236

DAN CHURCHILL

Dan Churchill was born and bred on Sydney's beautiful Northern Beaches. He comes from a family of three active boys who were always out in the backyard or down at the beach. He grew up with a strong interest in health, cooking and education, nurtured by the interest his family took in cooking. He is a natural entrepreneur and established his first business as a health coach at the age of 17.

Dan completed a Bachelor of Sport and Exercise Management and a Masters in Exercise Science (Strength and Conditioning) at the Edith Cowan University, Perth. He then started a personal training business and continued to work as a health coach. He self-published his first cookbook, *DudeFood*, when he was 19. He has since published *The Healthy Cook* and another edition of *DudeFood*.

Dan appeared on *MasterChef* in 2013. Since then he has coached athletes in strength and conditioning and nutrition, contributed a regular food column to *Men's Health* magazine and produced a cooking series on YouTube. He has also appeared on *Good Morning America* and been nominated as a *Cleo* Bachelor of the Year.

Dan's approach to food is based on bringing people together – 'whacking a board of something wicked and tasty on the table and having your mates tuck in!' Because he is also a health coach, he favours whole foods and no refined sugar. But the joy of food is what counts. He says, 'My number one rule is that it must be delicious! My number two rule is that it must be bright and colourful and full of nutrients.'

He learned many useful professional lessons from doing *Surfing the Menu – Next Generation*. He says, 'I'm used to working with a single lens for YouTube videos and looking straight to camera. So, I had to learn new skills for TV. I was given great direction on facial expression and how to hold things on camera. I'm super passionate when I'm cooking and laugh and use my hands a lot, so I had to learn to pull back and build up to the big moment when the dish is ready. That was hard, but a fantastic challenge.'

@churchill_dan

facebook.com/danthehealthycook

youtube.com/danchurchillcooks

+danchurchillcooks

dudefoodseries

HAYDEN QUINN

Hayden Quinn grew up surrounded by the ocean, great food and a crazy bunch of mates. From early in his life he has displayed a restless sense of adventure.

Hayden completed a Bachelor of Science in Marine Biology at the University of Technology, Sydney, after which he became a professional lifeguard for nine years. He still does the odd shift on the beach today. He loves to be active and is the co-owner of the Cube Gym on Sydney's Northern Beaches.

Since appearing on *MasterChef* in 2011, Hayden has appeared on the TV shows *The Dinner Project* (LifestyleFOOD, Australia) and *Hayden Quinn South Africa* (SABC3, South Africa). He is the author of *Dish It Up* and two eBooks. He has developed the innovative YouTube series of visual food adventures, *Unrefined*, and *Baking with Nutorious*. He has also joined forces with the philanthropic Kooks Wine label.

Hayden loves to create and share food that is alive with flavour and demands to be eaten. For him, even if a recipe looks fancy, the ingredients should be readily available at the local supermarket. Food is not just about creating special occasions, it is also about healthy, delicious, everyday sustenance for busy people. He is not above a sneaky little treat and thinks that eating refined sugar occasionally is OK. He says, 'At the end of a massive day when we were shooting I'd be up for a beer and Doritos. Dan has more self-control! But I'd still be awake early to exercise the next day.'

When asked what he learned the most from appearing on *Surfing the Menu – Next Generation*, Hayden says, 'There's a lot more to Australia that those of us in the big cities know about. There are many places out there that are more beautiful than anywhere I've been in the world. It's changed my insular Sydney-centric view of the world, even though I've been to wild places like Mozambique. I loved learning about the different types of people there are in Australia and what they do for a living. I understand much more about the amazing country we live in.'

@hayden_quinn
facebook.com/haydenjquinn
youtube.com/HaydenQuinnTV
+HaydenQuinn
mrhaydenquinn

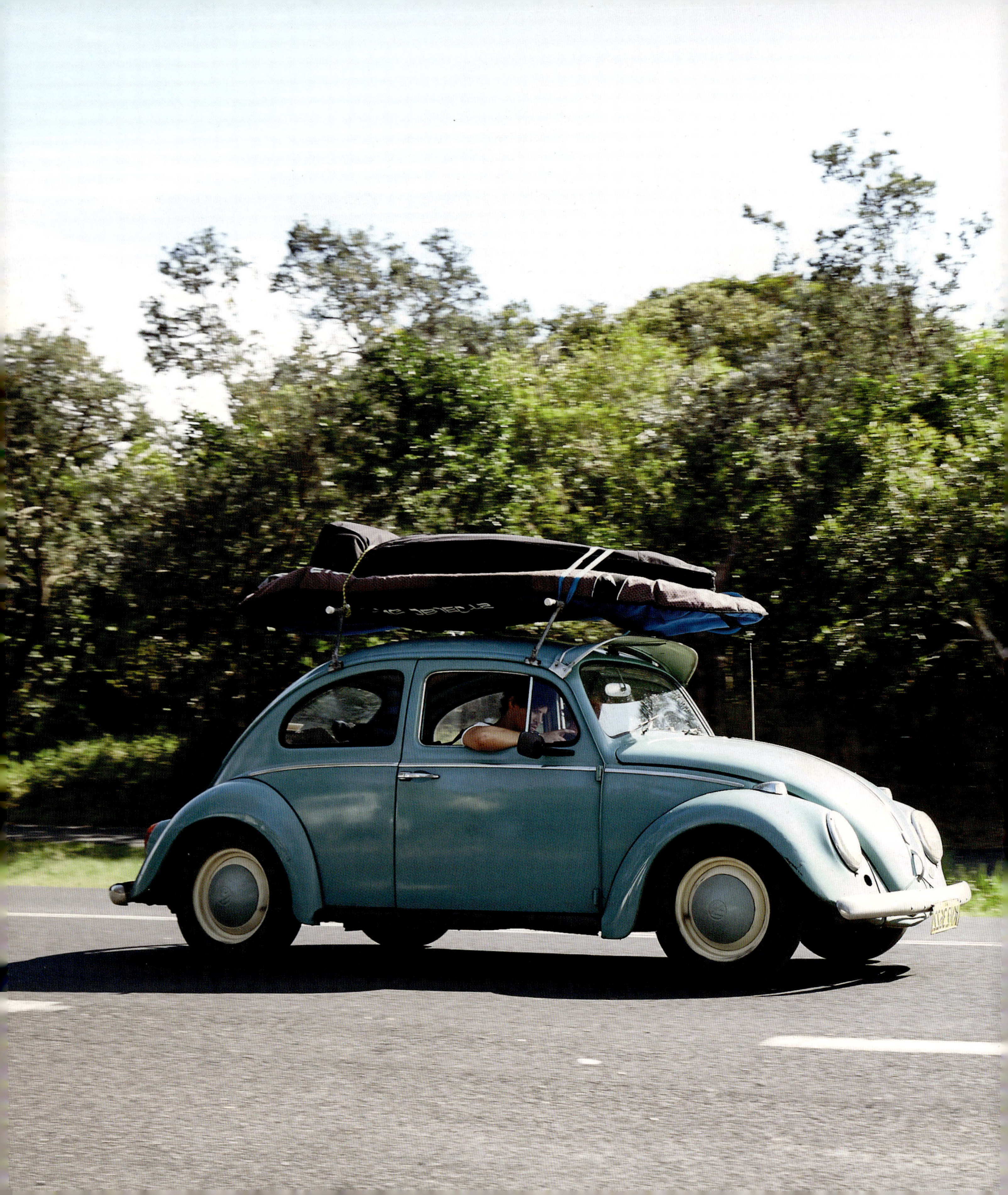

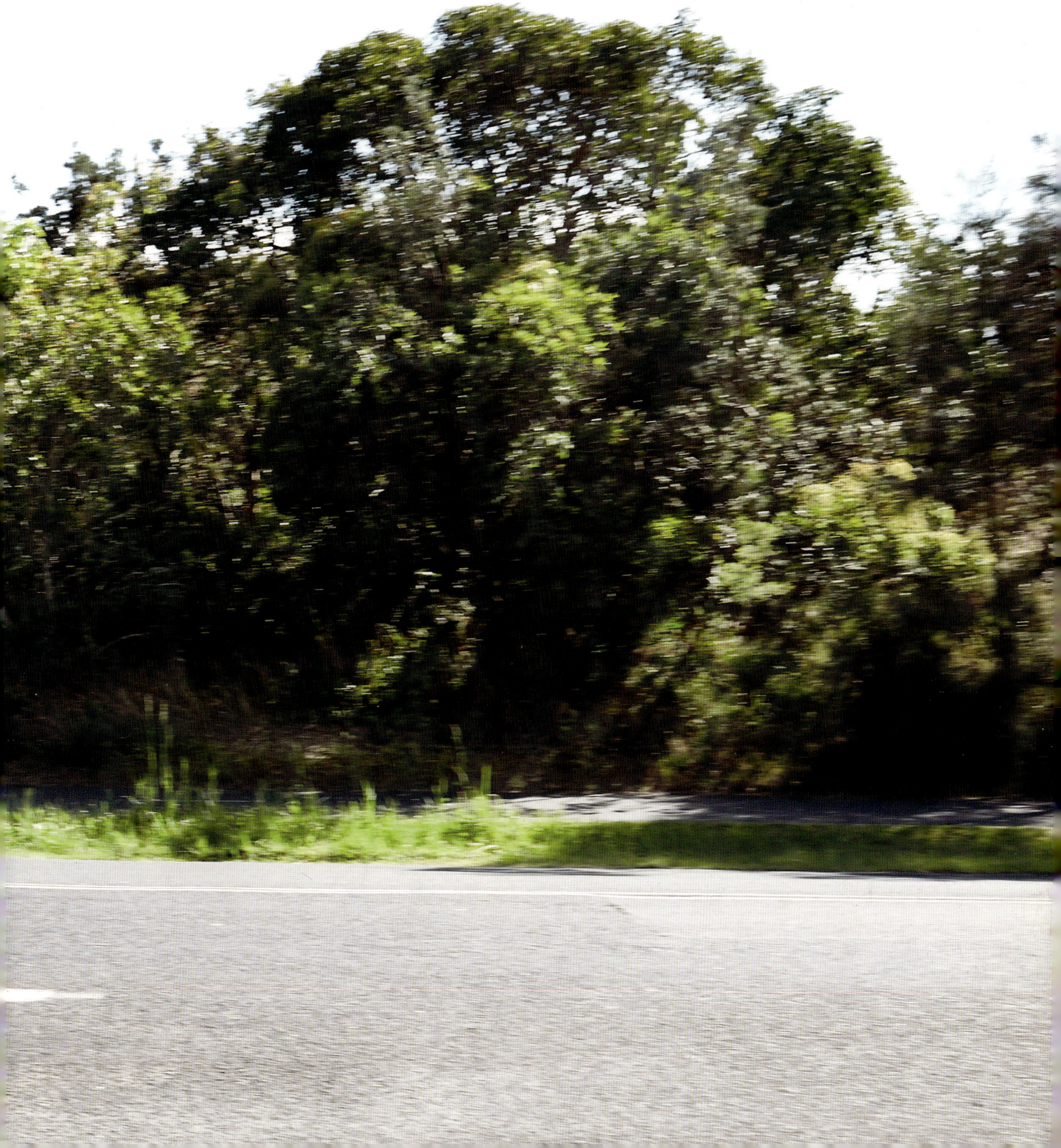

Meet Dan and Hayden

Two boys from Sydney's Northern Beaches were raised in families that love to cook. They both spent all their time at the beach and grew up to be keen surfers. They became mates because they both appeared on *MasterChef*, although not at the same time. And then, they were brought together to head off in Gigi, an intrepid vintage VW beetle, to explore what's cooking across northern Australia from the west to the east coasts. Of course, being surfer dudes, they caught the odd wave on their travels! And that's how *Surfing the Menu – Next Generation* came to be.

Surfing the Menu is the popular ABC TV cooking show. The first two series introduced us to Curtis Stone and Ben O'Donoghue. Now it's time to hit the surfing trail again with a new generation of food lovers – Dan Churchill and Hayden Quinn – and to discover the glorious fresh produce that can be found all over the north of this exciting country.

EARLY COOKING ADVENTURES

HQ: I come from a big family with two sisters. My mum is a home economist, so I grew up around a foodie. I'm always meeting people who say, 'Your mum taught me how to cook!' In fact, Tracy Rutherford – our recipe editor and food stylist – learned to cook with my mum. We never went out to dinner because she cooked such amazing food. I still prefer to entertain friends at home and I don't go to restaurants much.

I started cooking for the family and kept experimenting, then I moved on to cooking for friends and girlfriends. When I went overseas at 18, I found that discovering new food is a big part of travelling. People communicate by sharing food – it's such an enjoyable thing to do.

DC: Our family time reflected our love of food. I used to enjoy watching Jamie Oliver on TV when I was 12 and talking about flavours and cooking skills with my parents. We had a dinner timetable and I cooked for the family twice a week – my parents did a lot of smiling through gritted teeth! Later, I found my mates would get jealous when their girlfriends wanted to talk about cooking with me. That was when I wrote my first cookbook, *The Healthy Cook*, which I self-published. It was about encouraging guys to get into the kitchen more. I organised the whole book – testing recipes, organising the photography, getting print quotes, the lot. I went into bookshops myself to sell it, starting on the Northern Beaches. I promoted it through my social media networks and luckily had a supportive community around me. All my hard work paid off when a big publisher took notice and picked it up.

FROM MASTERCHEF TO SURFING THE MENU

HQ: I was on the third series of *MasterChef* when it was still a fresh thing. At the time I was a professional lifeguard, a beach surfers supervisor. I was responsible for 9 beaches and had a staff of about 40. Best job in the world. I like cooking shows on TV, and one day I was watching *MasterChef* and thinking 'I could give this a run, I know how to cook'. So I grabbed the laptop and tapped away on the lengthy application, whacked in a photo and thought 'This will be sick!' Then I got the call up. I was in the top 50 and then the top 24 … I didn't care about being on TV, my life was an epic adventure and there was nothing holding me back. Many people on *MasterChef* are running away from a horrible job or trying to change their life. I didn't have a sob story, instead I was running towards something and I was there to learn. I came 6th and stayed to the final week. I was happy with that – the people I was with by then were pretty damn good.

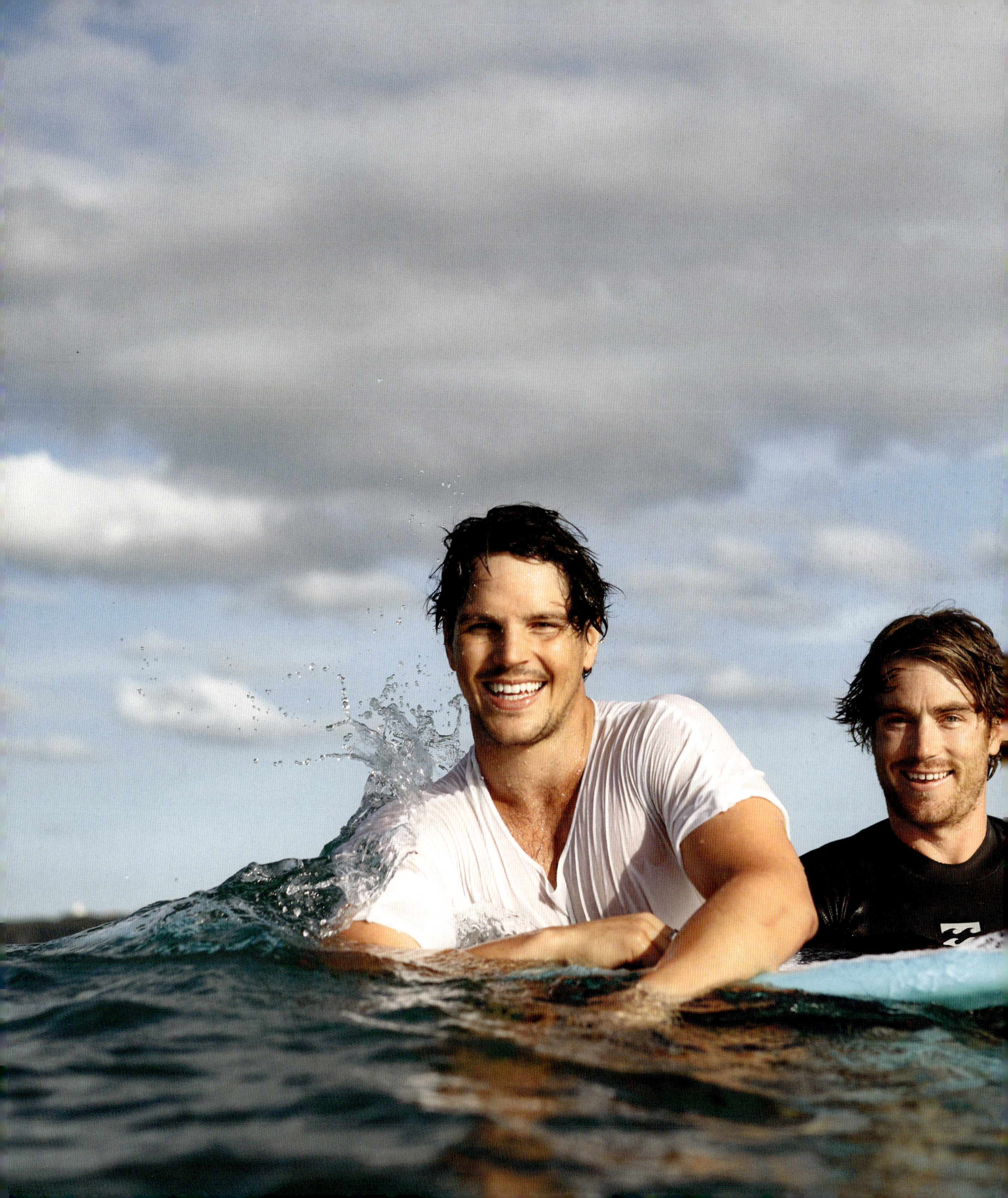

DC: I used to watch *MasterChef* with my girlfriend at the time and I watched Hayden on the show. I was producing my book, I was a health coach and I had a personal training business, and I was doing a Masters in exercise science. I was doing things I wanted to do; I wasn't trying to be 'successful'. But I wanted to learn more. *MasterChef* is about bringing home cooks together and I thought I could have a crack at it. So I secretly put together a video and applied (Hayden had it easy with a photo!). I got the call when I was finishing a session with a client – 'Hey Dan, it's *MasterChef*, you've been accepted!' It was pretty hectic. From week to week on the show, I would write up what I'd learned. I'd pull Matt, Gary and George aside and I'd talk to the other chefs on the series about their techniques. I was aware life would go on at the end of the show and I was always planning for what would come after. I'm utterly grateful for *MasterChef* – the whole thing started us off on our cooking careers – but it was a few years ago and a lot has happened since.

HQ: Dan got my number from a mutual friend and spoke to me about the show when he got the call-up. We kept in touch throughout and finally met when he finished the show. We're from the same area in Sydney – we would see each other when we were out – and eventually we became friends.

DC: My manager, Lance, had the idea to put us together. The format of *Surfing the Menu* fits so well with what we both stand for when it comes to food and surfing. The first couple of series took the world by storm and we're fortunate to take that legacy and give it a next-generation kick in the butt! I had a pinch-me moment when I was on a plane in Western Australia and realised we were doing the same thing as Curtis Stone and Ben O'Donoghue.

THIRTEEN DESTINATIONS – FAVOURITE LOCATIONS

HQ: The community of Beswick to the south-east of Katherine in the Northern Territory was an eye-opener. It was the first time I'd been to a place like that in Australia, although I've been to similar communities in Africa. For someone who grew up by the ocean, it was completely different for me to go somewhere so remarkable in the bush.

DC: I didn't know anything about the north-west of Western Australia. It's magical! The Ningaloo Reef at Exmouth with the migrating humpback whales, phenomenal sunsets and good surf breaks is a special memory. I'd never heard of Kununurra and didn't know what to expect, but the red riverbanks by the Ord River are so beautiful. We went 'skirfing' on the river on a speedboat and then sailed home at sunset with the local lads we'd met that day. I was remembering every sight and sound on purpose and I'll have those memories for the rest of my life. It was gorgeous! And seeing my lovely grandmother, Nunna, again in Ingham and cooking with her was an amazing experience.

At the end of the series, people asked me if I was exhausted, but I was buzzing! I could have done another 13 episodes straight up!

EXPLORING NEW TASTES – FAVOURITE FOOD MOMENTS

HQ: One of my treasured moments was a meal in Katherine of freshwater prawns and catfish cooked in the ground by a couple of locals, Manuel Pamkal and Ben Lewis. We ate lots of food that was buried in coals on the journey: damper, roo tail, barramundi, corned beef … really simple stuff, cooked straight up with nothing added to it. All the flavour came from the smoke and the fire and the leaves the food was wrapped in. We discovered that, according to cultural laws, in some cases certain proteins had to be cooked with specific leaves.

DC: Some of the really cool food moments were off-script and give me chills just thinking about them. In Carnarvon, the whole crew was invited to a wonderful traditional Vietnamese party held by Duc Nguyen, a local tomato grower. In Kununurra I put on a dinner for the crew. The shooting days were very long, and at the end the camera guys had another couple of hours of equipment cleaning to do. So I put on a spread for them with roasted eggplant, a beetroot board with spiced carrots, my One-Pan Chicken (recipe on page 135) and a Middle Eastern lamb dish. The boys were stoked and I had the satisfaction of putting in for the crew.

One incredible meal made for the show was my harissa bream recipe, cooked for Hayden on the back of a boat in the Whitsundays. It was so simple but so delicious. And a drop dead, kill-me-now moment was biting into my Goat's Cheese Chocolate Tart in Byron Bay! (Recipes on pages 166 and 232.)

SURFING THE MENU – THE BEST SURFING SPOTS

HQ: We didn't have much luck with surfing! It became a running joke, but you never know what Mother Nature is going to provide. Whenever we turned up at a new spot, the locals would say 'you should have been here yesterday' or 'the swell's coming tomorrow'. Classic comments! The best surfing locations were on the east coast at Noosa and Ballina, south of Byron Bay. At Noosa we were going to surf at Little Cove on the main break, but the waves were tiny and it was really windy. So we checked out Sunshine Beach and there was no wind, the water was sparkling and green, there were fun little two- or three-feet waves. It was perfect! I got to do a few turns and I saw a turtle in the water. That was my number one highlight, surfing-wise.

DC: When you're out on the surf, you're usually alone – you have the waves and maybe a couple of dolphins if you're lucky. But when you're surfing for the show, you've never had so much attention! You've got a Go-Pro on the front of your surfboard, you've got drones flying over you, there's a guy taking stills … The other surfers are thinking 'Who are these guys?!' But whenever surfing was part of the storyline, we were stoked. Being paid for going for waves was ridiculous!

500 km
Darwin
Katherine
Kununurra
Broome
Port Hedland
NORTHERN
Exmouth
WESTERN
AUSTRALIA
Carnarvon
Wooramel
Shark Bay
Geraldton

QUEENSLAND

- Cairns
- Townsville
- Whitsundays
- Bundaberg
- Noosa Heads
- Brisbane
- Toowoomba
- Byron Bay

TERRITORY
- Alice Springs

SOUTH AUSTRALIA

NEW SOUTH WALES

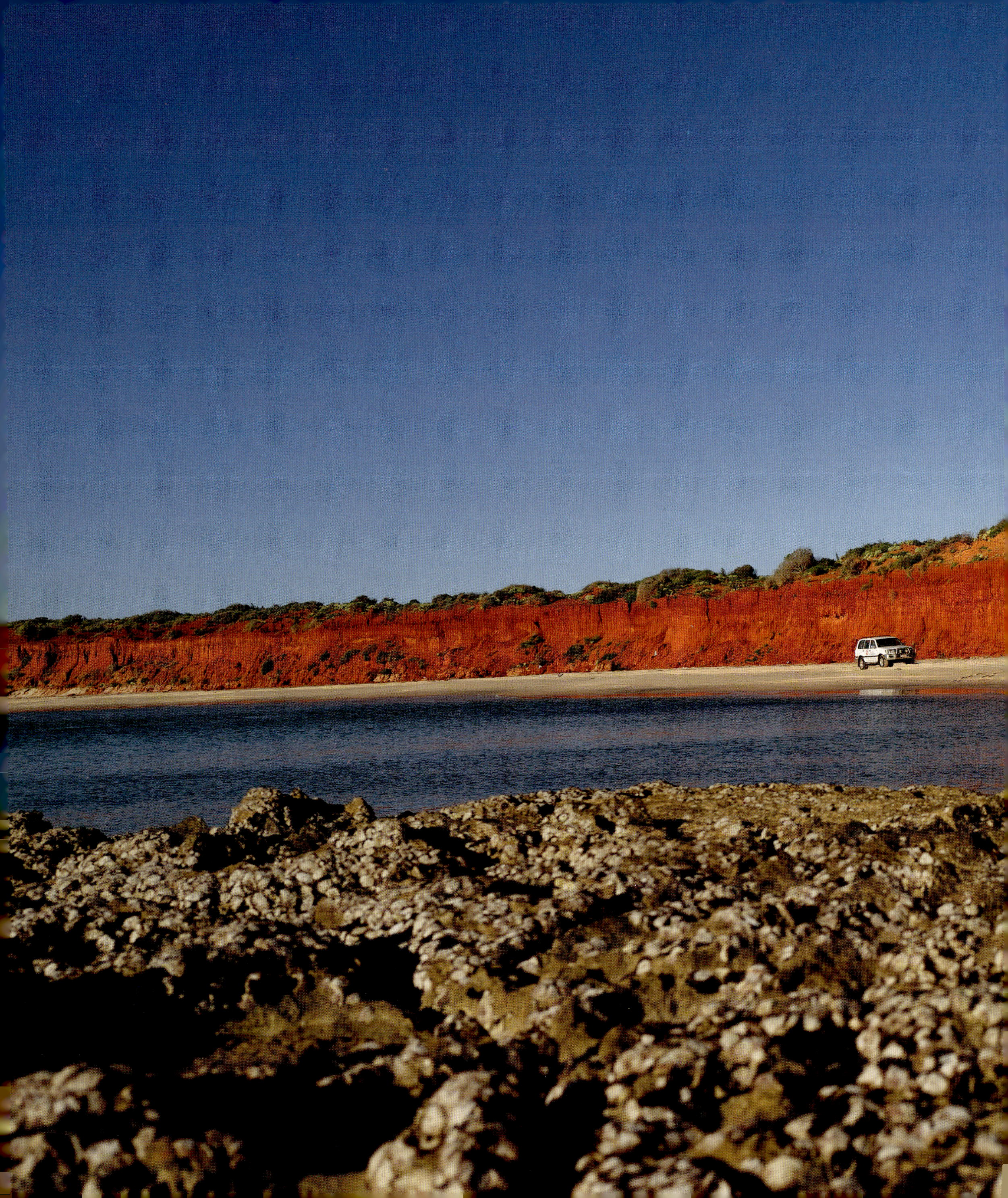

The FAR WEST

Fill up the tank and strap on the surfboards! The journey in Gigi begins in the Mediterranean warmth of the Coral Coast of Western Australia. First stop is Shark Bay, which is inscribed in the UNESCO World Heritage list in recognition of its outstanding natural beauty, biological diversity, fascinating ecology and unique insights into the planet's history. By far its most spectacular attraction is Monkey Mia, where the wild dolphins come to shore. Then we travel inland to the Gascoyne region to visit the vast Wooramel Station with its large herds of livestock, abundant wildlife and majestic river gums on the Wooramel River. So far deep in the outback, the night sky is sprinkled with countless stars. Next stop is Carnarvon, a subtropical oasis where top quality fresh fruit, vegetables and seafood are plentiful and bursting with flavour. On to Exmouth, and the turquoise waters glistening in the sun are the clearest you'll ever see. The Ningaloo Reef is one of the most biologically diverse marine environments on Earth, a true underwater paradise. And finally to Broome, the gleaming pearl of north-west Australia and the coastal gateway to the stupendous wilderness of the Kimberley region.

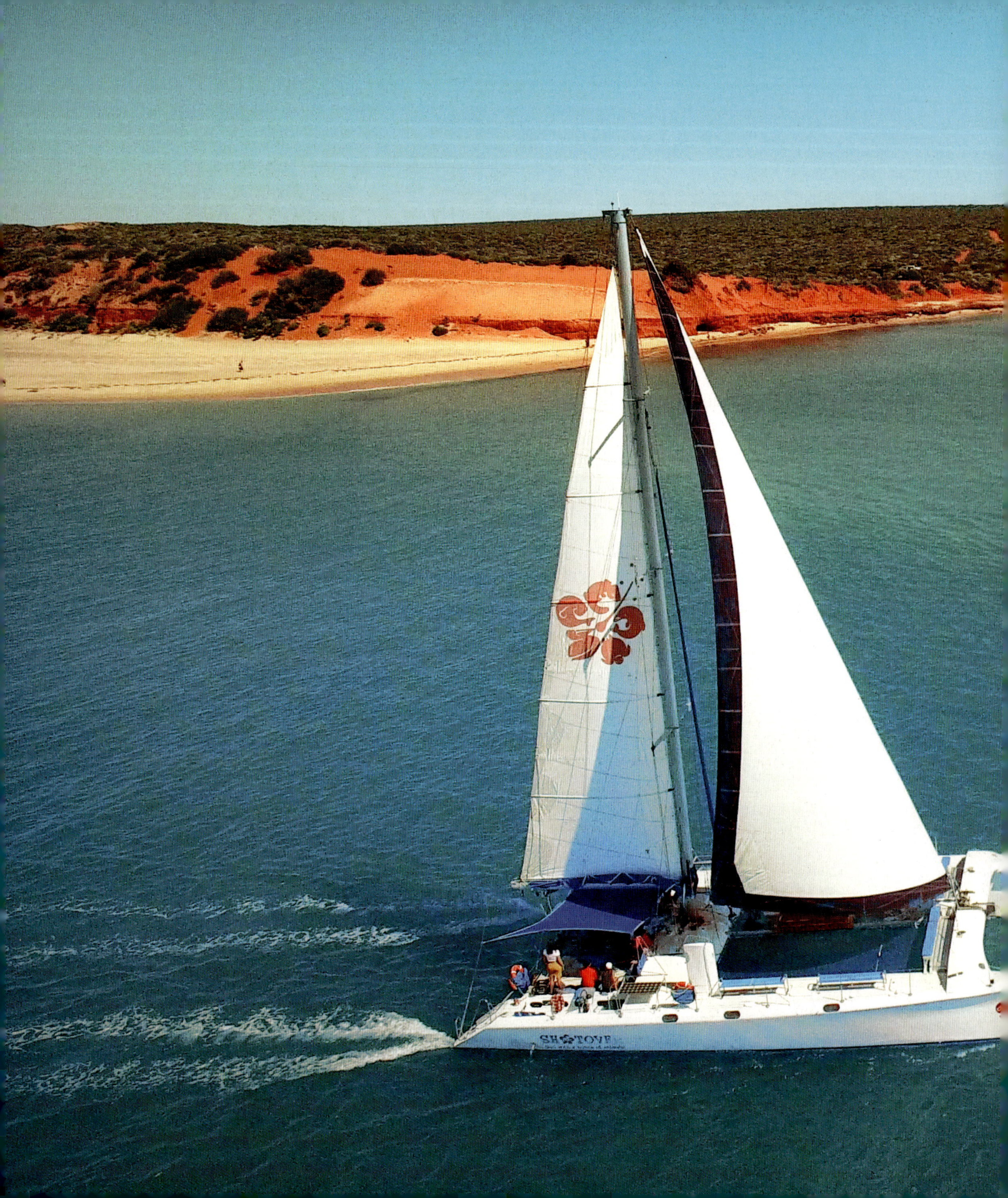

Shark Bay

Woohoo! The adventure begins … Well, if this is where we're starting the series, the bar has been set very high. Flying over Shark Bay reminded me of those coloured marbles we used to have as kids. The contrast between the crystalline royal blue of the water and the red of the sand is intensely beautiful.

Shark Bay revolves around the tourism industry with many people travelling there to glimpse the aquatic life, particularly the wicked dolphins. Our first destination was Monkey Mia, home to a research centre that studies the lifespan and activities of dolphins and other sea life such as turtles, sharks and whales. There we met Dr Ewa Krzyszcyk, a scientist who works on the Shark Bay Dolphin Project, and we boarded a catamaran with the excitement of 1000 dogs wagging their tails.

Despite the depth to the ocean floor we could still see the bottom. We came across the odd turtle doing its thing, just chilling in the water. We sailed up the coast with nothing but blue below us and the red rock and white sand sitting patiently on our left. We learned that the orange colour in the rock is the result of winds blowing the white sand across the red dirt. I'm accustomed to seeing green on the shoreline, so this was a fascinating sight.

Dr Ewa had fellow researchers on board from all around the world. One hilarious moment was when we came across a pod of dolphins. One of the girls super casually said, 'Oh yeah, that's Snoop.' To put it in perspective, we were 30 metres away and the dolphin didn't exactly jump out of the water and hand over its licence! I was impressed by the way the girls knew which dolphin was which. This is because they have a logbook in which they regularly post photos of each one's dorsal fin, like a fingerprint. Think of a folder of mug shots and replace it with hundreds of dorsal fins! Dolphins are not necessarily born with distinctive chips or markings but they acquire them through battles with sharks.

Even better was some of their names. My favourites were the food-related ones, like Cinnamon, Chilli and Spice.

I was also interested to learn about the gannets, those birds that dive into the water to catch their food before surfacing and flying off. The dive puts tremendous pressure on their eyes and over time this causes them to go blind. Then they can no longer eat, and they die – so the activity that they must do in order to survive also leads to their death. Talk about the circle of life!

Can I just say that HQ and I are no fishermen! We were very unsuccessful with our crab potting. We dropped in six, but there was nothing to take home. But being out on the water was memorable. The sky was so clear you could be forgiven, when looking into the horizon, for thinking the water was the sky. Not a bad day in the office!

Later it was time to get a taste of 'country', as the Indigenous people refer to the land. Capes, a famous local Indigenous man, welcomed us to his land by a riverbank. It was remarkable to hear the way he spoke. He frequently said 'Everything has life and spirit'. When we washed our hands in the stream, we first had to throw sand into it as if to say, 'We are coming from land and we respect the life of the water.'

Capes showcased some fantastic bush tucker. He walked us through his local area and talked about medicines and nuts and what his people use to flavour their dinner. We were fortunate to enjoy kangaroo tail the Indigenous way, cooked over coals. I have tasted roo tail before and I loved the simplicity of this particular method. The texture of the flesh and the way it absorbed the smoke created such a distinctive sensory experience. And to think the Indigenous people from around here have been doing this for thousands of years – the first celebrity chefs!

DC

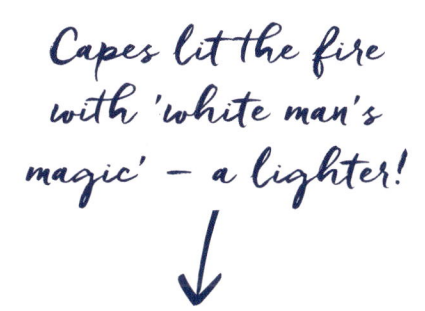

Capes lit the fire with 'white man's magic' — a lighter!

Roo tail and damper cooked over coals →

Broome

WA

Shark Bay

Geraldton

Perth

WA CLAMBAKE (HQ)

750ml bottle fruity chardonnay

6 sprigs thyme

1 head of garlic, cut in half

4 celery stalks, cut on the diagonal in large chunks

1kg new (chat) potatoes, left whole

4 corn cobs, husk and silk removed, cut in half

4 chorizo, cut in half

3 x 350g blue swimmer crabs, cleaned and quartered

750g green prawns, peeled and deveined, heads and tails left on

500g pipis, purged

1kg black mussels, cleaned and de-bearded

½ cup flat-leaf parsley leaves, roughly chopped

½ cup dill leaves, roughly chopped

250g butter, melted

2 lemons, cut into wedges

SPICE SPRINKLE

1 tablespoons celery salt

2 teaspoons mustard powder

1 teaspoon ground ginger

1 teaspoon smoked paprika

½ teaspoon ground black pepper

½ teaspoon ground allspice

½ teaspoon chilli flakes

¼ teaspoon ground nutmeg

¼ teaspoon ground cloves

¼ teaspoon ground cardamom

pinch ground cinnamon

Traditionally, a clambake requires you to build a large fire in a pit on the beach in which to cook it. But unless you are particularly adventurous, or live close to a beach, then doing it at home is the next best thing. This spicy recipe makes it really easy.

1. To make the spice sprinkle, combine all the spices in a small dry frying pan and cook, stirring, over medium heat for about 1 minute or until fragrant. Transfer to a bowl and set aside until ready to serve.

2. Pour the wine and 6 cups of water into a large pot, and bring to the boil. Add the thyme, garlic and celery. Add the potatoes and cook, covered, for 10 minutes.

3. Add the corn and chorizo and cook for a further 5 minutes. Lift out and drain. Set aside, covered, to keep warm.

4. Add the crabs and prawns and cook for 2 minutes, then add the pipis and mussels and cook just until the shellfish open.

5. Lift out the seafood and drain, leaving the broth in the pot. Arrange everything on a large platter or board and sprinkle with the spice mix and herbs. Serve with the cooking broth on the side, along with melted butter for dipping and lemons to squeeze over.

Serves 8

If the pipis haven't been cleaned, soak them in cold water for 1 hour before cooking.

If you have a pasta cooking insert for your pot, use that as it makes it easy to lift out the cooked food. Or use tongs and a slotted spoon.

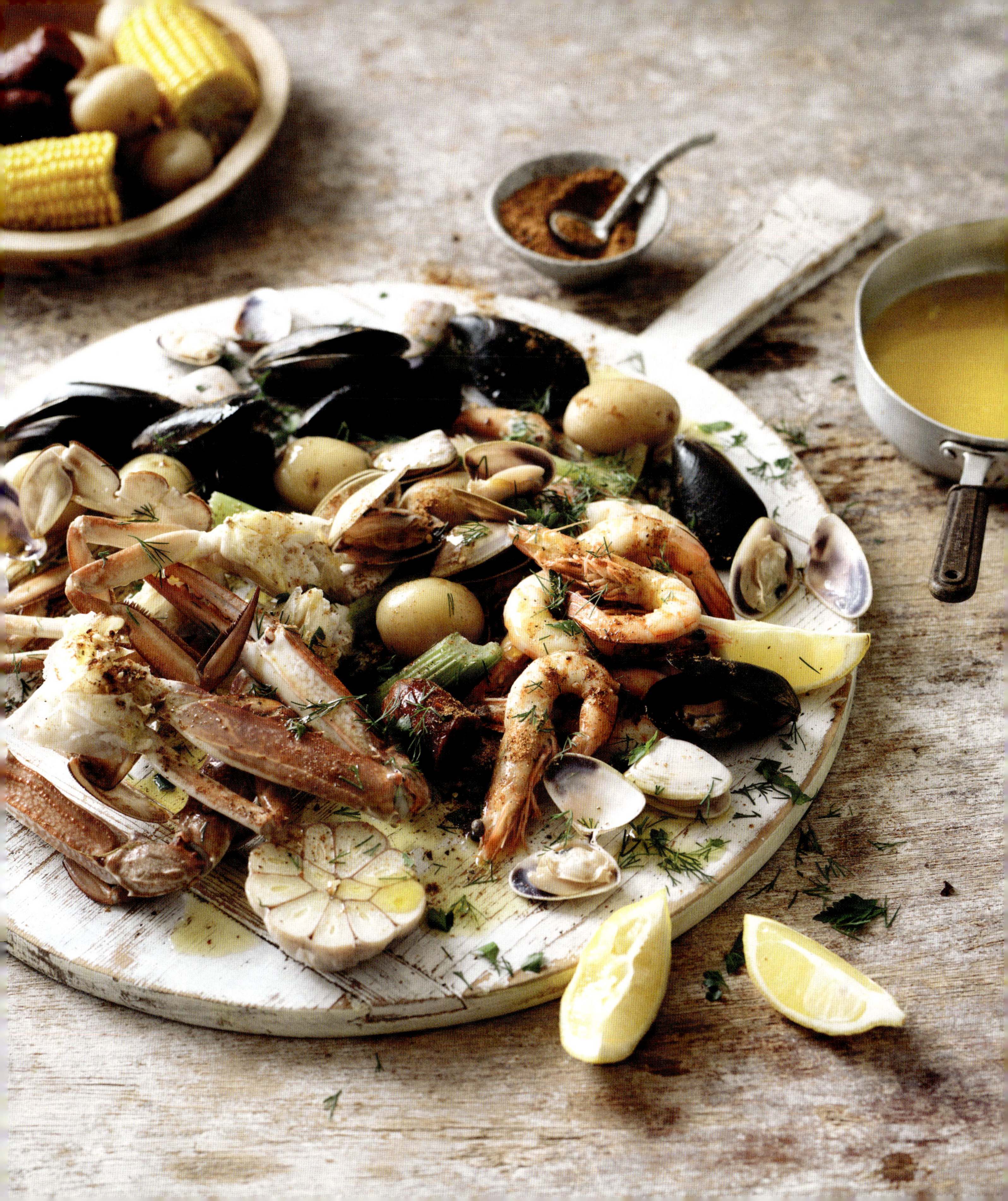

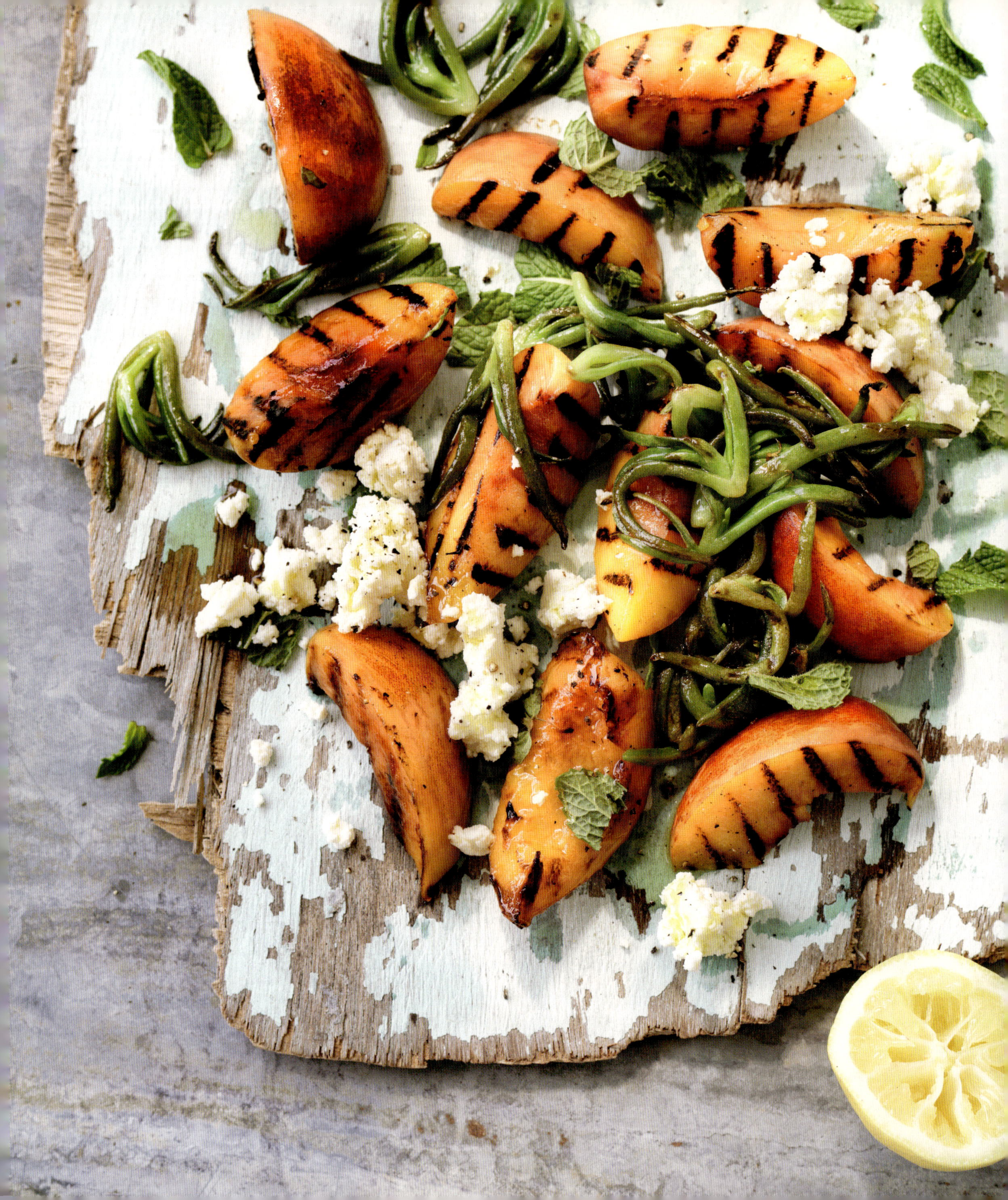

CHARRED PEACH, SAMPHIRE AND RICOTTA SALAD (DC)

4 peaches, stones removed, quartered

¼ cup olive oil

100g samphire or asparagus

½ cup mint leaves

½ cup firm ricotta (from the deli)

1 tablespoon lemon juice

1. Preheat a BBQ grill plate over medium-high heat and brush the flesh of the peaches with a little olive oil. Put onto the BBQ on one of the flesh sides. Cook for 1–2 minutes or until charred, then turn to the other flesh side until charred. Transfer to a plate and set aside. Increase the heat to high.

2. Toss the samphire with 1 tablespoon of the olive oil and cook on the BBQ for 1–2 minutes, constantly rotating until slightly charred all over. Transfer to a board. If you are using asparagus, slice on an angle into little spears.

3. Tear half the mint leaves and place into a large bowl with the peaches and samphire. Season with salt and pepper, and toss to combine. Transfer to a big serving plate or board.

4. Dollop with ricotta, sprinkle with the remaining mint and drizzle lemon juice and a little olive oil over.

Serves 4 as a starter

> Samphire is a native plant with a succulent texture and salty flavour. Jump online to find a supplier.

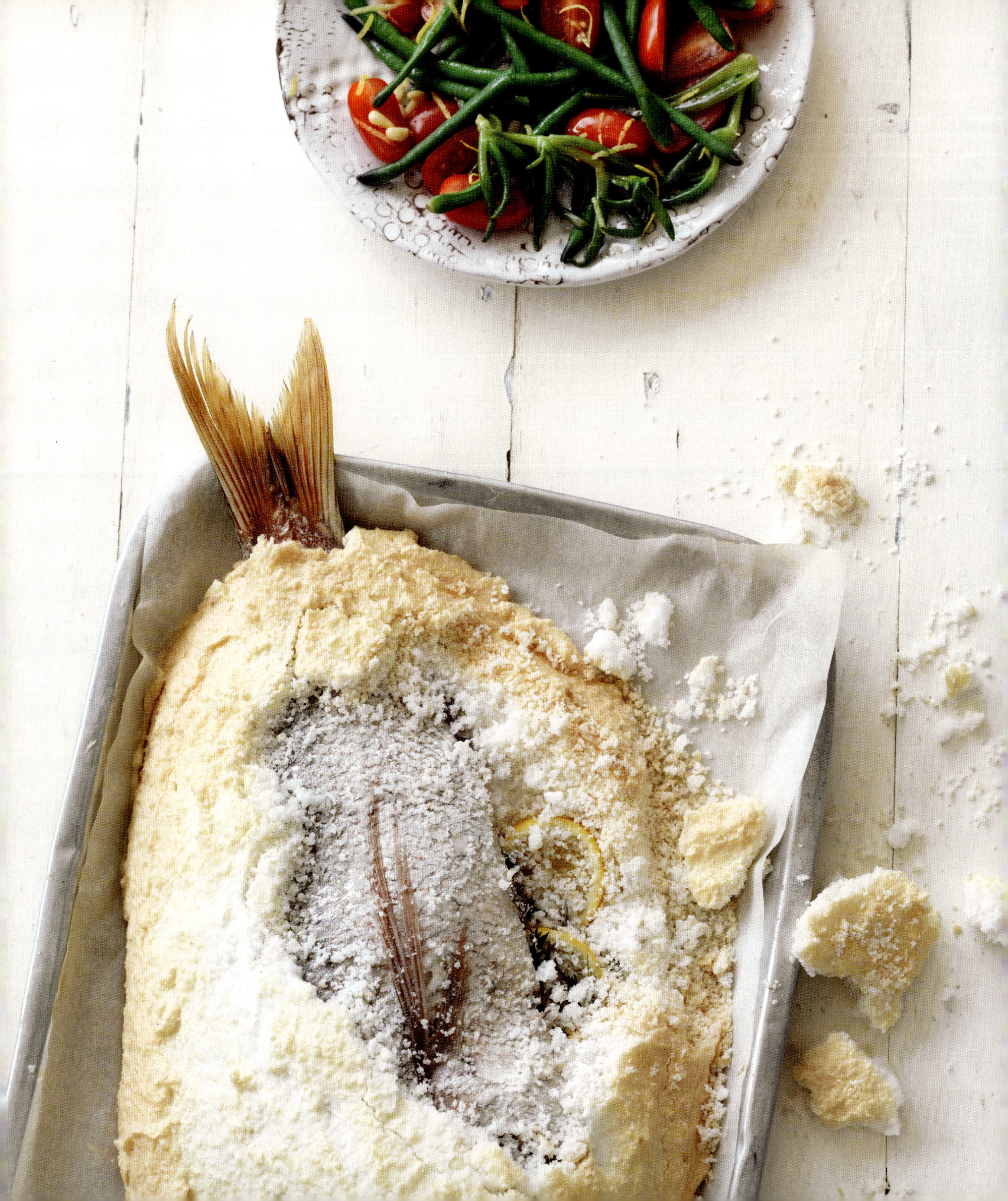

SALT BAKED FISH WITH SAMPHIRE SALAD

The salt bake looks wicked, but it's easy to make – trust me! Samphire is sometimes known as 'the asparagus of the sea' and thin asparagus spears are a suitable substitute here. They will take another minute to cook.

1 tablespoon olive oil

2kg coral trout or snapper, cleaned

1 lemon, cut into slices

handful dill sprigs

4 thyme sprigs

6 egg whites

2 kg cooking salt

SALAD

200g snake beans

¼ cup olive oil

100g samphire

250g grape tomatoes, halved

2 tablespoons pine nuts, toasted

1 teaspoon finely grated lemon zest

1 tablespoon lemon juice

1. Preheat the oven to 200°C (180°C fan-forced) and line a large baking tray with baking paper.

2. Drizzle olive oil on both sides of the fish and rub inside the cavity. Pop the lemon wedges inside the cavity, giving them a gentle squeeze first to release some juice. Tear the dill and thyme and stuff into the cavity. Season with pepper.

3. Use electric beaters to beat the egg whites to soft peaks, then add the salt gradually, beating until the mixture has increased in volume. It should be thick and coarse (it doesn't matter if the salt hasn't dissolved).

4. Using a spoon or a spatula, spread one-third of the salt mixture onto the tray to make a 1cm thick layer. Lay the fish on top and cover with remaining salt mixture, about 1cm thick. Make sure you seal any cracks – have a good look and make sure it is completely covered.

5. Bake, ideally in the centre of the oven, for 30-35 minutes. You can check by inserting a knife or fork into the thickest part of the fish (or where you think it would be as you can't see it) and touching it to your bottom lip. If it is cold, keep it going. If it is hot, then it is done.

6. Meanwhile, for the salad, blanch the snake beans in boiling water for 3 minutes. Rinse under cold water. Cut into 6cm lengths.

7. Heat 1 tablespoon of the oil in a frying pan over medium-high heat. Cook the samphire for about 1 minute, until glossy and slightly wilted. Transfer to a bowl and add the snake beans, tomatoes, pine nuts and zest. Drizzle with the juice and remaining olive oil and season with salt and pepper. Toss to combine.

8. To serve, take the fish to the table. Crack the salt crust to expose the fish, and serve with the salad.

Serves 4–6

SALT AND PEPPER ROO TAIL (DC)

Face it, it's not every day we have kangaroo tail. But these days ox tail is easily found, and it's just as awesome if you can't get roo. My family and I love a good salt and pepper squid. In fact, there is one Vietnamese restaurant where we would go especially for that dish. Here's to mixing Australian bush food with a family favourite. Nothing beats a bit of nostalgia!

1 kangaroo tail, cut into pieces

1 litre beef stock

3 bay leaves

3 garlic cloves, crushed

1 onion, finely chopped

3 thyme sprigs

1 tablespoon Sriracha sauce

⅔ cup maple syrup

1 tablespoon Szechuan peppercorns

1 tablespoon salt

2 teaspoons freshly ground black pepper

1½ cups dry breadcrumbs

1 cup plain flour

2 eggs, beaten

rice bran oil, to deep fry

1. Combine the roo tail, stock, bay leaves, garlic, onion, thyme and Sriracha sauce in a large pot. Season with salt and pepper. Cover and bring to the boil. Turn the heat to low and simmer for 1½ – 2 hours or until tender, then remove the tail from the pot and allow to cool.

2. To make the glaze, transfer the liquid to a wide frying pan and add the maple syrup. Bring to the boil over high heat and cook uncovered until it is reduced to one-third of the volume and is syrupy. Set aside to cool.

3. Dry-fry the peppercorns until aromatic, then grind in a mortar and pestle with the salt and pepper. Combine the mixture with the breadcrumbs on a plate.

4. Put the flour onto a plate and whisk the eggs in a shallow bowl. Pour enough oil in a deep frying pan to be about 3cm deep (the pan should be no more than half full). Heat the oil to 180°C or until a wooden skewer bubbles when inserted.

5. Toss the tail pieces in the flour and shake off the excess. Dip into the egg, shake off the excess, then roll in the breadcrumbs, pressing on gently.

6. Pop a few pieces into the oil and cook, turning occasionally, for about 2 minutes or until golden brown and crispy. Repeat with remaining tail, keeping in mind the more you have in the oil the lower the heat, so don't overcrowd the pan. Drain on paper towels and season with salt and pepper. Serve with the sticky glaze poured over.

Serves 4

Use Panko breadcrumbs to make these extra crunchy.

Sriracha is a Thai hot chilli sauce that you can buy in most supermarkets.

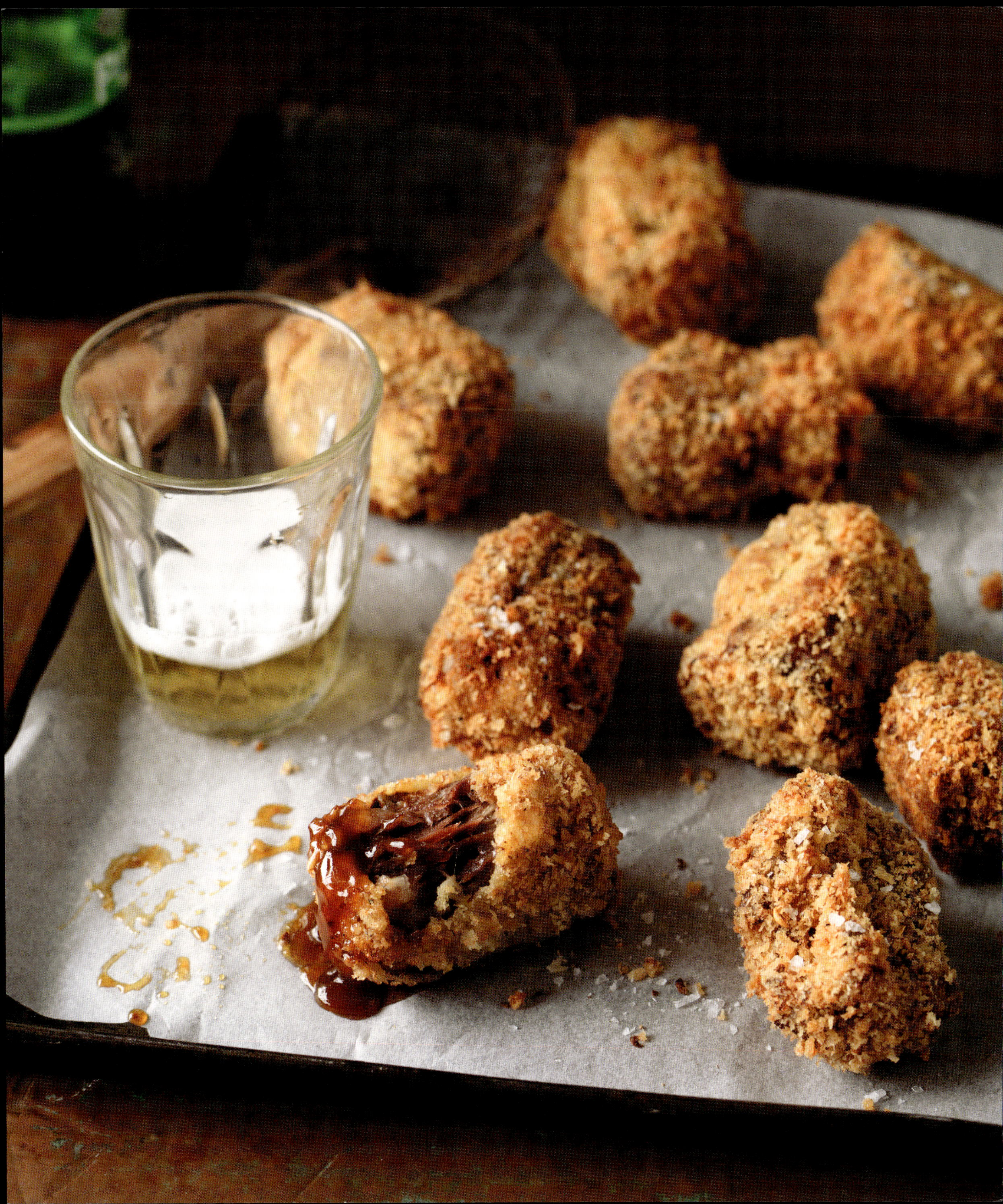

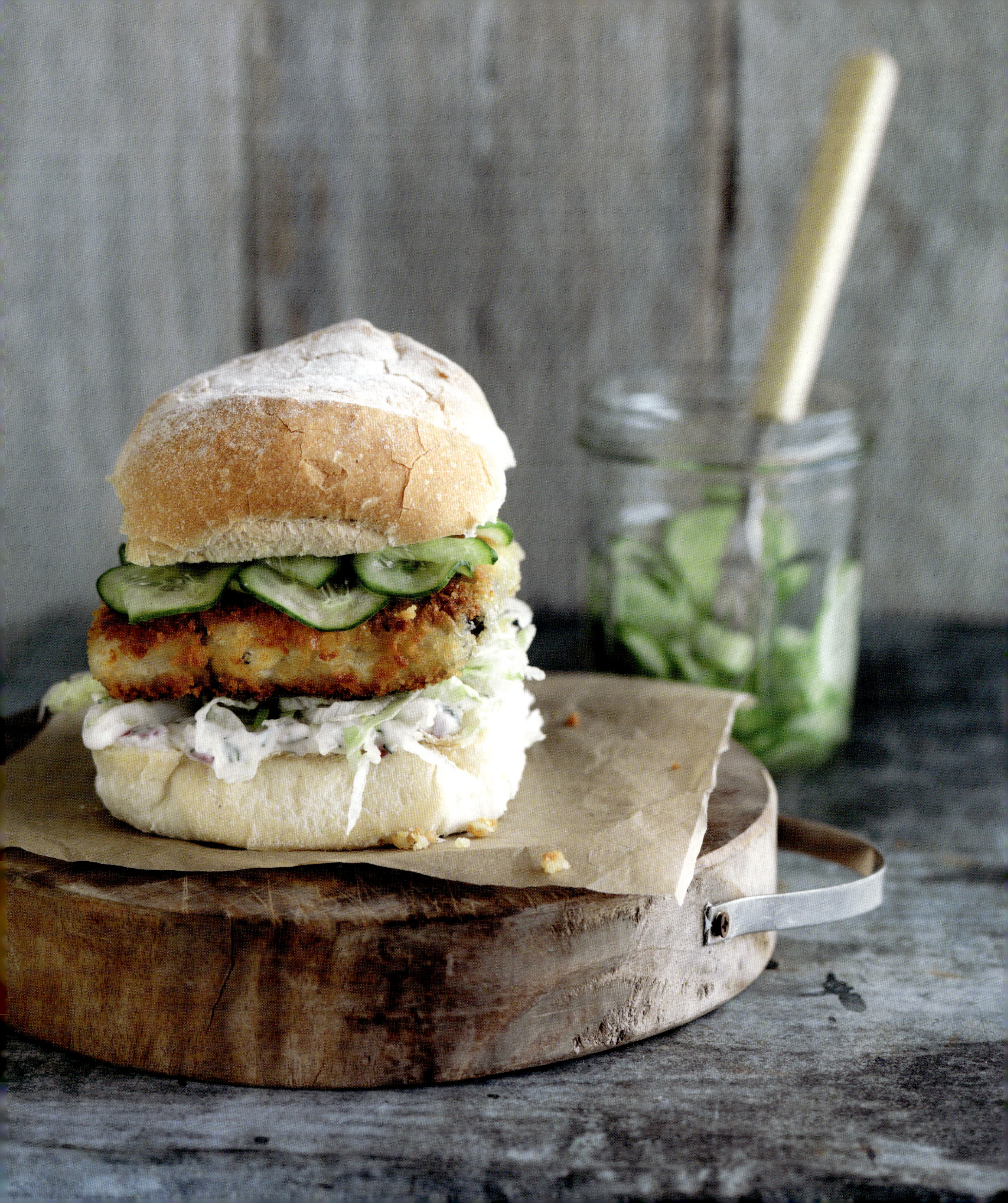

FISH BURGERS (HQ)

Whether it's burgers, kebabs, sushi or skewers, there's nothing like tucking into food that doesn't require knives and forks. This appealing burger is up there with my fave types of handheld food. Share them with friends and wash them down in the sun with an ice cold drink!

2 eggs

¼ cup plain flour

¾ cup dried breadcrumbs

4 x 150g white fish fillets, skin and bones removed (about 1.5cm thick)

¼ cup rice bran oil, for frying

4 soft round buns, split

¼ iceberg lettuce, shredded

QUICK PICKLE

1 large Lebanese cucumber, cut into 5mm discs

¼ cup apple cider vinegar

1 teaspoon sugar

1 teaspoon salt

¼ teaspoon cayenne pepper

HERBED MAYO

½ cup mayonnaise

finely grated zest of 1 lemon

¼ cup dill leaves, finely chopped

½ small red onion, finely diced

1. Whisk the eggs in a shallow bowl and place the flour (seasoned with salt and pepper) and breadcrumbs onto separate plates. Dip a fish piece into the flour, shake off the excess, then dip into the egg and shake off the excess. Coat in breadcrumbs, pressing on gently. Place onto a tray, and continue until all fish is coated.
2. To make the quick pickle, combine the cucumber, vinegar, sugar, salt and cayenne pepper in a medium glass or ceramic bowl. Cover and place into the fridge until ready to serve.
3. For the herbed mayo, combine all the ingredients in a small bowl or jar. Cover and refrigerate until ready to serve.
4. Heat half the oil in a non-stick frying pan and cook 2 pieces of fish over medium heat for 2–3 minutes each side, until golden and cooked through. Drain on paper towel, and repeat with the remaining fish.
5. To assemble the fish burgers, spread the bottom half of each bun with a generous helping of the mayo. Make a layer of lettuce, then the fish and finally the pickle and bun top.

Serves 4

I suggest snapper, kingfish or mahi mahi, but you could use any fish in season or local to your area.

Fish can be crumbed 1 day in advance and kept, covered, in the fridge until cooking time.

Cut the fish fillet to a size that's suitable for the bun.

BLUE SWIMMER CRAB NACHOS

- 2 corn cobs, husk and silk removed
- 200g bag blue tortilla chips (or regular corn chips)
- ½ cup grated tasty cheese
- 1 ripe avocado, cut into small dice
- 2 baby radishes, thinly sliced
- 400g blue swimmer crab meat
- 2 green shallots, cut on angle
- ¼ cup coriander, roughly chopped, to garnish
- 2 limes, cut into wedges, to serve
- sour cream and hot sauce, to taste

1. Drop the corn into a large pot of boiling water and cook for 10 minutes. Preheat a BBQ grill plate or chargrill pan to medium-high heat.
2. Drain the corn and cook on the BBQ, turning occasionally, until charred. Set aside to cool slightly before using a small knife to slice off the corn kernels.
3. Preheat the oven to 180°C (160°C fan-forced). Spread the tortilla chips out onto an ovenproof platter. Scatter the cheese evenly over the chips. Place into the oven for 5 minutes or until the cheese has melted.
4. Top with avocado, corn, radish, crab meat and green shallots, and garnish with coriander. Serve with lime wedges, sour cream and hot sauce to drizzle over.

Serves 4

Use any type of crab meat locally available, or from a tub in the fridge at the supermarket.

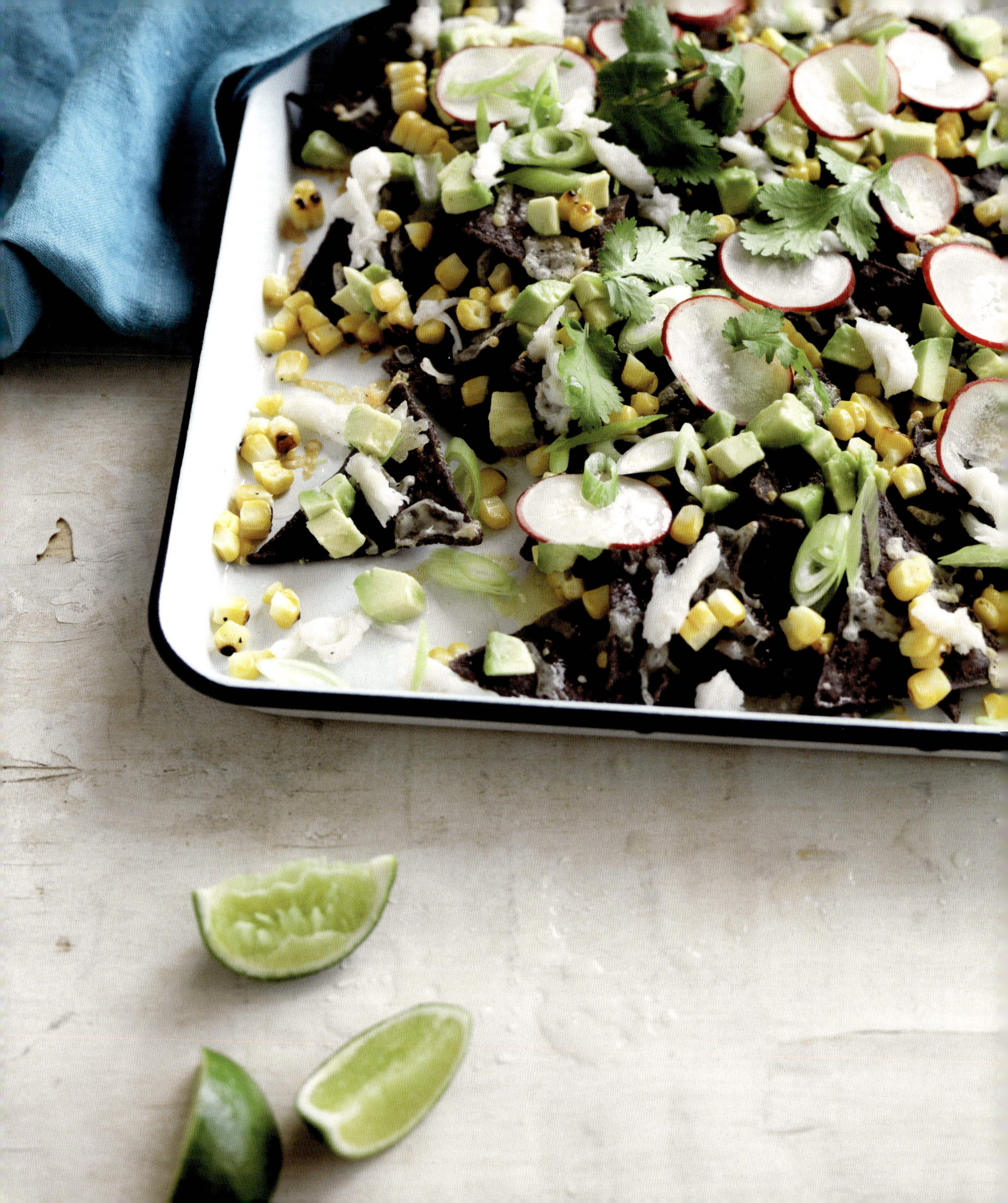

BLUE SWIMMER CRAB OMELETTE (HQ)

Who doesn't love a sweet, salty, chunky and flavoursome crab omelette? I used blue swimmer crab, but feel free to use crab meat local to you.

4 eggs

2 teaspoons chopped chervil leaves

2 teaspoons chopped chives

2 teaspoons chopped flat-leaf parsley leaves

1 tablespoon butter

2 teaspoons olive oil

100g picked blue swimmer crab meat

extra virgin olive oil, to serve

lemon juice, to serve

microherbs and crusty sourdough bread, to serve

1. Whisk the eggs with the herbs and 2 tablespoons water. Season with salt and pepper. Heat a medium (20cm base) non-stick heavy-based frying pan over medium heat. Add half the butter and oil to the pan, and heat until the butter begins to bubble.

2. Pour in half the egg mixture. Once it begins to cook, start pulling the cooked egg to the centre of the pan, so the uncooked egg runs out to the edges. It should set in nice fluffy folds and should still be a little runny on top.

3. Scatter half the crab meat onto one half of the omelette. Fold the omelette over, and using a spatula flip omelette out onto a warm plate. Repeat for the second omelette.

4. Drizzle with olive oil and lemon juice, scatter with microherbs and serve with the bread.

Serves 2

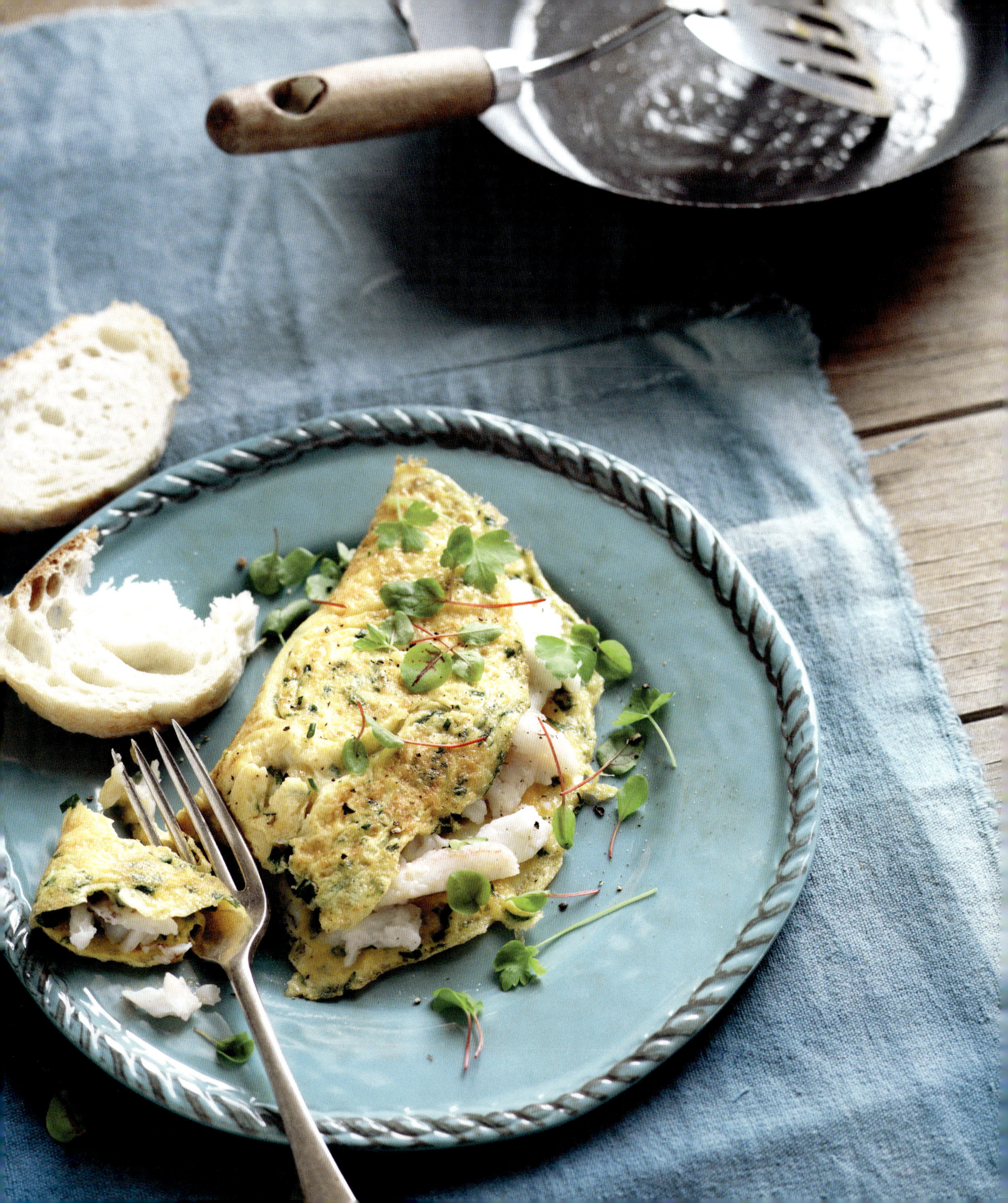

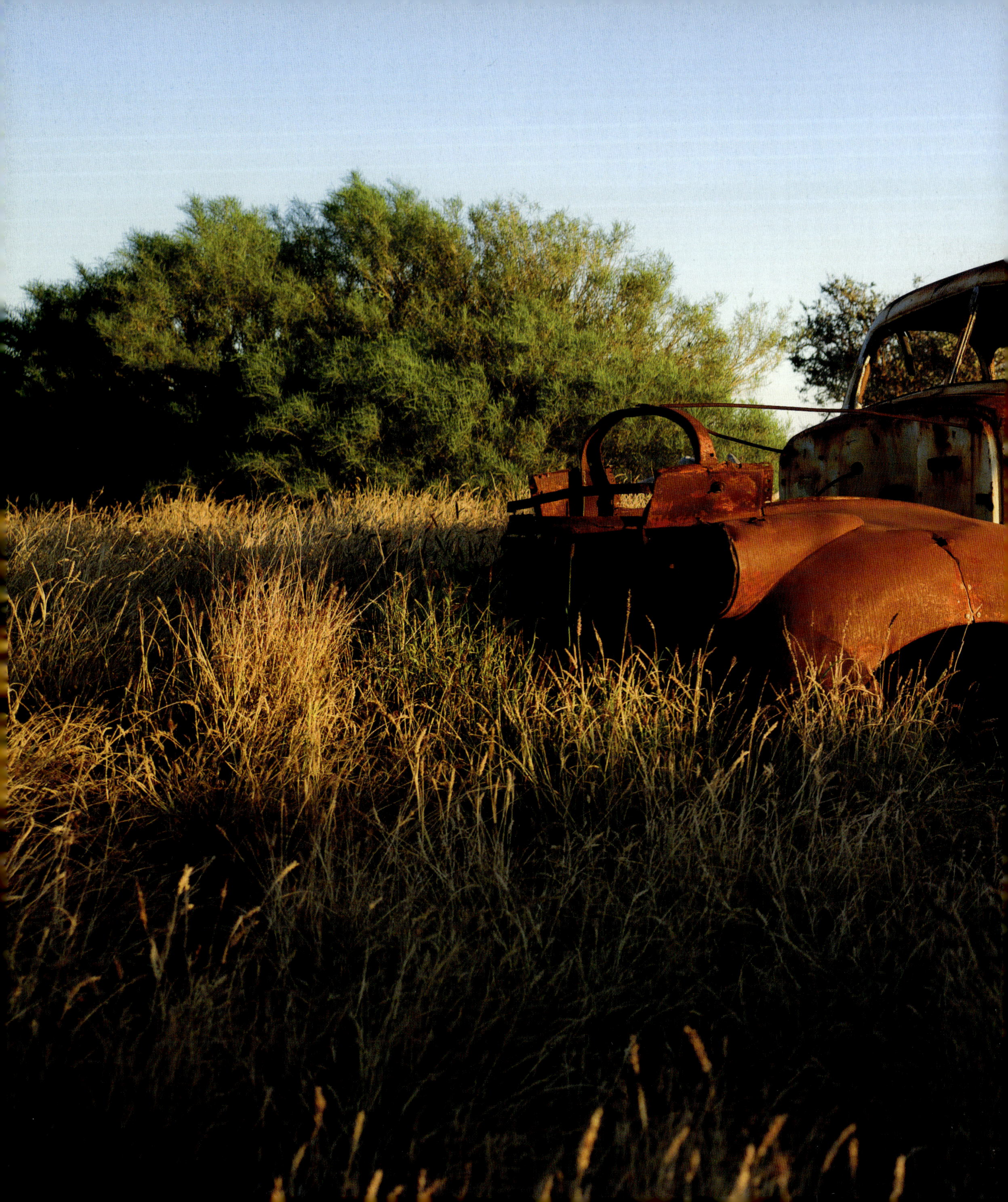

Wooramel

Before we hit Wooramel Station, we took a quick detour to check out Hamelin Pool Marine Nature Reserve, home to one of only two stromatolite ecosystems in the world. These living fossils date back over 3.5 billion years. Yeah, no joke! As a result, geologists research these bad boys to comprehend the first forms of life on earth. The natural saltiness of the water and its temperature – up to 43 degrees C – provide the perfect environment for the bacteria that create the structure of the stromatolites to grow. Fun fact: every year they grow 3mm ... And we thought tortoises were taking it easy!

Life on a station is far from what I'm used to on the Northern Beaches of Sydney, where everything is at your disposal within a 1 kilometre radius. That wouldn't even get you to the letterbox on a station! Wooramel Station was everything I expected it to be and more. There was plenty of pasture, livestock, sheds and yards, but also a plane, spas, glamping tents and artwork-like statues made out of old car parts.

Let me ask you this ... What do you think is the quickest way to muster cattle? Horse, motorbike, perhaps a 4-wheel-drive? Nah – how about a 4-seater plane?! Quinny and I witnessed first-hand the fearless, modern-era farmwork that the station owner, Justin, calls 'mustering'. Occasionally we heard a plane overhead when we were driving through the paddocks, and I swear, if we'd put a hand up in the air, we'd only be cooking with one now!

After mustering the cattle, we got on with separating the goats into male and female using a steel divider. Hayden pushed them through and I sorted them. Man, they moved seriously quick and hard! As I let a few into the wrong pen, we had to retrieve them and put them where they belonged. To do this, we had to grab them by the horns, hold on tight and get a leg over them. Sounds weird, but that's what we were instructed to do!

I had a go first and went straight for the first male I could see. I gripped hard and his back legs roared into action. He kept jumping and kicking so his front legs were always up in the air, which made it very hard to put my leg over, let me tell you! After about 15 seconds of some tight gripping I got my leg over and squeezed my thighs together as if I was riding a bike. He didn't move so I squeezed my thighs a little tighter. He marched forward and I got him into the right pen.

Hayden went next, and his goat was a little more cooperative. Well, at least at first. Hayden grabbed the goat's horns and sat on him, job done. But then the goat started to back up, and you could see the growing strain on Hayden. Whenever he wanted the goat to go forward, he moved back. It was hilarious as the way Hayden positioned his hands, it looked like he was riding a Harley Davidson. He ended up getting the goat in after some throttle-pulling. Man, was that fun!

One of the things I love most in this life is cooking over an open fire. You are outdoors, there is the primeval smell of charring wood and smoke that gets the blood going, plus I like controlling the heat with intuition, not a dial. Hayden and I were treated to a great afternoon filled with rich smells, local cattle and the amazing view of the river in the background. Sitting with the boys around the campfire, having a couple of beers while the sun was setting ... there are no words to explain how we felt there and then. To think this is only our second stop!

DC

Cooking with intuition over a campfire ↓

Wooramel Station owner, Justin Steadman

BUSHMAN'S STEAK WITH OUTBACK SAUCE (HQ)

A tomahawk steak is just a rib-eye steak attached to a long rib bone that hasn't been cut down. They're pretty big, so if you don't have a huge frying pan, cook it on the BBQ and then transfer to a tray for its time in the oven. If you can't find this extravagant cut, then use regular rib-eye steaks from your favourite butcher. Either way, you're in for a treat!

2 x 1.5kg 'tomahawk' steaks

2 teaspoons rice bran oil

1½ tablespoons butter

3 garlic cloves, smashed (you can leave the skin on)

OUTBACK SAUCE

1 cup whole egg mayonnaise

¼ cup tomato sauce

¼ cup chilli sauce (not sweet chilli sauce)

2 teaspoons Worcestershire sauce

1 teaspoon smoked paprika

1 teaspoon garlic powder

1½ teaspoons chipotle chilli sauce

1. Take the meat out of the fridge 1 hour before cooking so it is at room temperature. Preheat the oven to 180°C (160° fan-forced).

2. Season steaks well with salt (I don't like to add pepper at this stage as the pepper just tends to burn in the high heat of the pan) and drizzle with the oil. Heat a large (and I mean big!) ovenproof cast iron frying pan over high heat until smoking. Cook the steaks in the pan for 3 minutes each side, turning once. Transfer pan to the oven for 15 minutes, turning the steaks halfway through.

3. Remove from the oven and add the butter and garlic to the pan. Spoon over the steak, then loosely cover with foil and set aside to rest for at least 10 minutes.

4. To make the outback sauce, combine all the ingredients in a bowl or large jar. If making ahead of time, cover and keep in the fridge.

5. Serve the steaks sliced on a large board with a good dollop of the sauce on the side. Season well with salt and pepper and serve with your choice of favourite sides.

Serves 4–6

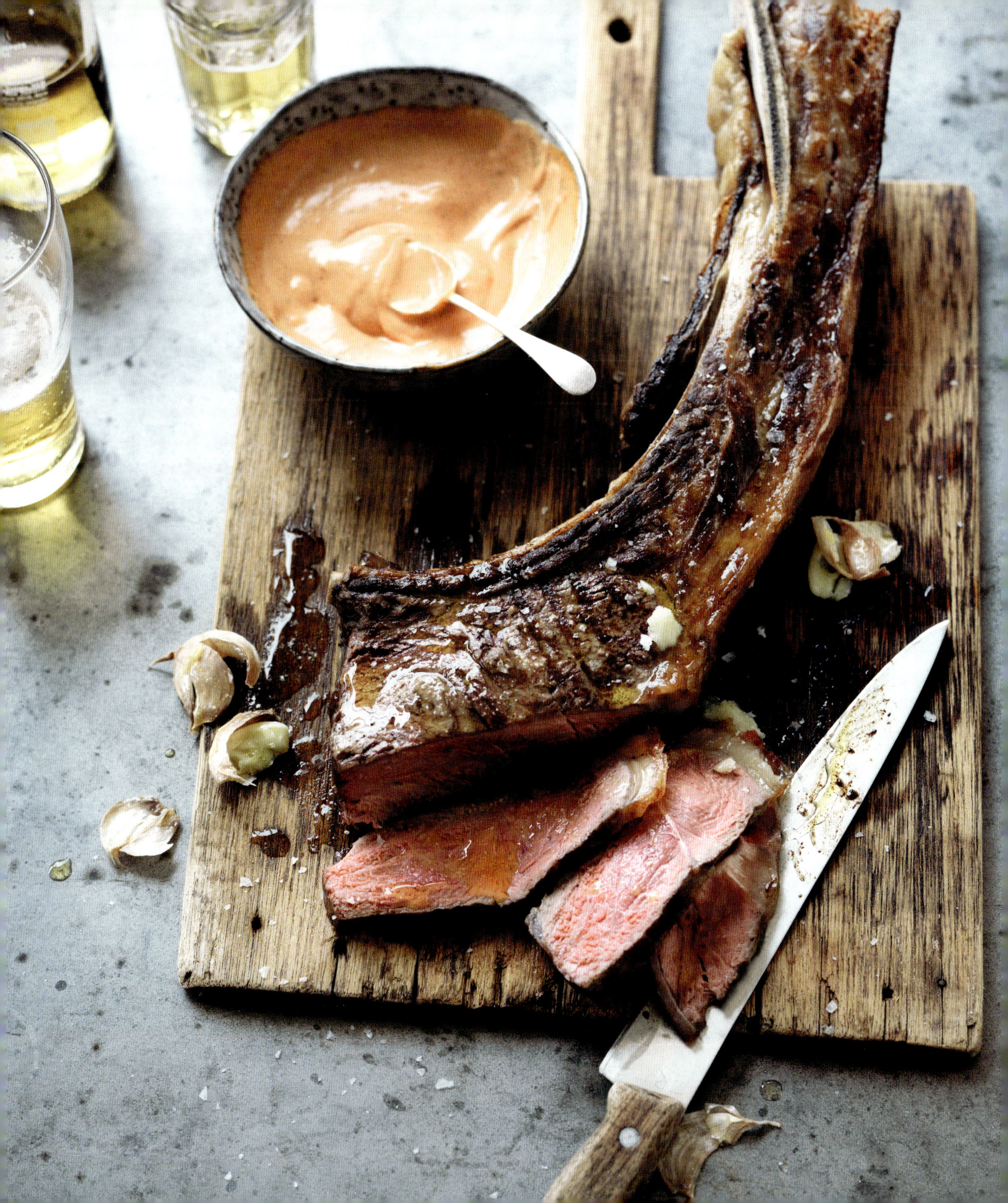

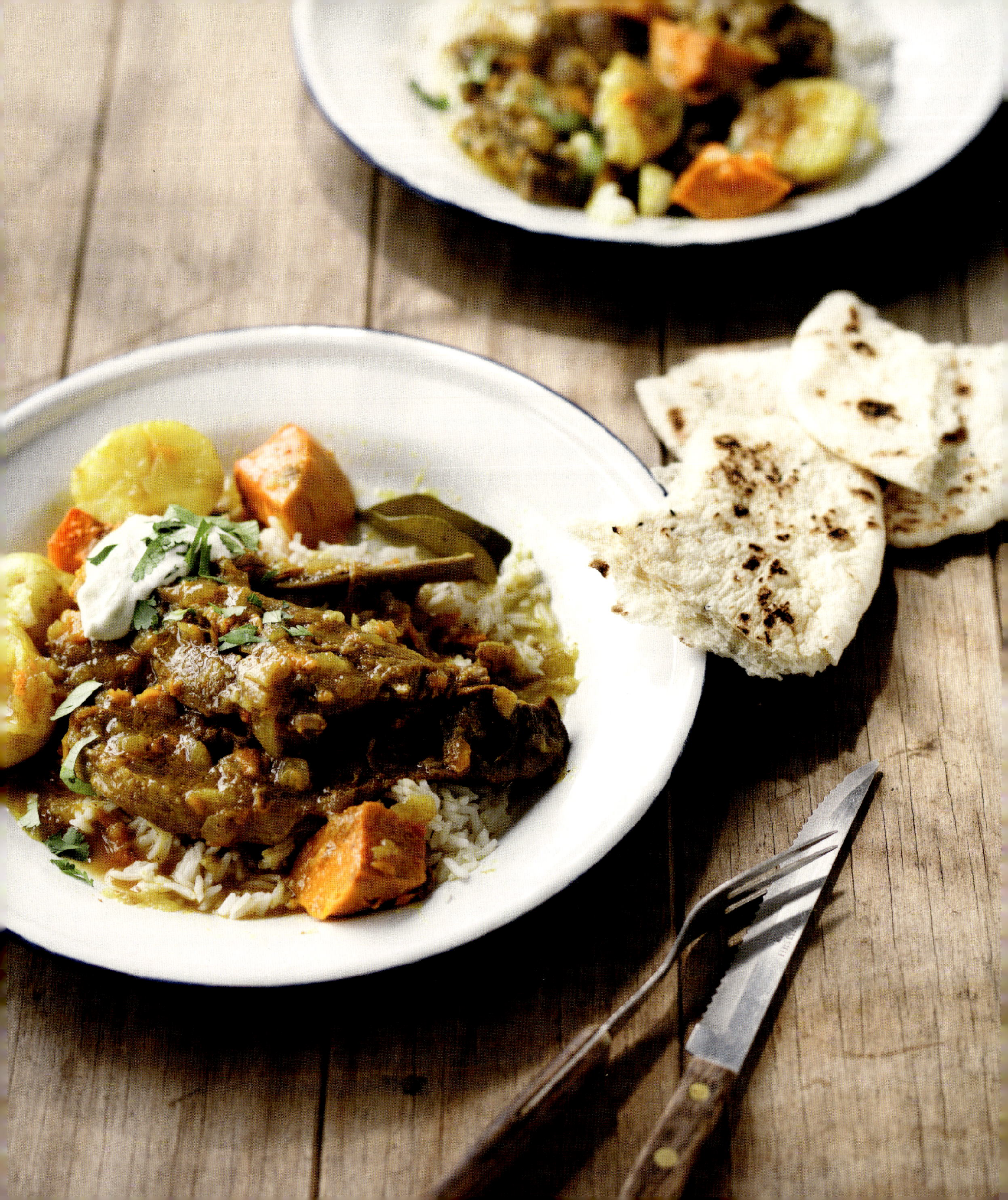

GOAT CHOP CURRY WITH FLATBREADS

We cooked our curry in a cast iron pot over campfire coals, but we had to be careful to maintain a steady heat. I've tweaked it here to cook slowly at home until the chops are super tender. You're welcome!

1kg goat chump, forequarter or neck chops

¼ cup rice bran oil

4 onions, roughly chopped

3 garlic cloves, crushed

3cm knob ginger, finely grated

2 lemongrass sticks, bruised

3 kaffir lime leaves, finely shredded

1 large sweet potatoes, peeled and cut into 4cm chunks

6 small new (chat) potatoes, halved

steamed basmati rice, flatbreads, Greek yoghurt and chopped coriander, to serve

SPICE RUB

1 tablespoon curry powder

2 teaspoons ground cumin

2 teaspoons ground coriander

1½ teaspoons ground turmeric

1 teaspoon chilli powder

1. To make the spice rub, combine all the spices in a large bowl and season with salt and pepper. Add the goat and toss to coat. If you have time, cover and refrigerate for a few hours, or even overnight.

2. Heat the oil in a large heavy-based pot over medium heat. Cook the onion, garlic, ginger, lemongrass and kaffir lime leaves for about 5 minutes or until the onion is golden brown. Add the meat and enough water to just cover. Bring just to the boil, then reduce the heat to very low and simmer, covered, for 1 ½ hours.

3. Add the sweet potatoes and potatoes and simmer for a further 45 minutes. Season with salt and pepper. Serve with rice, flatbreads, yoghurt and coriander.

Serves 6

Use lambchops if goat isn't available.

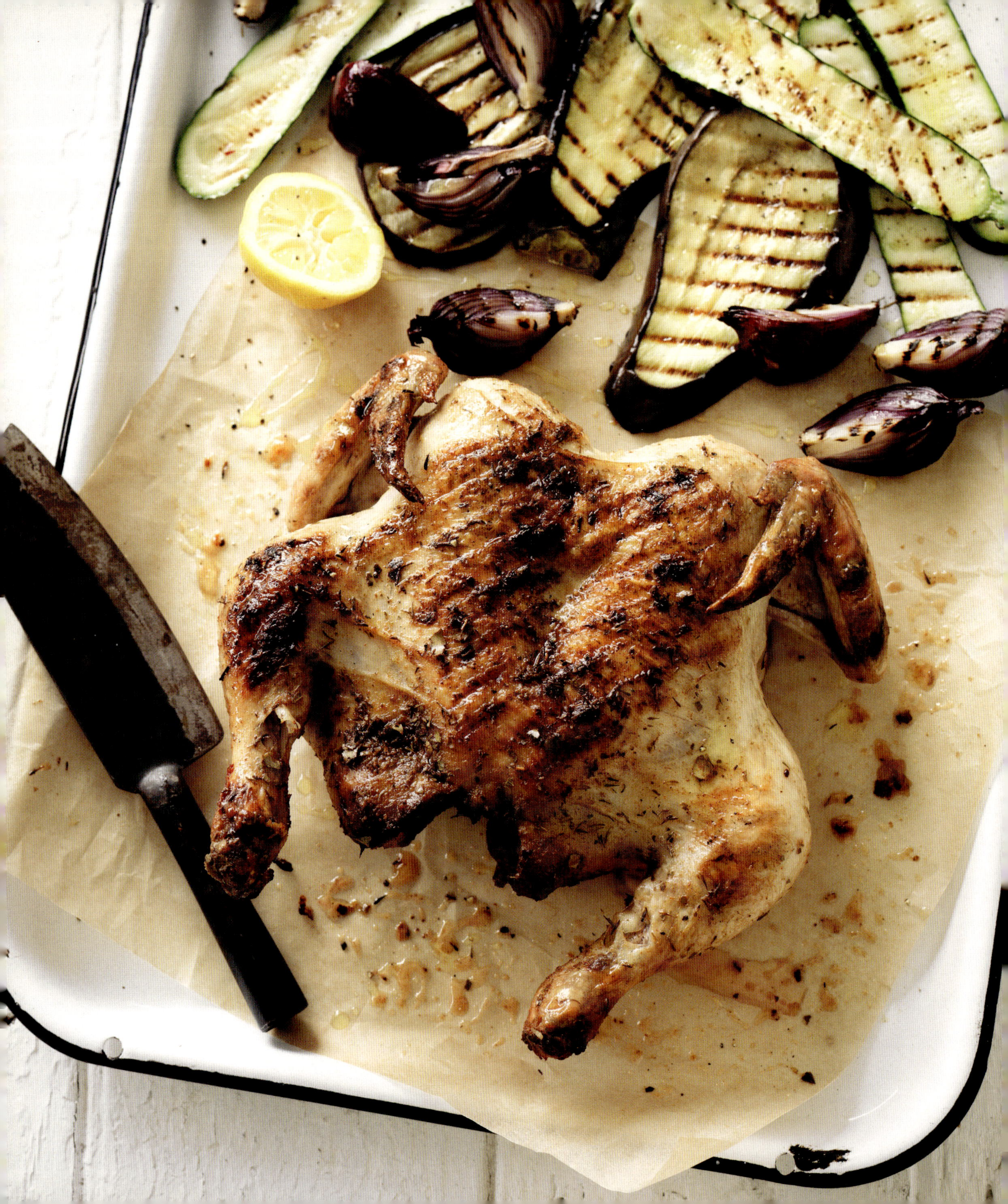

BUTTERFLIED SALTBUSH CHOOK WITH CHARRED VEG ⓓⓒ

Get your butcher to butterfly the chook for you, or do it yourself. Use good poultry shears or sturdy kitchen scissors, and cut down either side of the backbone. Discard the bone and flatten out the chook by pressing down on the breast area.

¼ cup dried salt bush or bay leaves

2 teaspoons ground cumin

1 teaspoon garlic powder

1 teaspoon cayenne pepper

2 teaspoons dried thyme

2 tablespoons lemon juice

⅓ cup olive oil

1 whole chicken (about 1.8kg), butterflied

2 red onions, quartered (with root end on)

2 eggplant, sliced 5mm thick lengthways

4 zucchini, sliced 5mm thick lengthways

1. Use a mortar and pestle or spice grinder to grind up the salt bush (or bay leaves). Combine in a bowl with the cumin, garlic powder, cayenne pepper, thyme, 1 tablespoon of the lemon juice and half the oil. Season with salt and pepper.

2. Rub the marinade all over the chicken on both sides, getting into all the hidden joints. Marinate in the fridge for a minimum of 30 minutes, or overnight.

3. Preheat a covered BBQ grill plate to medium-high heat. Bring the chicken to room temperature for 20 minutes, then add it to the grill skin side down. Cover with the lid (or a large upside down saucepan if your BBQ doesn't have a lid). Cook for about 8 minutes or until the skin is golden. Turn chicken over, cover again and cook for a further 15–20 minutes or until the juices run clear when you pierce a skewer into the thigh. Transfer to a tray, cover with foil and set aside to rest.

4. Brush the vegetables with the remaining oil. Start cooking the onions (they take the longest) on the BBQ for 5 minutes or until charred on both sides. Add the eggplant and zucchini, and cook for 2–4 minutes or until charred. Season the vegies with salt and pepper, and squeeze the remaining lemon juice over them. Serve them with the chook.

Serves 4

Saltbush is an Australian native plant. The dried leaves give a herbal, salty flavour in cooking. Jump online to find a supplier.

WOORAMEL | 45

OUTBACK LAMB RIBS WITH STICKY SWEET AND SOUR SAUCE (DC)

Lamb ribs are seriously naughty. Touching them up with some sour and sweet notes makes them even more delectable. #NextLevel!

3 lamb rib racks
1 tablespoon ground allspice
¼ cup tamarind pulp, roughly chopped
½ cup honey
2 teaspoons finely grated ginger
½ teaspoon chilli powder
2 tablespoons lemon juice
2 coriander stalks, stems finely chopped, leaves set aside
2 teaspoons sesame seeds

1. Preheat the oven to 150°C (130°C fan-forced).
2. Remove the fat and sinewy membrane from the lamb ribs (or get your butcher to do it for you). Rub both sides of the ribs with the allspice and season with salt and pepper. Place them on an oiled rack in a large roasting pan with 2cm water in the bottom. Cover tightly with foil and cook for 1 ½ hours or until the meat can easily be pierced with a knife. Set aside to rest.
3. Combine the tamarind pulp and 2 tablespoons boiling water in small saucepan over medium heat. Bring to the boil, then turn heat to low and simmer for about 5 minutes until thickened slightly. Turn up the heat to medium and add the honey, ginger and chilli powder. Bring to the boil and cook until reduced to ½ cup. Take off the heat and stir in the lemon juice and coriander stems.
4. Preheat a BBQ to high heat. Brush the glaze over both sides of the lamb ribs and cook for 2 minutes on each side or until slightly charred. Baste with more glaze as they cook.
5. Serve with a final drizzle of glaze, and sprinkle with sesame seeds and coriander leaves.

Serves 4

You can use 2 tablespoons of tamarind puree instead of the pulp.

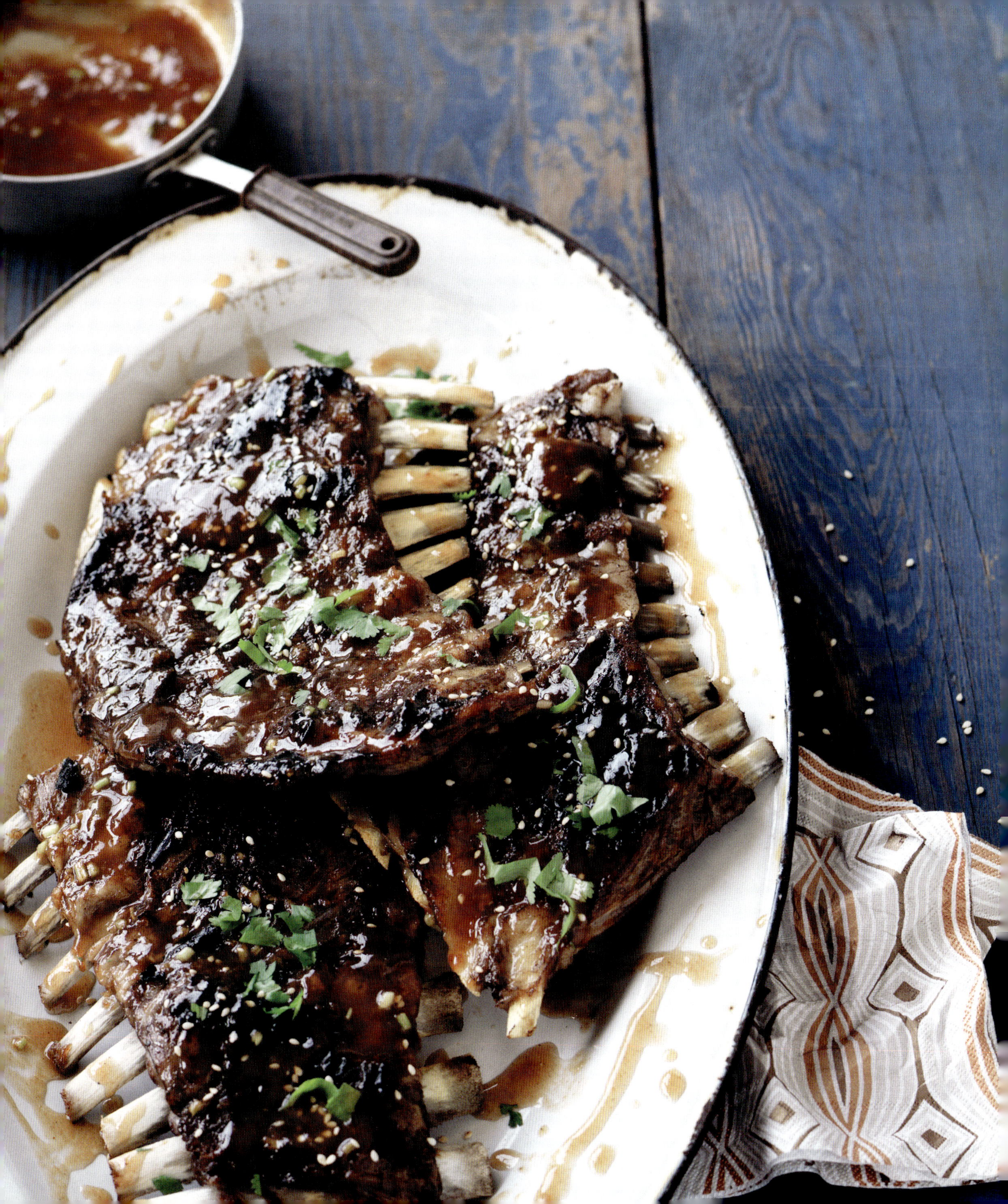

CAMPFIRE LAMB SHOULDER WITH SIMPLE SLAW (HQ)

120g butter, softened
1 tablespoon coriander seeds, ground
1 tablespoon cumin seeds, ground
1½ teaspoons smoked paprika
2kg lamb shoulder, bone in, excess fat trimmed
1 head of garlic, halved
¼ cup olive oil
flatbreads, to serve

SIMPLE SLAW

½ red cabbage, core removed, thinly sliced
2 carrots, grated
1 cup flat-leaf parsley leaves, roughly chopped
¼ cup whole-egg mayonnaise
1 tablespoon sesame seeds

1. Preheat the oven to 190°C (170°C fan-forced). Combine the butter, spices and a good pinch of salt and rub all over the lamb shoulder. Place in a large roasting pan along with garlic, olive oil and ¼ cup water.

2. Cover tightly with foil and roast for 2½ hours. Remove the foil, baste with pan juices and cook uncovered for a further 1 hour. The meat should be very tender and falling off the bone. Set aside to rest for 10 minutes, loosely covered with foil.

3. To make the slaw, place all the ingredients into a serving bowl. Season with salt and pepper and mix well so that the mayo is evenly combined.

4. Take the lamb to the table on a large board. Pull off chunks and serve with the slaw, and flatbreads for wrapping.

Serves 6

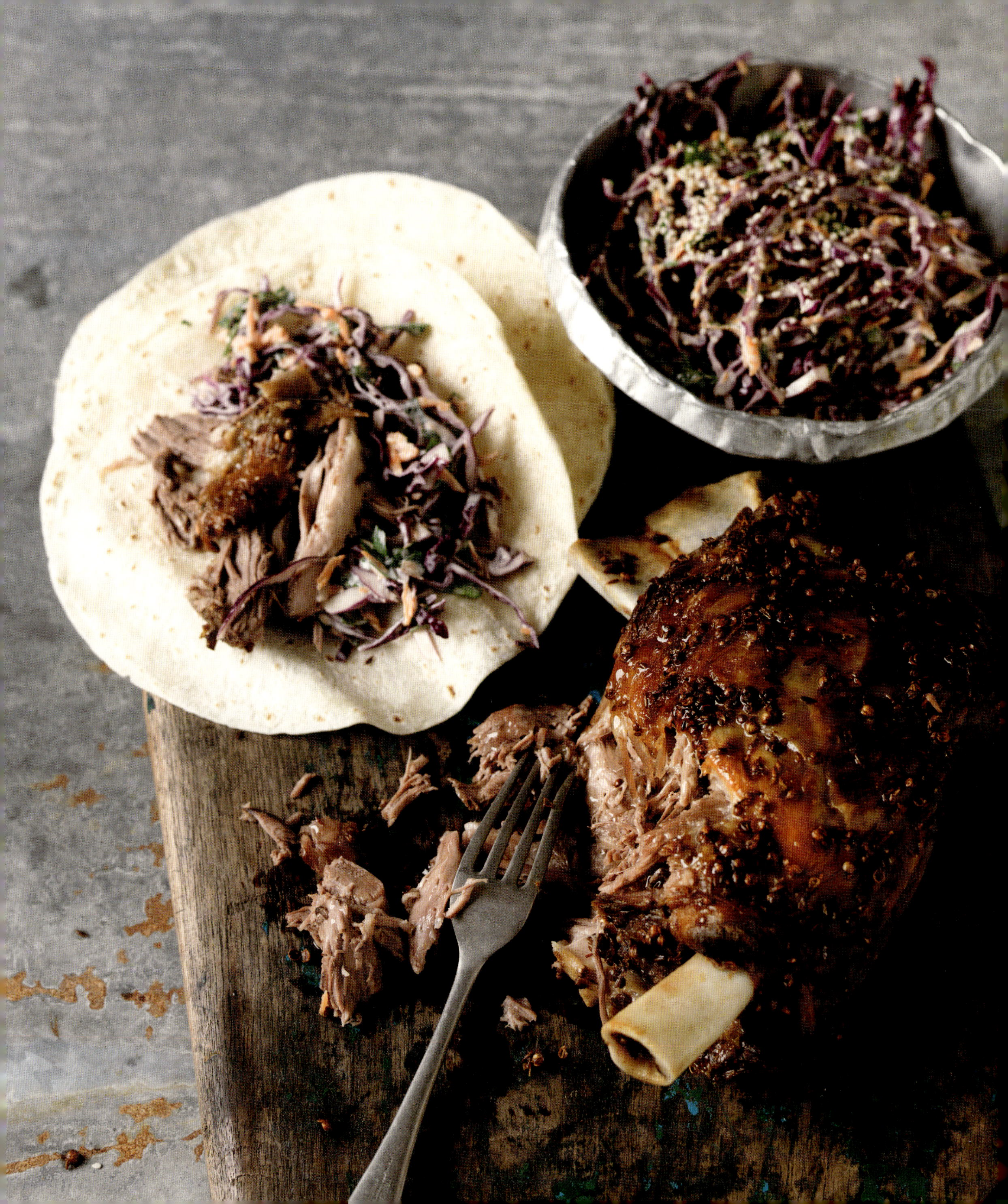

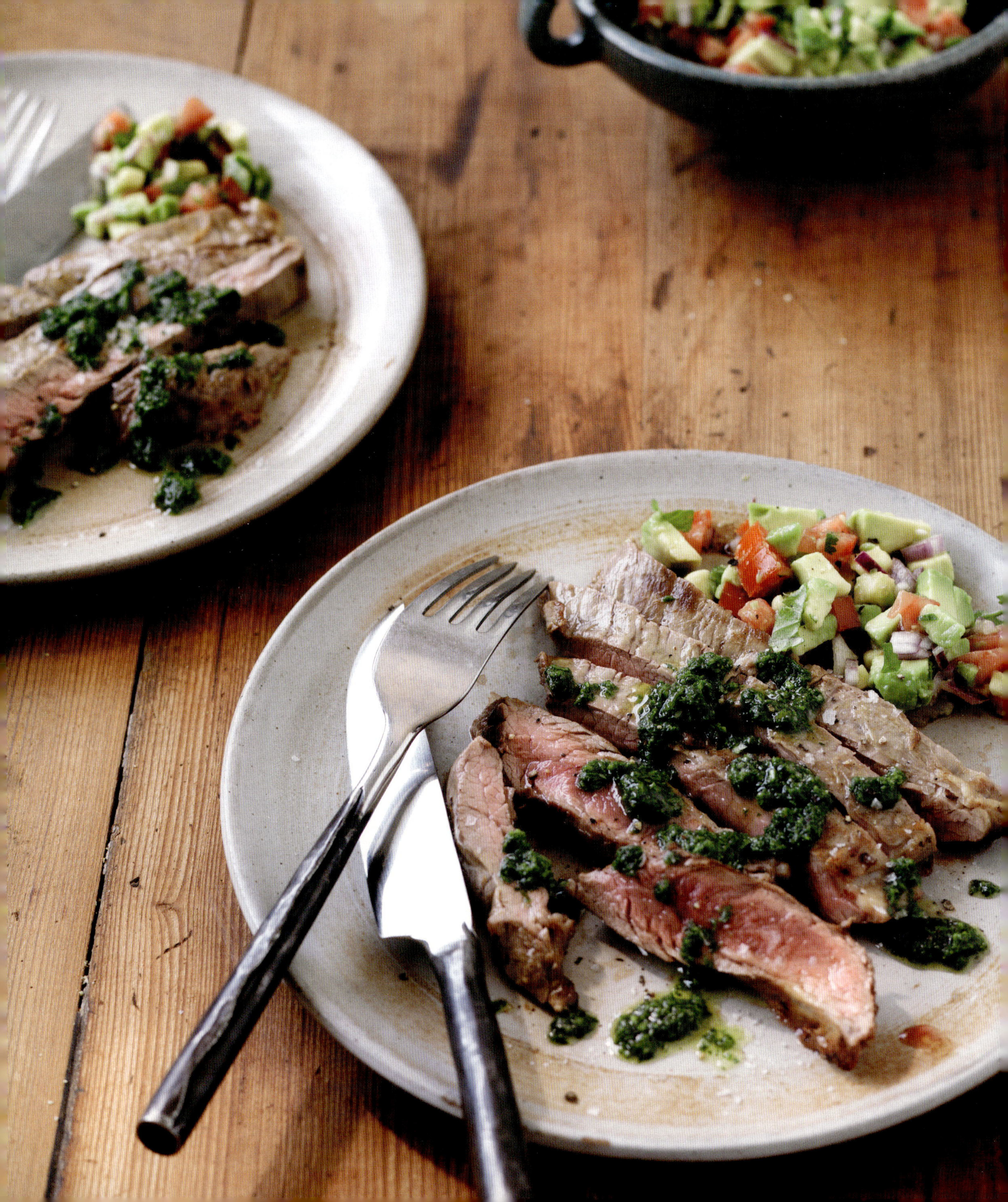

STOCKMAN'S SKIRT STEAK WITH AVO SALSA AND CHIMICHURRI

500g piece skirt steak

1 garlic clove

2 tablespoons olive or macadamia oil

2 rosemary sprigs

3 thyme sprigs

CHIMICHURRI

1 bunch flat-leaf parsley, leaves picked

1 bunch coriander, leaves picked

200ml olive oil

2 garlic cloves

finely grated zest and juice of 1 lemon

AVO SALSA

juice of ½ lemon

1 red onion, diced

1 tomato, diced

1 cucumber, diced

1 avocado, mashed

3 coriander stalks with leaves, finely chopped

1. For the chimichurri, put all the ingredients into a mortar and pestle or food processor and grind to a paste.

2. For the avo salsa, squeeze the lemon juice over the onion in a bowl and stand for 20 minutes. Mix in the remaining ingredients and set aside.

3. Season both sides of the steak with salt and stand at room temperature for 15–20 minutes. This means the steak doesn't hit the BBQ when it is cold, and helps to create a great crust.

4. Use a mortar and pestle to crush the garlic with a pinch of salt and pepper. Mix into the oil. Tie the rosemary and thyme sprigs together with string. Place the tips into the mortar and crush with the pestle to release flavour into the oil. Set the herbs aside.

5. Preheat a BBQ grill plate over high heat and get it really hot. Using the herbs as a brush, dip into the garlic oil and slather over the steak.

6. Cook the steak for 3–5 minutes, turning every 15 seconds or so, continually brushing with the oil. The cooking time will vary depending on the thickness and fat content of the steak. Take off the heat and cover with foil to rest for 5 minutes. This will keep in all the juices and all the flavour.

7. Slice the steak to your desired thickness and serve with the chimichurri and avo salsa.

Serves 4

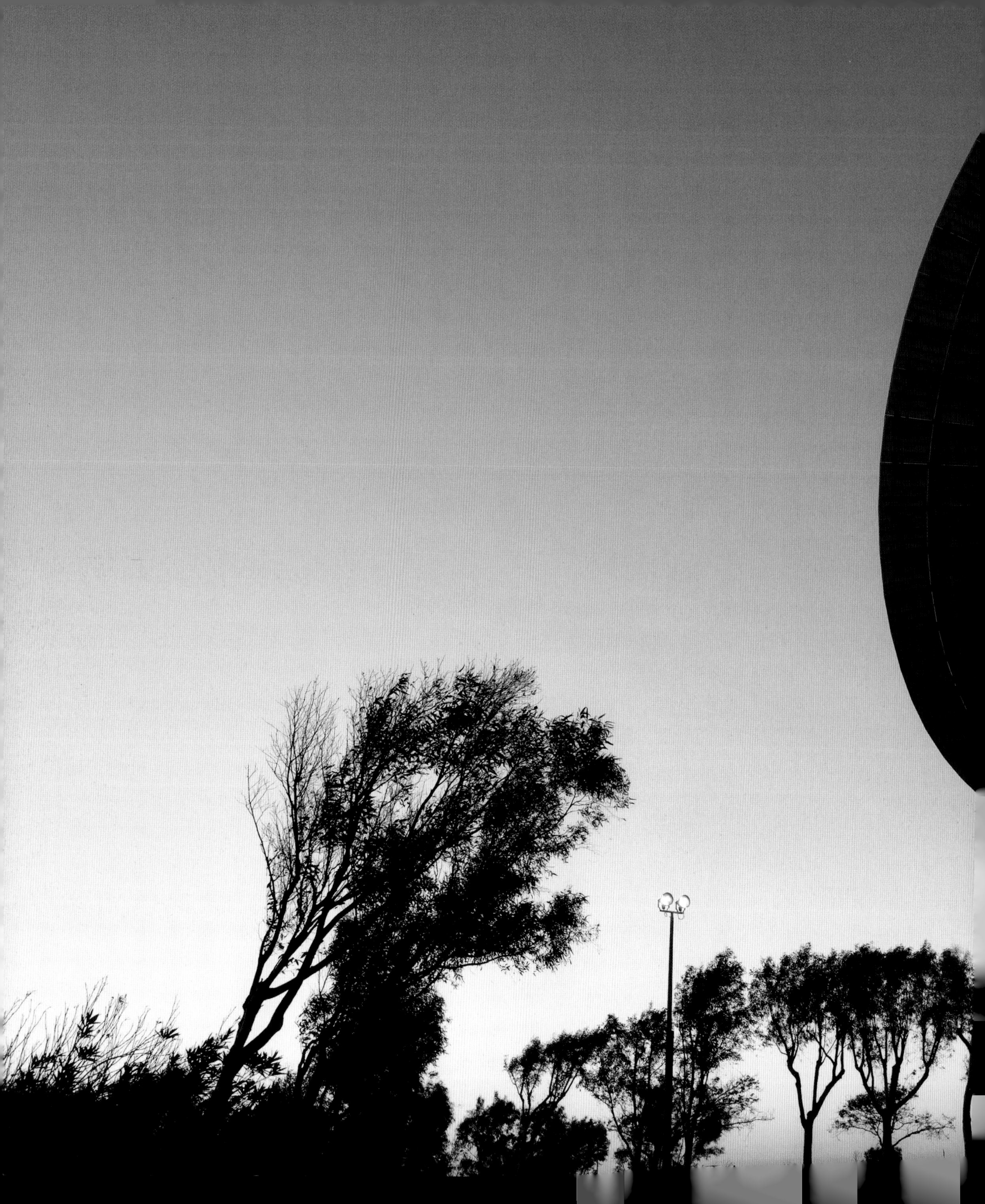

Carnarvon

Carnarvon is a beautiful coastal town, one of the many fruit bowls around this area that are fed by the Gascoyne River. The dry, semi-tropical climate makes it perfect for growing fresh produce and there are many thriving food businesses, plantations and farms that we were lucky to discover.

The first thing I want to say about Carnarvon is that the name is hard to say. Dan and I both struggled with it, but after hanging with the locals we had it down pat!

Our first stop was Morel's Orchard where we met Jean and Doris Morel. They are originally from the Seychelles and are famous locally for their beautiful fruit and vegetables. Our favourite – and something neither of us had never tasted before – was the black sopote fruit. I'm not much of a fruit lover, but this was pretty cool, with a chocolate-like taste (which I definitely do love!), and a mushy soft texture. Another highlight was the frozen mango ice cream. This part of Australia is bloody hot, so anything cool is like a dream, and the little popsicles we ate were a refreshing treat. All mango, nothing added, just puréed, frozen – and dipped in chocolate! I grabbed a whole heap of watercress from the Morels to use for my Watercress Pesto Orecchiette (page 60) and Wild Wicked Watercress Juice (page 68), and Dan took a handful for his Watercress Orange Pinenut Salad (page 64), and then we were off to Duc Nguyen's tomato plantation.

Duc is a great Aussie with a fun sense of humour and a wicked laugh. His rows and rows of tomatoes show us how hard work can create something special – he produces 630 tonnes each year from 90,000 plants. He came to Perth from Vietnam with his family as refugees on a tiny boat through South-East Asia in 1981. They settled in Carnarvon in 1990 and made a life for themselves here, with his dad starting up the business from scratch. Stories like these are what make Australia special. Our multiculturalism means we have a diversity of people, beliefs, cultures and languages that I think sets us apart from many other countries around the world.

Duc insisted on inviting the whole crew (10 of us in total) the birthday party of his friend's daughter, so that night we ended up at the most extravagant party for a toddler I have ever seen! Two long tables seating at least 30 people each were set up in the back garage, men on one side and women on the other. Each one was laden with vibrant, colourful and aromatic food. We shared traditional Vietnamese dishes, had a few beers and celebrated the second birthday of a girl we had never met. It was one of those extraordinary moments you have when meeting great people on the road.

The next day the food didn't stop coming. We were invited to an umu, which is a Tongan style of cooking where the food is baked in the ground on hot rocks and then covered with leaves, blankets and sand. We drove Gigi out to the river where the festivities were in full swing – the fire was raging, the pig was spinning on a spit, and our new Tongan friends were cooking and preparing the meal, with the men looking after the fire and the pig, and the women preparing the food to go into the umu.

Everyone was welcoming and friendly and we were made immediately to feel part of the community. They insisted on Dan and me eating first and we chose pieces of roast pig and the umu itself, which included a homely corned beef with a classic cream sauce and onions, plus prawns, taro, sweet potato and fish. All washed down with the sweetest fruit coconut punch ever! After a good time eating and chatting, it was time to work off some of our lunch with a little sing-a-long and a dance for Dan 'Rubber Hips' Churchill (I was happy to accompany the percussion with a few choice claps!). Again, another warm example of multicultural Australia.

HQ

Sampling the wares at Morel's orchard

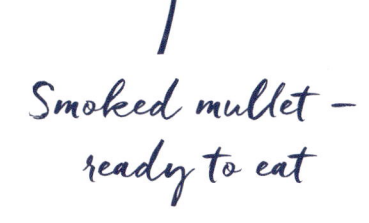

Working off lunch, Tongan-style!

Smoked mullet – ready to eat

FISH PIE (HQ)

Even though we were in super hot Carnarvon, I couldn't help thinking up a dish that would be perfect for those nights when you want to get all warm and cosy with a hearty meal! The peas, dill and lemon make this pie taste fresh and vibrant while still giving you that welcome comfort.

2 chorizo sausages, roughly chopped

2 potatoes, cut into 1.5cm chunks

1 onion, diced

2 garlic cloves, crushed

1 medium fennel bulb, thinly sliced

500g white fish fillets, skin and bones removed, chopped

1–2 sheets frozen puff pastry, just thawed

1 egg, lightly beaten

SAUCE

½ cup fish stock

½ cup cream

2 teaspoons Dijon mustard

2 tablespoons plain flour

¼ cup dill leaves, chopped

½ cup frozen peas

juice of ½ lemon

1. Preheat the oven to 200°C (180°C fan-forced). Heat a large frying pan over medium heat. Add the chorizo and potato (the chorizo will release oil for cooking) and cook for 5 minutes, or until the chorizo is lightly browned.

2. Add the onion, garlic and fennel. Cook, stirring often, until the vegetables are soft. Add the fish and fold through. Set aside.

3. Meanwhile, to make the sauce, combine the fish stock, cream and mustard in a small saucepan. Put the flour into a small bowl and add a little bit of water. Stir to a smooth paste, then add to the pan. Whisk over medium-low heat until the sauce simmers and starts to thicken. Stir in the dill, peas and lemon juice.

4. Transfer the fish mixture to a 6–7 cup capacity pie dish or shallow baking dish. Season with freshly ground black pepper, and pour the sauce over. Top with the pastry, joining and trimming as needed to cover the dish. Press around the edges to seal. Brush the pastry with the egg, and cut a small slit for steam to escape.

5. Bake for 25–30 minutes or until the pastry is puffed and golden.

Serves 4

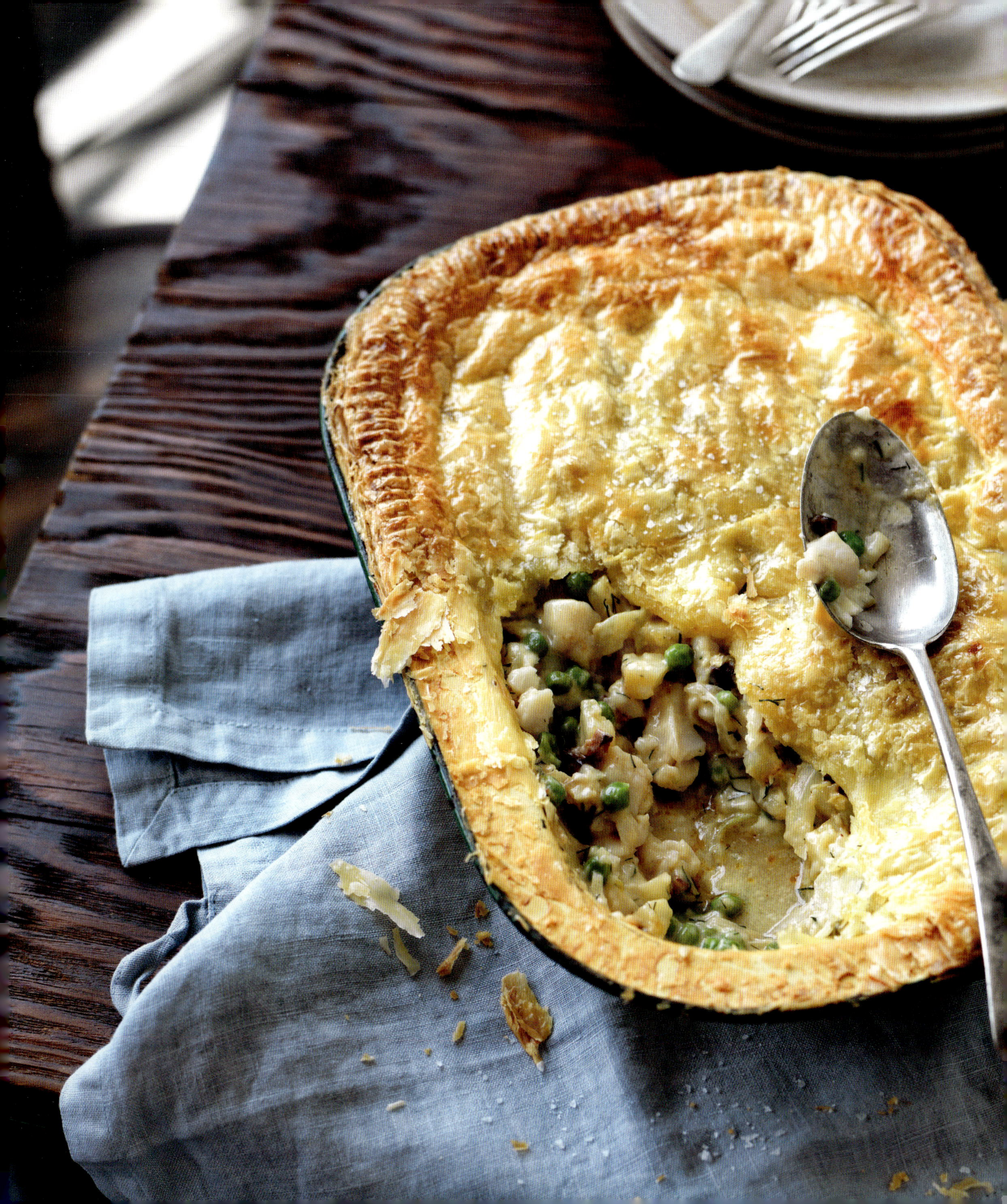

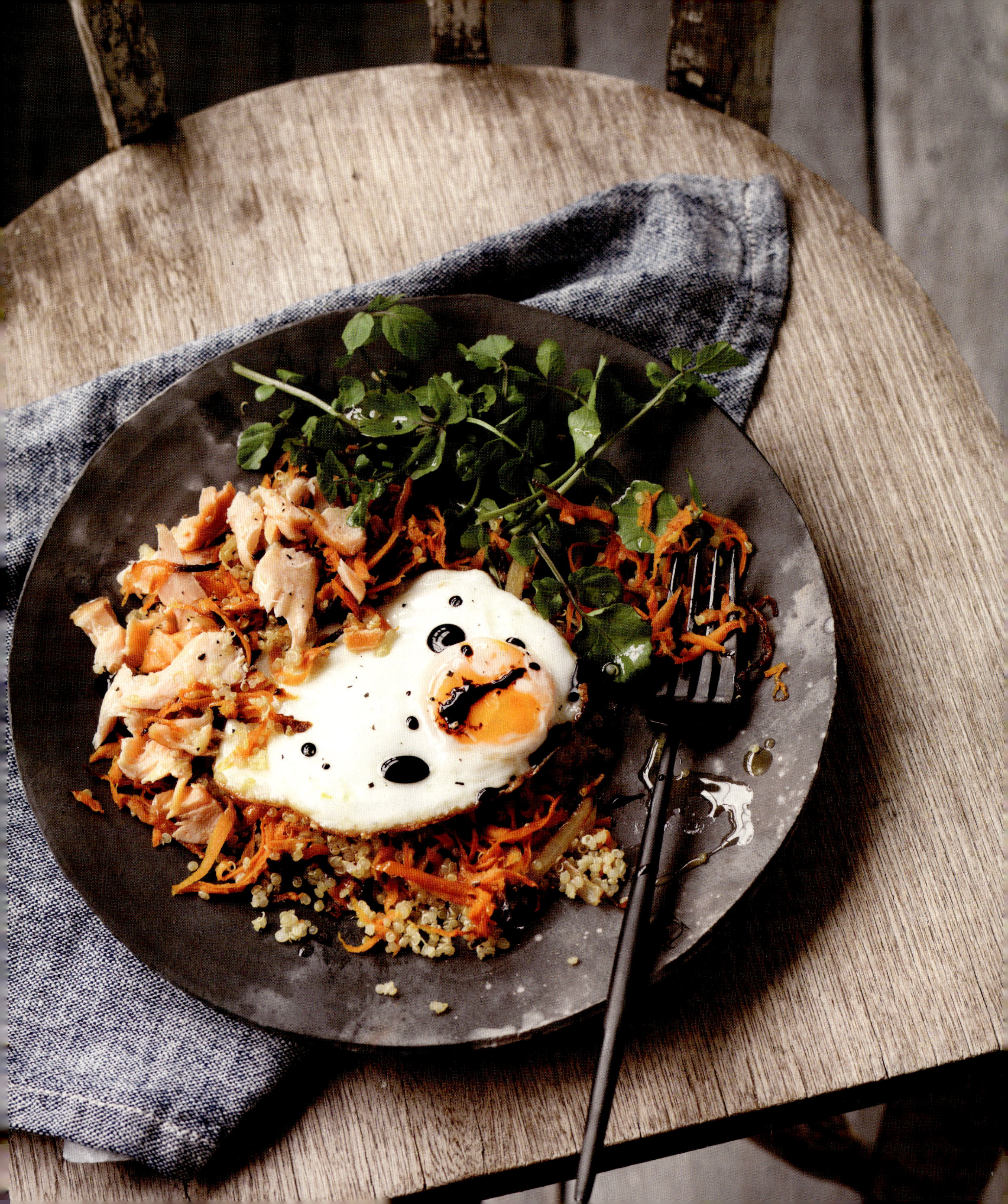

SMOKED FISH HEALTHY HASH

1 large sweet potato (about 500g), peeled and grated

2 tablespoons olive oil

1 cup quinoa, rinsed

knob of butter

1 onion, sliced

4 eggs

1 cup watercress sprigs

200g hot smoked fish (such as barramundi or salmon)

juice of ½ lemon

AGRODOLCE
2 cups balsamic vinegar

¼ cup honey

1. Preheat the oven to 180°C (160°C fan-forced). To make the agrodolce, place the balsamic vinegar into a small saucepan over medium heat. Bring to the boil, then reduce the heat to low and add the honey. Simmer until the mixture has reduced to ⅓ of the volume. Take off the heat and set aside.

2. Put the sweet potato into a large bowl. Add 1 tablespoon of the oil and a pinch of salt and pepper. Mix well. Line a baking tray with baking paper and spread the sweet potato out evenly. Bake for about 30 minutes, rotating the tray every about 7 minutes, so it cooks evenly, until golden.

3. Combine the quinoa and 2 cups of water in a medium saucepan. Bring to the boil, then reduce the heat to low. Cook, covered, for 10–12 minutes or until quinoa becomes translucent and is light and fluffy. Set aside.

4. Melt the butter in a large frying pan over medium heat. Cook the onion for 5 minutes or until golden brown, then carefully fold through the sweet potato, quinoa and 1 tablespoon of the agrodolce. Heat the remaining oil in another frying pan and fry the eggs sunny side up.

5. To serve, divide the quinoa mixture between 4 bowls. Top with an egg, the watercress, smoked fish and a drizzle of lemon juice and agrodolce.

Serves 4

Grating the sweet potato can be hard work, so I like to use the grating attachment on the food processor for this.

Keep leftover agrodolce to use in salad dressings or to drizzle over just about anything!

CARNARVON | 59

WATERCRESS PESTO ORECCHIETTE WITH SMOKED FISH

Dan and I sourced the smoked fish for the recipes in this chapter from the Carnarvon wharfs. The rich oily smokiness adds so much to a simple dish like this pasta. I used fresher-than-fresh watercress from the Morel's Orchard as well. Can't beat the taste of just-picked produce!

1 cup watercress leaves, roughly chopped

½ cup basil leaves, roughly chopped

50g pine nuts, toasted

⅔ cup finely grated Parmesan, plus extra to serve

2 garlic cloves, crushed

½ cup olive oil

3 teaspoons lemon juice

400g dried orecchiette

1 small smoked mullet, flaked

1. Place the watercress and basil leaves (save some small leaves for garnish), pine nuts, Parmesan, garlic, olive oil and lemon juice into a food processor and pulse until you get an almost smooth, slightly chunky pesto. You may need to add a little extra liquid here, either water or more olive oil. Season with salt and pepper. Transfer to a bowl.
2. Cook the orecchiette in a large pot of rapidly boiling salted water according to packet instructions, or until al dente.
3. Drain the pasta and toss with a generous quantity of the pesto. Serve in large pasta bowls, topped with flaked fish, extra Parmesan, watercress and basil leaves, and the remaining pesto on the side to be added to taste.

Serves 4

As an alternative to pine nuts, use walnuts, cashews or macadamias. Different nuts give the pesto a different taste and texture.

If you can't get watercress, use all basil, or replace with another soft green herb.

As an alternative to smoked mullet, use hot smoked salmon or trout.

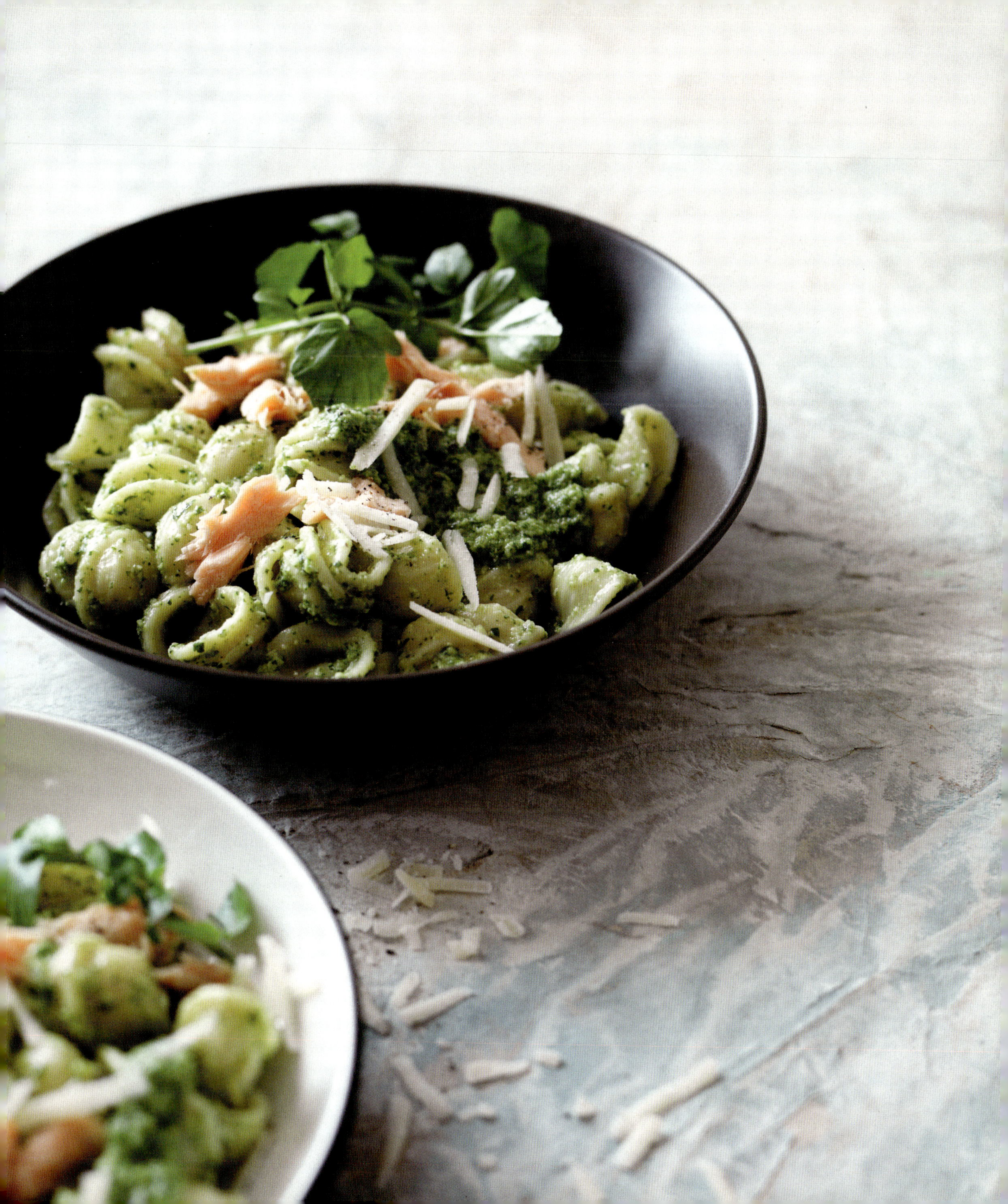

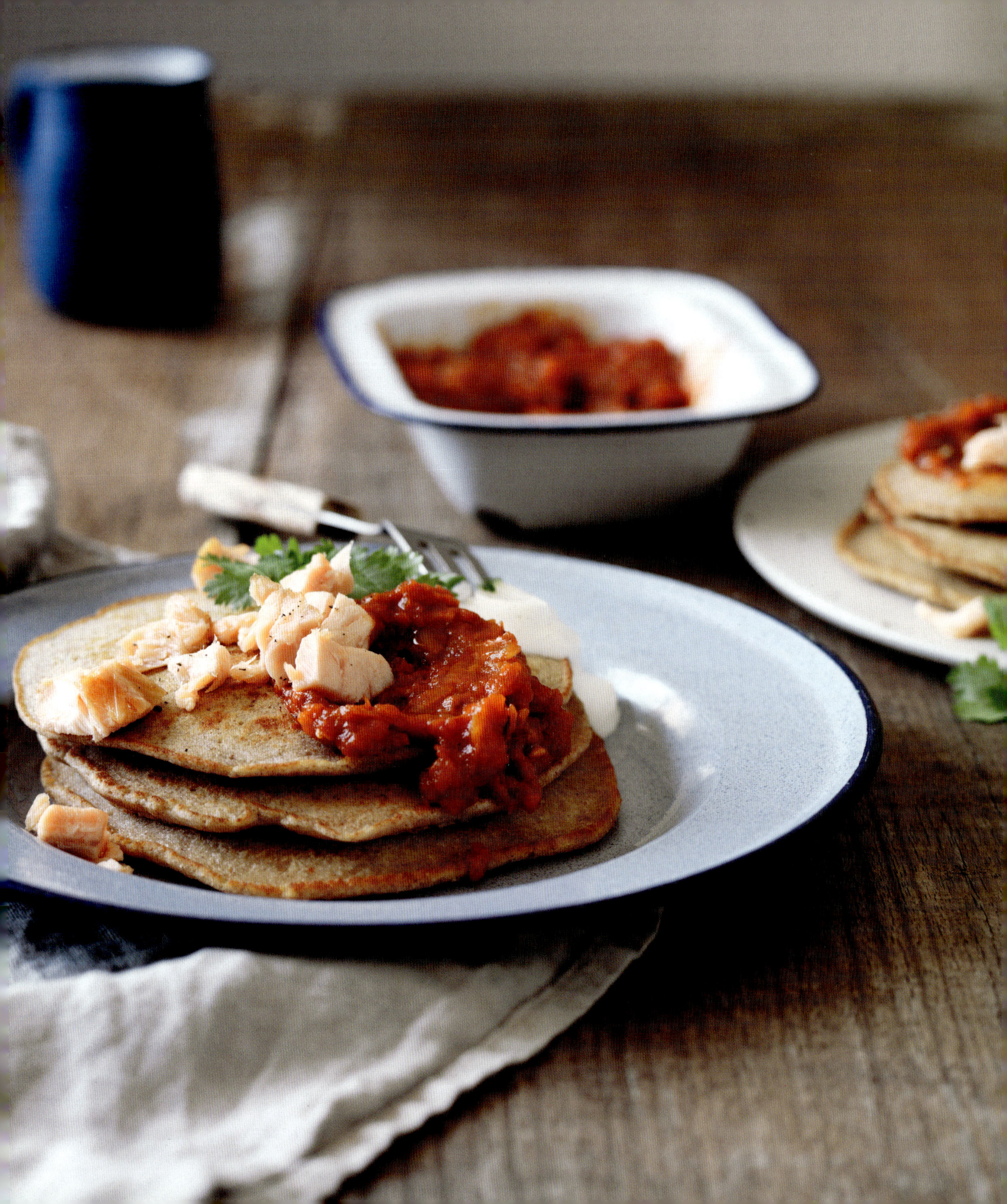

SAVOURY PANCAKES WITH SMOKED FISH AND TOMATO CHUTNEY (DC)

I do love my sweet pancakes, but these little wonders are for those of you who are keen on some savoury fluffiness to start your day. You can substitute self-raising flour for the buckwheat, but here I wanted to showcase a nutty, gluten free option.

1⅓ cups buckwheat flour
1 teaspoon gluten free baking powder (or regular is definitely fine)
1 teaspoon ground allspice
½ teaspoon chilli powder
¼ cup desiccated coconut
2 green shallots, finely sliced
2 eggs
1¾ cups milk (cow, almond or soy - up to you)
40g butter
200g hot smoked fish (such as barramundi or salmon)
natural yoghurt and coriander leaves, to serve

TOMATO CHUTNEY

6 roma tomatoes, halved
¼ cup olive oil
3 garlic cloves, crushed
3 thyme sprigs
1 onion, sliced
2 tablespoons honey
1 teaspoon dried chilli flakes
finely grated zest and juice of ½ lemon

1. To make the tomato chutney, preheat the oven to 200°C (180°C fan-forced) and line a baking tray with baking paper. Arrange the tomatoes cut side up on the tray, drizzle with 2 tablespoons of the olive oil and sprinkle with the garlic and thyme. Season with salt and pepper and bake for about 20 minutes or until super soft and jammy. Transfer to a blender and pulse until smooth (or you can use a stick blender in a pot). Heat the remaining oil in a frying pan over medium-high heat and caramelise the onion for 3–5 minutes.

2. Add the tomato mixture to the frying pan, along with the honey, chilli flakes and lemon zest. Reduce the heat to medium and cook for 10 minutes, or until reduced to a thick chutney-like spreadable consistency. Season with lemon juice and salt and pepper, if needed. Transfer to a jar, allow to cool, seal and store in the fridge.

3. Sift the flour, baking powder, allspice and chilli powder into a large mixing bowl. Season with salt and pepper, and stir in the coconut and green shallots. Whisk the eggs and milk in a jug. Gradually add to the dry mixture, whisking until combined.

4. Melt a little butter in a large frying pan on medium heat. Add ¼ cups of pancake batter to make 11cm diameter circles (you'll probably only be able to cook 2 at a time; if possible, get 2 large frying pans going at once). Cook for 1½ minutes until bubbly on top and golden underneath, then flip and cook for a further 30 seconds on the other side. Repeat with remaining batter to make 12 pancakes.

5. Serve with the tomato chutney, smoked fish, yoghurt and coriander.

Serves 4

Any leftover chutney will keep for up to 1 week in the fridge.

WATERCRESS, ORANGE AND PINE NUT SALAD ⓓⓒ

In my eyes, simplicity is always the best when it comes to food, so what's better than a mix-and-eat situation in a large bowl? The pop of colour, the silky and crunchy textures and the bright flavours are too good to miss.

½ cup pine nuts

1 orange

1 tablespoon lemon juice

¼ cup extra virgin olive oil

2 big handfuls of watercress, ends trimmed

1 Toast the pine nuts in a small dry frying pan over medium heat for 2 minutes or until aromatic and golden. Be sure to constantly shake the pan so they cook evenly.

2 Finely grate the zest from half the orange, then cut off the skin and cut the flesh into segments.

Using a mortar and pestle (or in a bowl), mash one quarter of the orange segments with the zest and lemon juice. Season with salt and pepper. Gradually whisk in the olive oil until combined.

3 Put the watercress, half the pine nuts and half the remaining orange segments into a large bowl. Drizzle in half the orange vinaigrette, then turn out onto your favourite board, bowl or serving dish. Top with the remaining orange segments and pine nuts, and drizzle with the remaining vinaigrette and a healthy touch of black pepper.

Serves 2

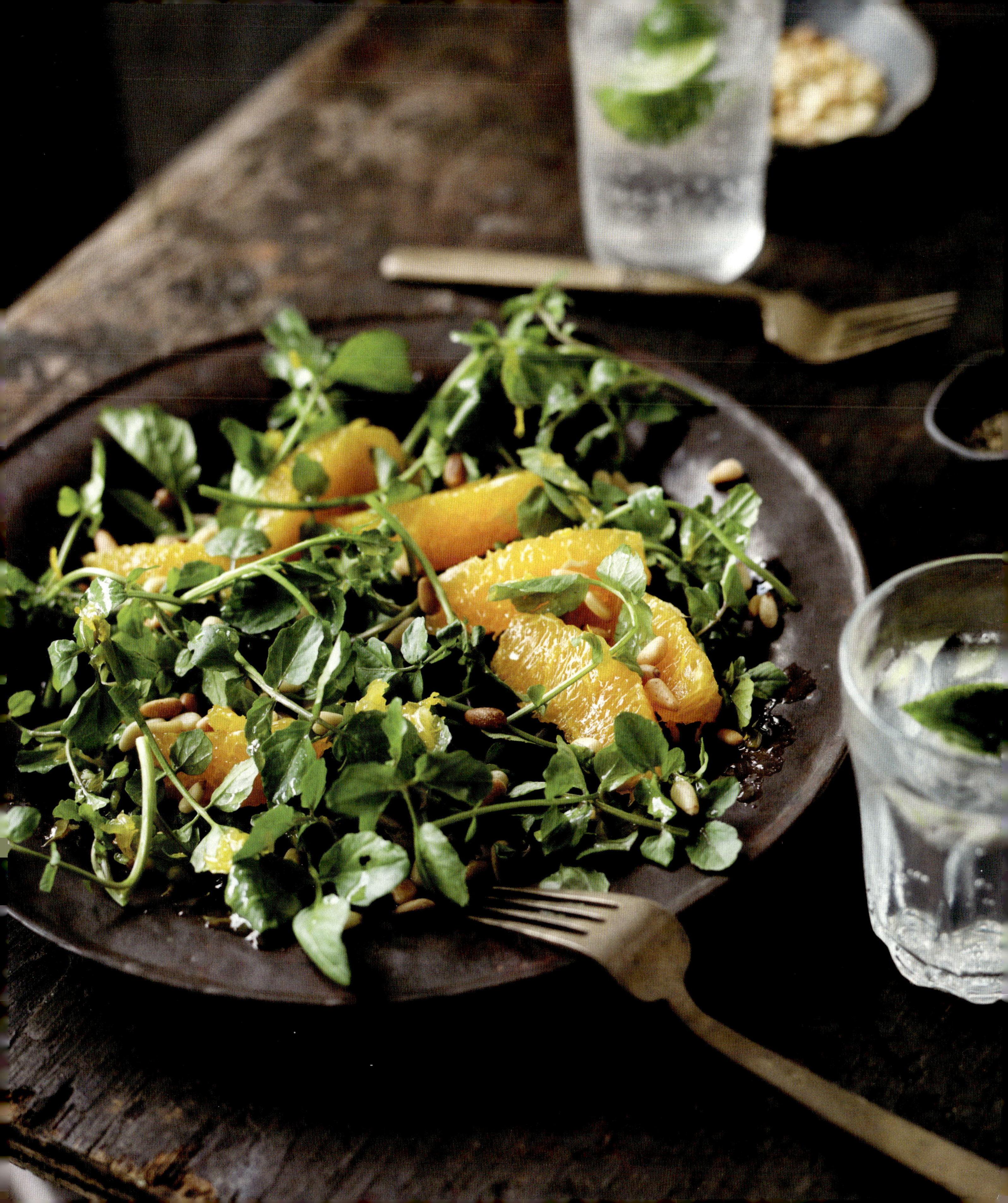

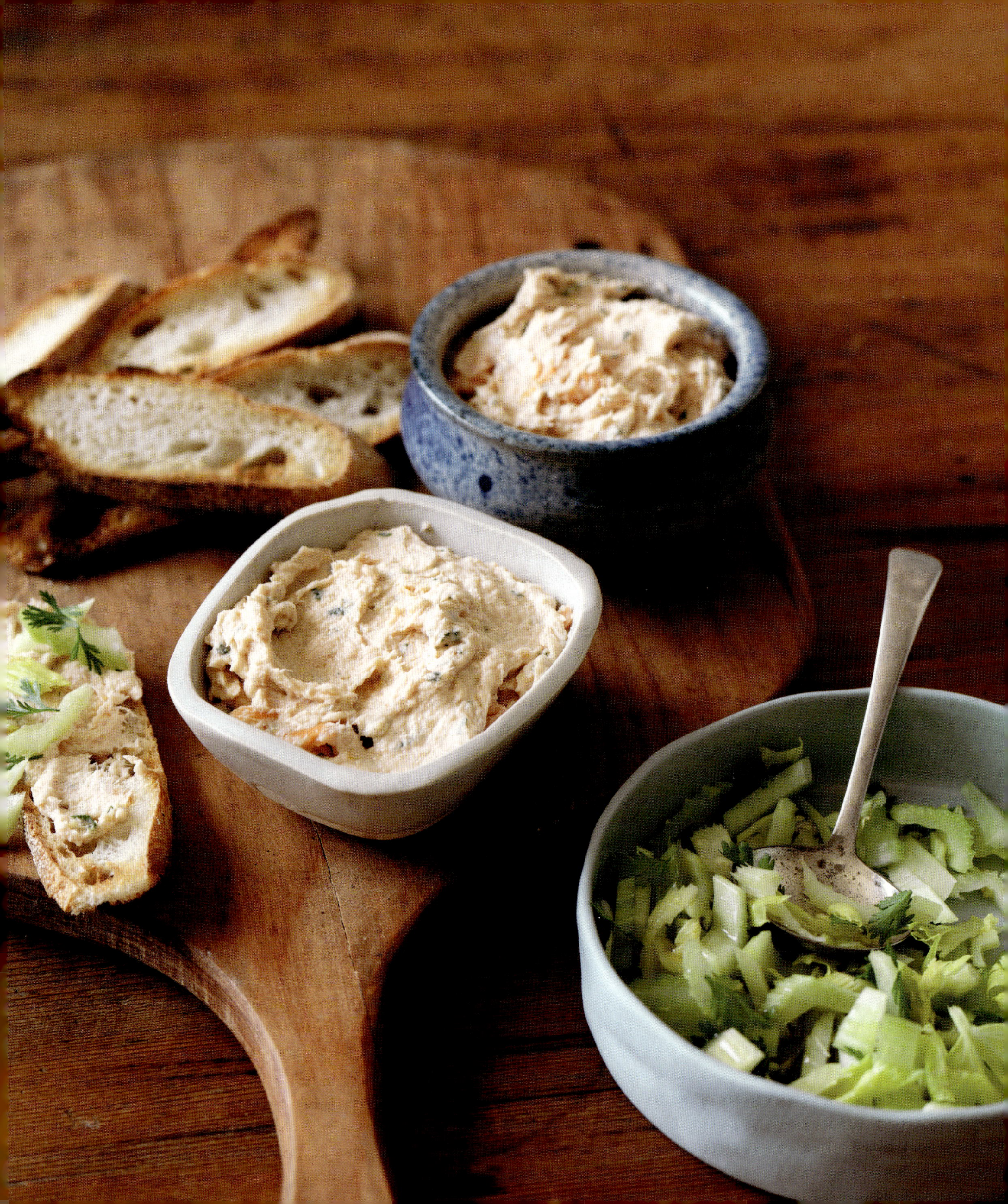

SMOKED FISH PATÉ (HQ)

500g hot smoked salmon, skin removed

150g cream cheese

100g crème fraiche

1 teaspoon finely grated lemon zest

1 teaspoon lemon juice

¼ teaspoon cayenne pepper

¼ cup dill leaves, finely chopped

¼ cup chervil leaves

¼ cup sliced celery

extra virgin olive oil and lemon juice, to dress

thin slices sourdough bread, toasted

1. Place ¾ of the fish into a food processor with the cream cheese, crème fraiche, lemon zest, lemon juice, cayenne pepper and dill. Season with salt and pepper. Pulse until smooth, then transfer to a mixing bowl.
2. Flake the remaining salmon with a fork and mix through the paté. Put into a serving bowl.
3. Combine the chervil and celery in a small bowl and dress lightly with a little oil and lemon juice. Serve the paté with the toasts and the celery salad.

Makes 3½ cups

WILD WICKED WATERCRESS JUICE (HQ)

- 1 cup watercress leaves
- 1 Granny Smith apple
- 1 large Lebanese cucumber
- 3cm knob ginger
- 2 medium carrots
- juice of 2 limes
- crushed ice, to serve

1. Process all the ingredients (apart from the ice) through a juicer, preferably cold press. Serve over crushed ice.

Serves 2

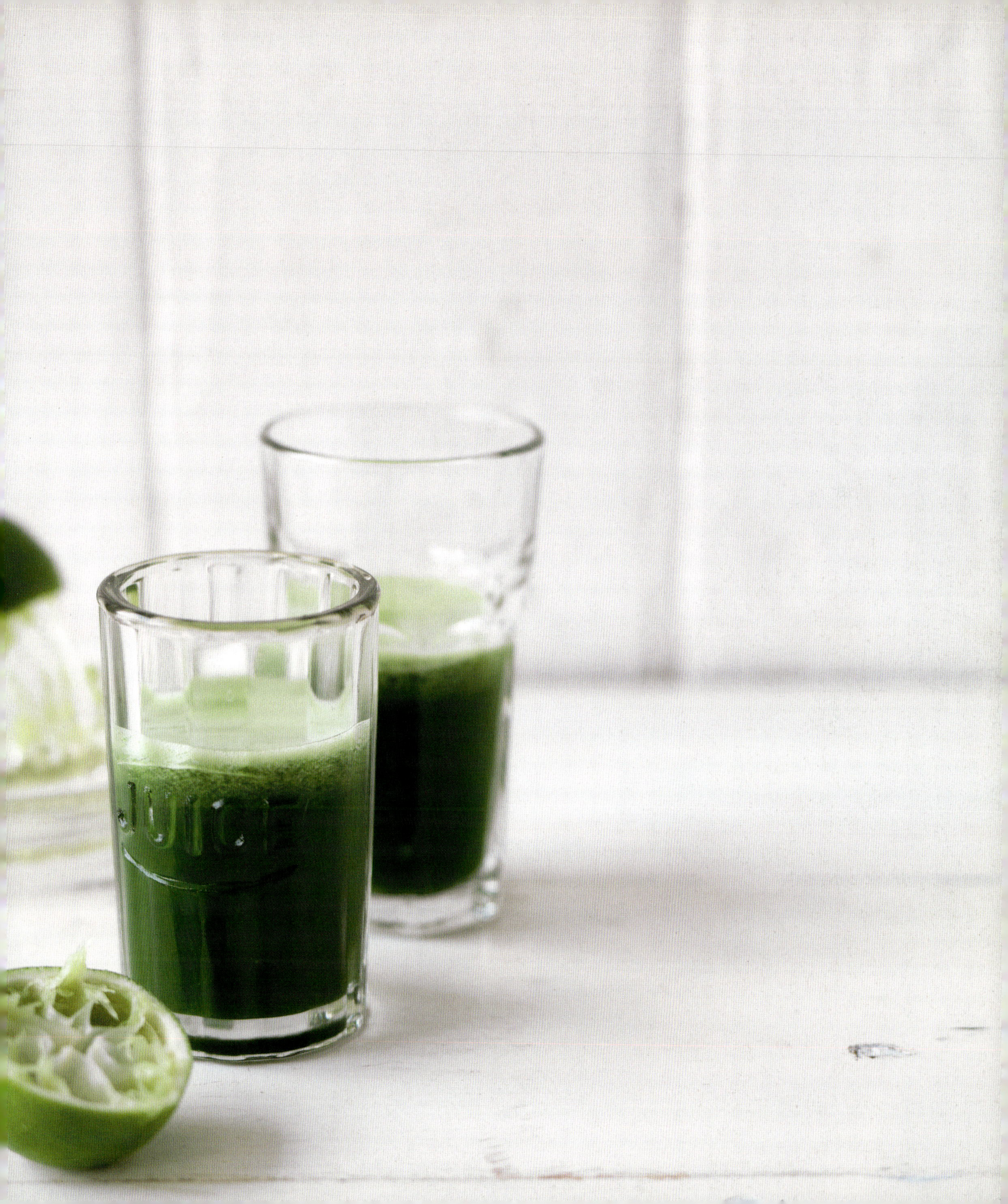
JUICE

Exmouth

Exmouth is an undiscovered treasure. If you've visited it, you'll know what I'm talking about. If you haven't, book a ticket, as it offers some of the most beautiful sights in the country.

Upon our arrival into Exmouth, HQ and I were lucky to nab a fresh catch of magnificent prawns straight from a trawler just in from the ocean. Every year, my old man goes to the supermarket two weeks before Christmas to order prawns and oysters for the big day and I have years of prawn-peeling practice behind me. So when we saw all those just-caught prawns, we had to challenge Stefan, the captain, to a peeling competition … and guess who won?! It may not have been pretty, but I was the Stephen Bradbury of peeling, not by finishing first, but by having the best execution of peeled prawns – speed not an issue!

Exmouth was one of the few spots so far where Hayden and I could get the boards wet. The stretch of the coast around Exmouth is fringed by the pristine Ningaloo Reef, which meant the waves would creep up on us slowly. Ningaloo is the only barrier reef on the western side of a continent and it's home to some 500 species of fish, whales, whale sharks, turtles, manta rays and dugongs. Amazing!

A special experience is to hang out with humpback whales as they work their way up and down the coastline on the 'humpback highway'. Quinny and I caught up with Dave and Kirsten, two locals who told us we were in for a treat as they took us out on their boat. Not only did we see turtles and dive deep into the reef on legendary underwater scooters but we had some serious hang-outs with about 25 whales as it was their migrating season.

There are 50,000 humpbacks migrating up and down the west coast of Australia to breed every year, a far greater number than the 15,000 navigating the east coast. What's interesting about humpbacks is that their spray looks like a 'V'. Rather than shooting directly up, two streams spurt out in opposite diagonals. Super cool! They migrate north up the coast as the calves have insufficient blubber to survive in the cooler waters of the south. We learned that the mothers feed and build up their fat in the cold season in Antarctica in order to have enough stored for the long migration and to nourish the calf growing inside them. Then they give birth in the warmer northern waters and the cycle repeats.

You can't approach them, but if they approach you it's as if you were picked for the basketball team by your mates at school – and didn't they want to play with us! Watching them come up and spurt their unique V-shape was mesmerising. They were no more than five metres from us. What made it all the more special was when we encountered a whale with a black tail, apparently a rare sight. To top it off, I saw a whale breach right out of the water, trying to impress a female ready for mating. We were seriously that fortunate!

Living on the east coast, H and I have seen some amazing sunrises, particularly as we are up early, checking the waves. But finishing that day at the Vlamingh Head Lighthouse, watching the sun go down, was #NextLevel spectacular. It was the kind of moment you want to share with a loved one and a glass of wine … and I had Hayden! But it was epic to enjoy the moment with such a great mate.

DC

Hanging out on the reef ↓

The prawn-peeling comp! ↑

Broome
WA
Exmouth
Geraldton
Perth

#NEXTLEVEL CHILLI CRAB

In Exmouth we were introduced to Jim Alston who runs Wilderness Island, a wildlife retreat. Whenever he goes out crab fishing he always makes a catch, so we thought we were in safe hands with him. But no joke, we walked for eight kilometres on mudflats in 40 degree heat and didn't catch a single crab. It was ridiculous! Hope you have better luck finding a crab for this seriously delicious dish.

1 large mud crab or 2 blue swimmer crabs

2 onions, roughly chopped

3 long red chillies

1 tablespoon sesame oil

2 garlic cloves, crushed

3cm knob ginger, finely grated

1 tablespoon tomato paste

400g can diced tomatoes

2 tablespoons soy sauce

1 tablespoon honey

½ cup fish stock

juice of ½ lemon

steamed jasmine rice and coriander sprigs, to serve

1. Remove the top shell of the crab along with the finger-like gills, then cut the crab through the body into quarters (or halves if using blue swimmers). Using the back of the knife, crack the claws so the flavours can penetrate while cooking.

2. Puree the onions and chillies in a small food processor until smooth.

3. Heat the oil in a wok over high heat. When it starts smoking, add the onion mixture. Cook for about 3 minutes, stirring, until the moisture is gone, then add the garlic and ginger. Cook, stirring, for 2 minutes, then add the tomato paste, tomatoes, soy sauce, honey and fish stock.

4. Bring to the boil, then add the crab. Reduce the heat to medium and cook, covered, for 8–10 minutes or until the shells change colour and the meat is cooked. Drizzle with lemon juice, and serve with rice and coriander.

Serves 2

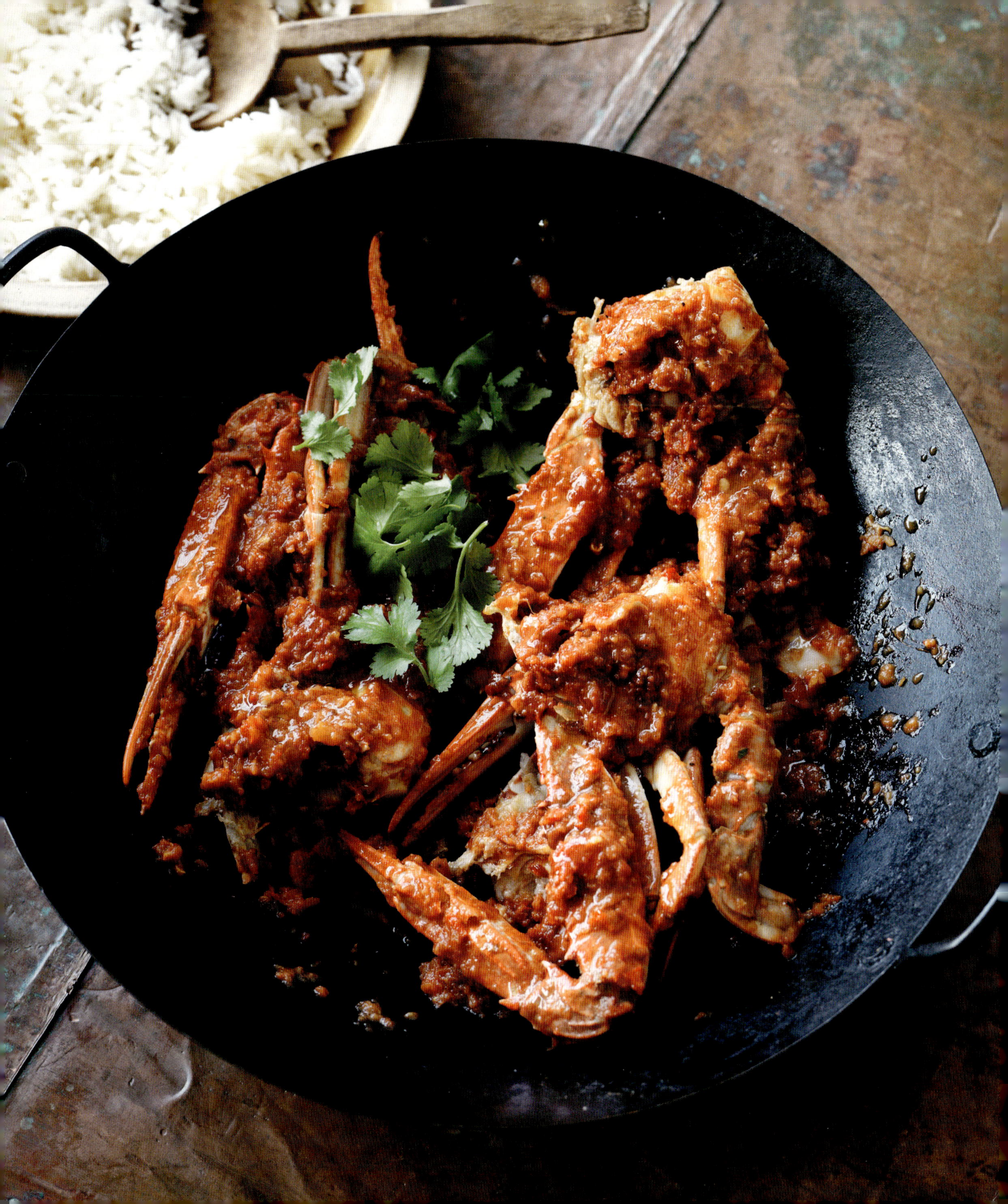

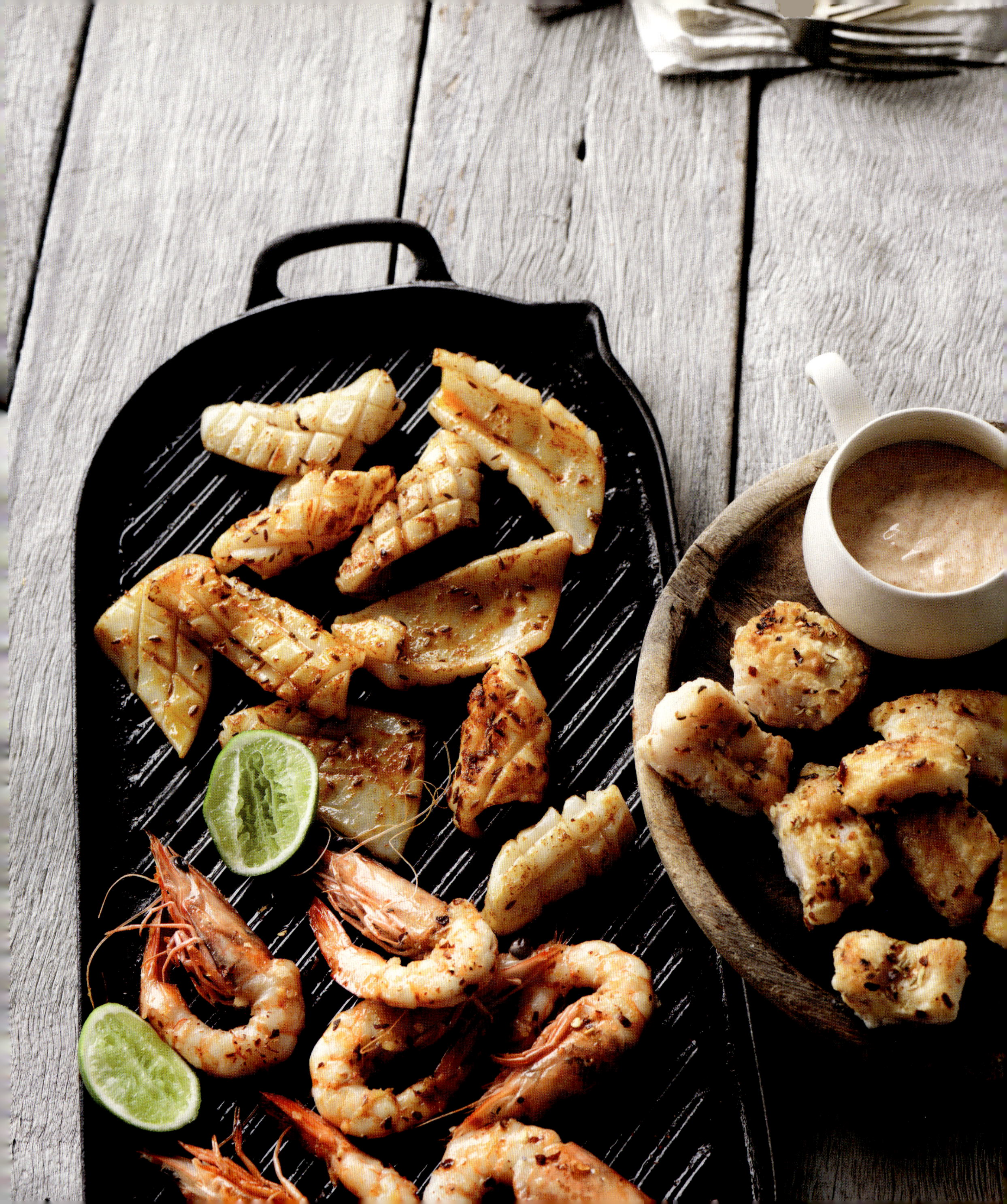

GRILLED SEAFOOD PLATTER (HQ)

SPICED YOGHURT

¾ cup natural yoghurt

1½ teaspoons smoked paprika

1 garlic clove, crushed

SNAPPER CHUNKS

2 tablespoons plain flour

1 tablespoon fennel seeds

2 teaspoons dried chilli flakes

500g snapper fillets, cut into bite-sized chunks

2 tablespoons grapeseed oil

CHILLI GARLIC PRAWNS

10 green king prawns, peeled and deveined, heads and tails left on

3 garlic cloves, crushed

½ teaspoon dried chilli flakes

2 teaspoons rice bran oil

PAPRIKA AND CUMIN SQUID

3 whole squid, cleaned, hood split and scored diagonally

1 tablespoon rice bran oil

2 teaspoons ground paprika

2 teaspoons cumin seeds

1. To make the spiced yoghurt, combine the ingredients in a small bowl. Cover and refrigerate until serving time.

2. For the snapper chunks, mix the flour, fennel seeds and chilli flakes in a bowl and season with salt. Toss the snapper in the seasoned flour. Heat the oil in a large frying pan over medium heat. Add the fish and cook for 2–3 minutes on each side, or until cooked through.

3. To make the chilli garlic prawns, preheat a BBQ grill plate or chargrill pan over medium-high heat. Combine all the ingredients in a large bowl and toss to coat. Cook the prawns, turning frequently, for about 4 minutes or until they change colour.

4. For the paprika and cumin squid, cut the squid into pieces and toss with the oil, spices and a pinch of salt. Cook on the BBQ grill plate or chargrill pan over medium-high heat, turning frequently, for about 4 minutes or until it changes colour.

5. Transfer the seafood to a board or platter and serve with the spiced yoghurt.

Serves 4

SUPER CLEAN MAHI MAHI TACOS (DC)

Living on the Northern Beaches with a bunch of mates means that our food has a hands-on approach, and build-your-own tacos are always a winner. These little babies are super clean and fresh. Lemon juice does amazing things to some ingredients, and in this recipe, the onions become naturally sweeter. Crack open the drinks and say hello to tastiness!

1 red onion, finely diced
juice of ½ lemon
2 tomatoes, deseeded and finely diced
1 Lebanese cucumber, finely diced
2 avocados
½ long red chilli, deseeded and chopped
small handful coriander leaves, roughly chopped
1 teaspoon finely grated lemon zest
2 teaspoons lemon juice, extra
2 tablespoons olive oil
450g mahi mahi or tuna, cut into 1cm thick slices
8 flour tortillas
mint and coriander leaves, to serve

1. Soak the onion in the lemon juice with a pinch of salt for a minimum of 30 minutes. Combine the tomatoes and cucumber in a bowl.
2. Use a fork to mash the avocado, chilli, coriander, zest and extra lemon juice. Set aside.
3. Heat the oil in a frying pan over high heat. Cook the mahi mahi on one side for 30 seconds (or 1 minute for tuna) until golden, and season with salt in the pan. Turn the fish over onto plate and allow the residual heat to cook the fish through.
4. Drain the excess liquid from the onion and combine with the cucumber and tomato. To serve, smear a tortilla with the avo mixture, add a spoonful of the tomato mixture and then some fish. Top with mint and coriander leaves and enjoy!

Serves 4

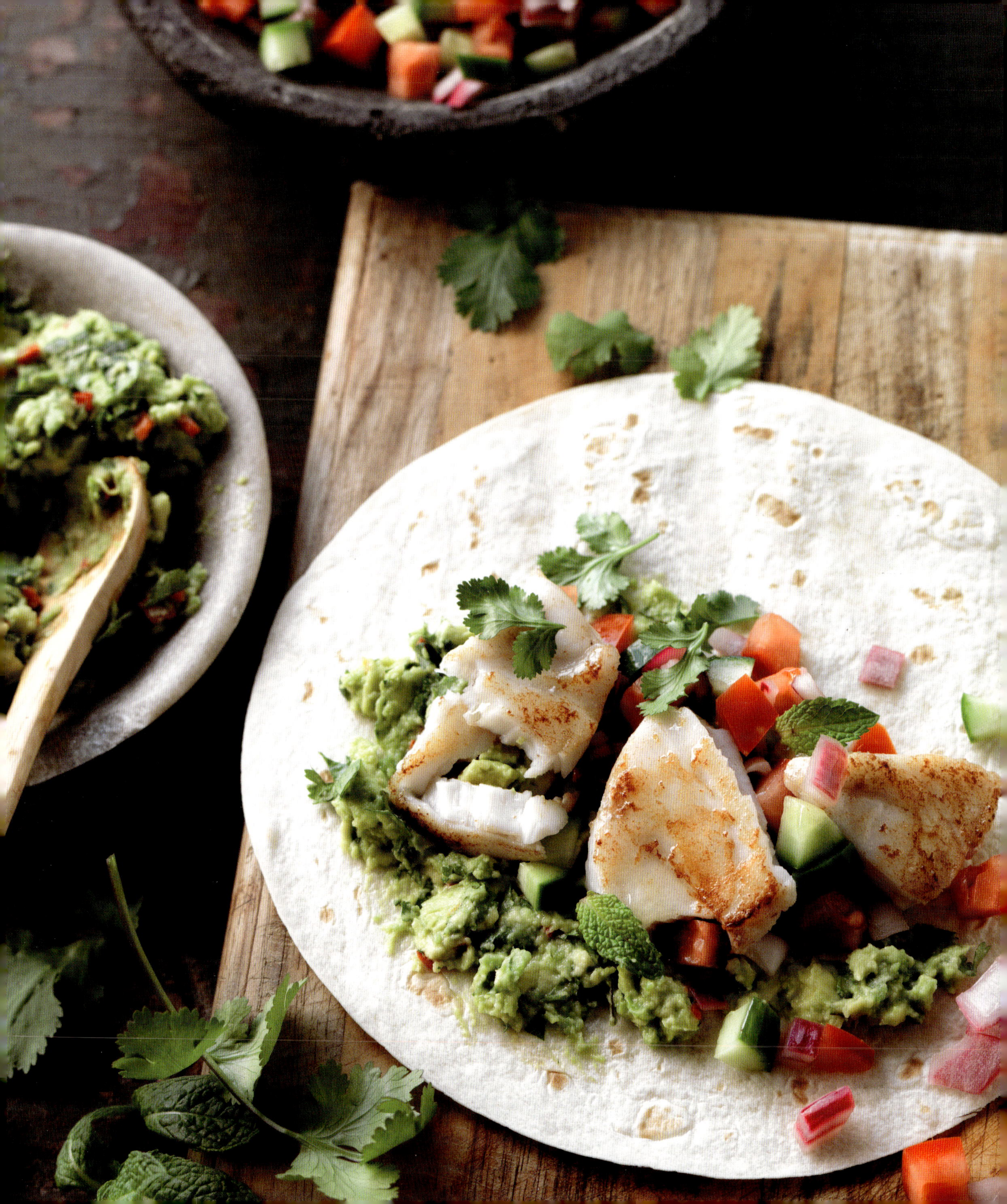

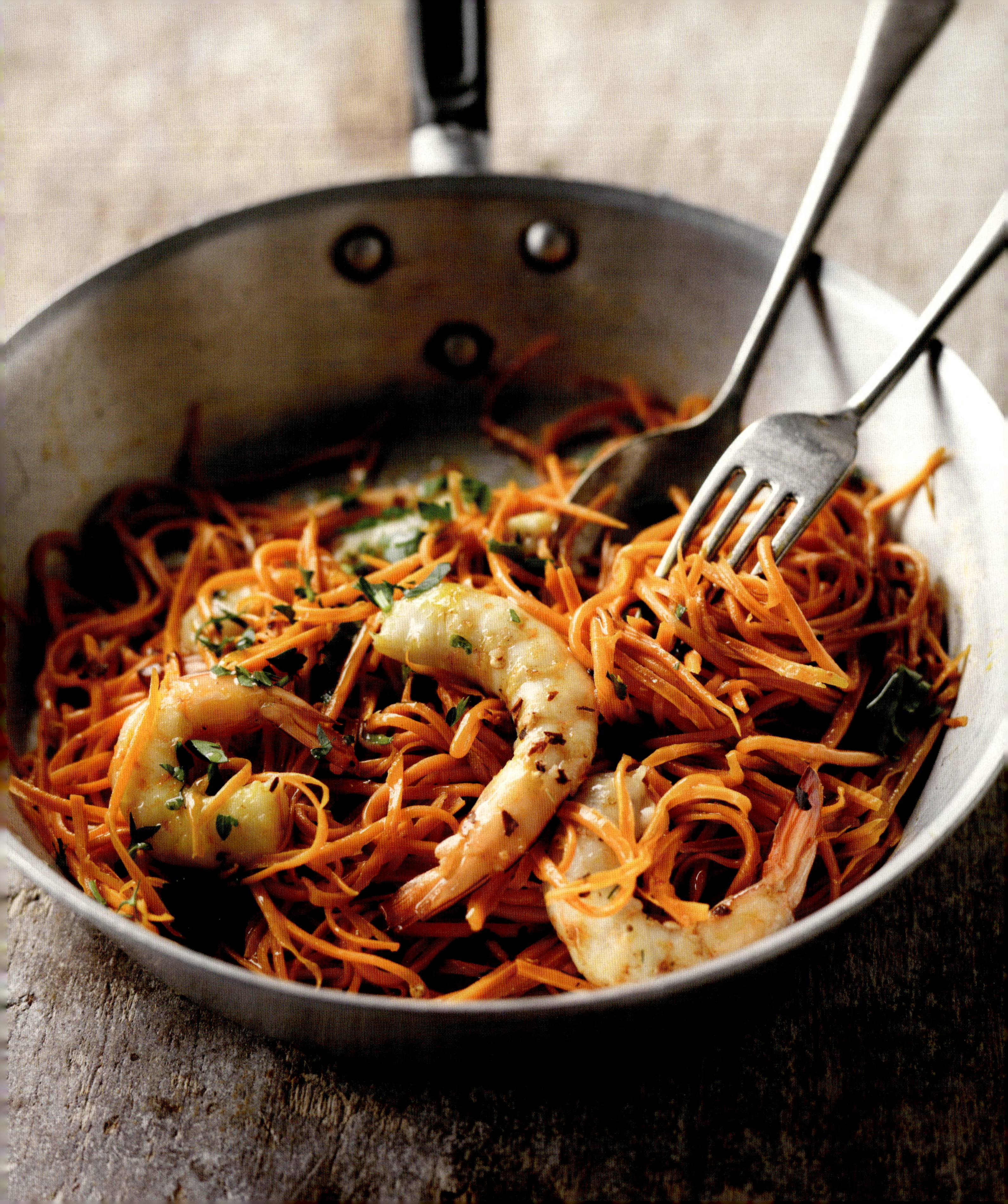

'SWAGHETTI' CHILLI PRAWN PASTA

I *love* everything about Italy, in large part because of the cuisine. This version of spaghetti bolognaise is about showcasing the versatility of the awesome sweet potato to achieve a #NextLevel flavour. It just also happens to be a gluten free, healthier version. If you prefer standard spaghetti, swap it in … otherwise, give this good-for-you number a go!

2 tablespoons olive oil

6 prawns, peeled and deveined, heads kept aside

2 garlic cloves, finely chopped

1 teaspoon dried chilli flakes

500g sweet potato peeled and coarsely grated

½ handful flat-leaf parsley, finely chopped

1 tablespoon lemon juice

1. Heat the oil in a large deep frying pan over medium-high heat and cook the prawn heads for 3–5 minutes or until they are red and the oil is aromatic. Use a slotted spoon to remove the heads and discard. Add the garlic and cook for 3–4 minutes or until golden brown.

2. Sprinkle in the chilli flakes, allowing it to add heat to the oil for a minute before adding the prawns. Slide them around to coat in the oil, and cook for 2–3 minutes or until they change colour.

3. Add the sweet potato and cook, tossing, for about 3 minutes to soften. Toss in half the parsley. Season with salt and pepper. Finish with the lemon juice, then divide between serving bowls. Top with remaining parsley and … dig in!

Serves 2

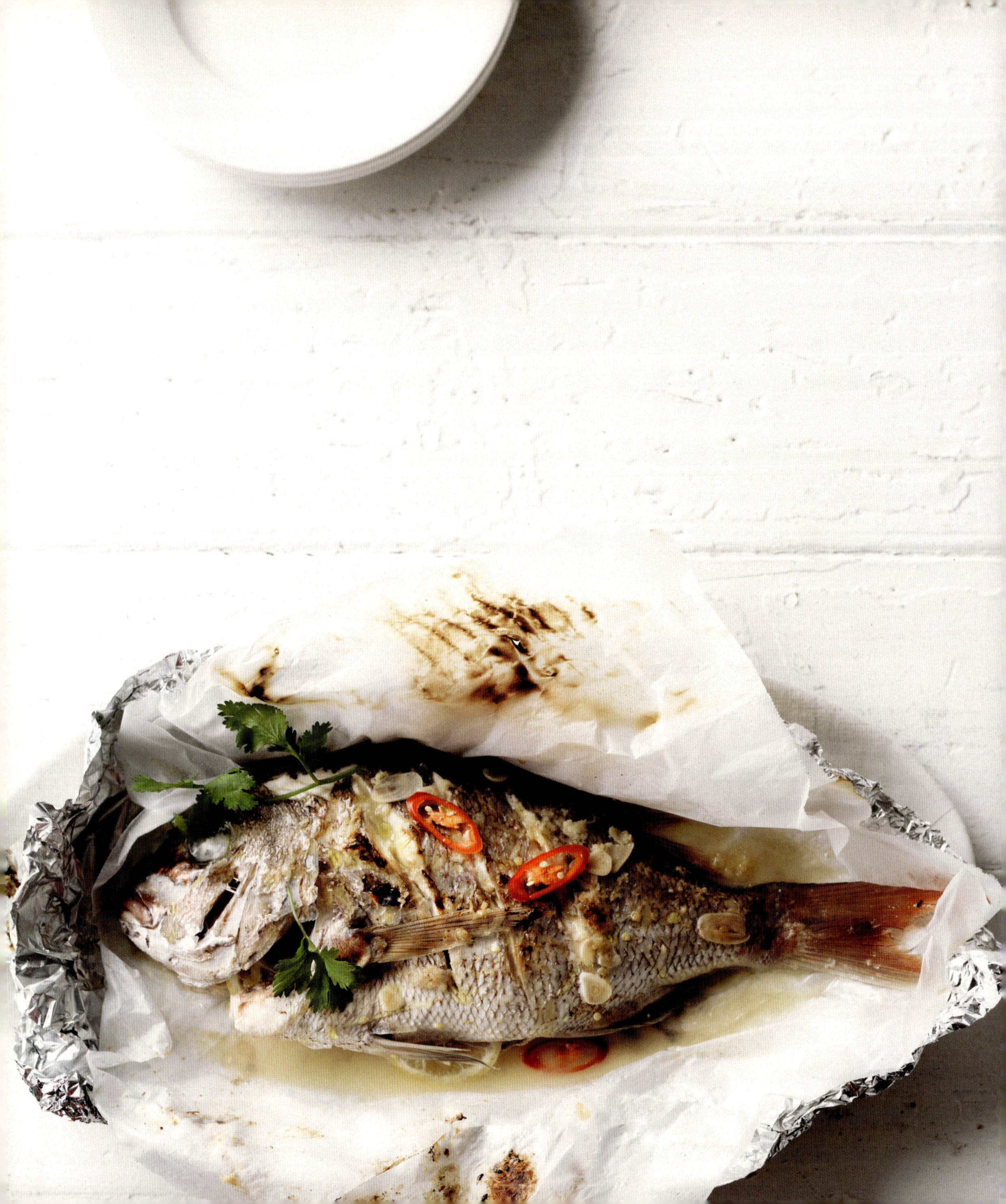

BBQ WHOLE FISH WITH GINGER, CORIANDER AND CHILLI

Exmouth is one place you don't want to leave, and this is the sort of cook-up that means your friends won't want to leave your BBQ! This recipe is all about the simplicity and beauty of fresh ingredients. Feel free to mix up the herbs and spice to give the fish your own touch.

1.5kg snapper, gutted and cleaned

2 tablespoon rice bran oil

1 lemon, sliced

1 long red chilli, sliced

3cm knob ginger, finely grated

3 garlic cloves, crushed

2 limes, cut in wedges

2 teaspoons sesame oil

½ cup coriander, leaves picked

2 long red chillies, sliced on angle

COCONUT RICE
2 cups jasmine rice

400ml coconut milk

1. Heat a BBQ over medium-high heat. Lay out a large sheet of foil and top with a large sheet of baking paper. Score the fish on both sides in the thickest part of the flesh. Place onto the paper and rub all over with the oil. Fill the cavity with the lemon slices, and then rub the chilli, ginger and garlic into the flesh of the fish. Season with salt and pepper. Wrap the fish by folding the baking paper and foil and then scrunching the foil tight to seal.

2. Cook the snapper on the BBQ for 30–35 minutes, turning over halfway through cooking. To check if it is cooked, unwrap and poke the flesh with a fork – it should flake easily.

3. Meanwhile, to make the coconut rice, combine the rice, coconut milk and 100ml water in a medium saucepan and bring to the boil. Reduce the heat and simmer uncovered for 10 minutes, stirring occasionally to prevent the rice sticking together. Once the liquid is almost all absorbed, remove from the heat, put the lid on and stand for 5 minutes to finish cooking.

4. Transfer the fish to a large platter and carefully open the foil (watch for steam). Squeeze some lime juice over, drizzle with sesame oil, and sprinkle with chilli and coriander. Serve with the rice.

Serves 6

BUTTERFLIED CRUMBED PRAWNS WITH GREEN AIOLI ⓓⓒ

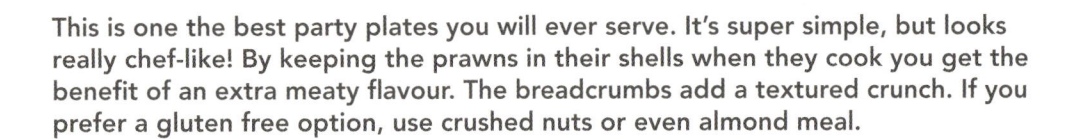

This is one the best party plates you will ever serve. It's super simple, but looks really chef-like! By keeping the prawns in their shells when they cook you get the benefit of an extra meaty flavour. The breadcrumbs add a textured crunch. If you prefer a gluten free option, use crushed nuts or even almond meal.

16 large green prawns, butterflied and deveined

80g butter, at room temperature

1 garlic clove, crushed

1 teaspoon thyme leaves

¾ cup fresh breadcrumbs

GREEN AIOLI

3 egg yolks

1 teaspoon Dijon mustard

1 large garlic clove, crushed

3 teaspoons lemon juice

⅔ cup light olive oil

small handful basil leaves, finely chopped

small handful mint leaves, finely chopped

1. To make the aioli, whisk the egg yolks, mustard, garlic and half the lemon juice in a bowl until combined. Whisking constantly, gradually add the oil in a thin stream. Make sure you add the oil very slowly or the mixture will split. Continue to whisk until all of it is combined and the mixture is thick. Season with salt and pepper and the remaining lemon juice to taste, then fold in the herbs. Cover and keep in the fridge until needed.

2. Preheat the oven to 200°C (180°C fan-forced). Line a baking tray with baking paper and spread the prawns out flesh side up. Mix the butter, garlic and thyme and season with salt and pepper. Place little dots of the butter onto the flesh of the prawns, distributing evenly.

3. Sprinkle the breadcrumbs onto the prawn flesh, then pop into the oven for 4–5 minutes or until prawns are cooked and breadcrumbs are toasted. Serve with the aioli. You will be surprised how easily the meat comes from the shell.

Serves 4 as a starter

To make fresh breadcrumbs, whizz up day-old crusty bread in a food processor.

Keep any leftover aioli in the fridge for up to 2 days.

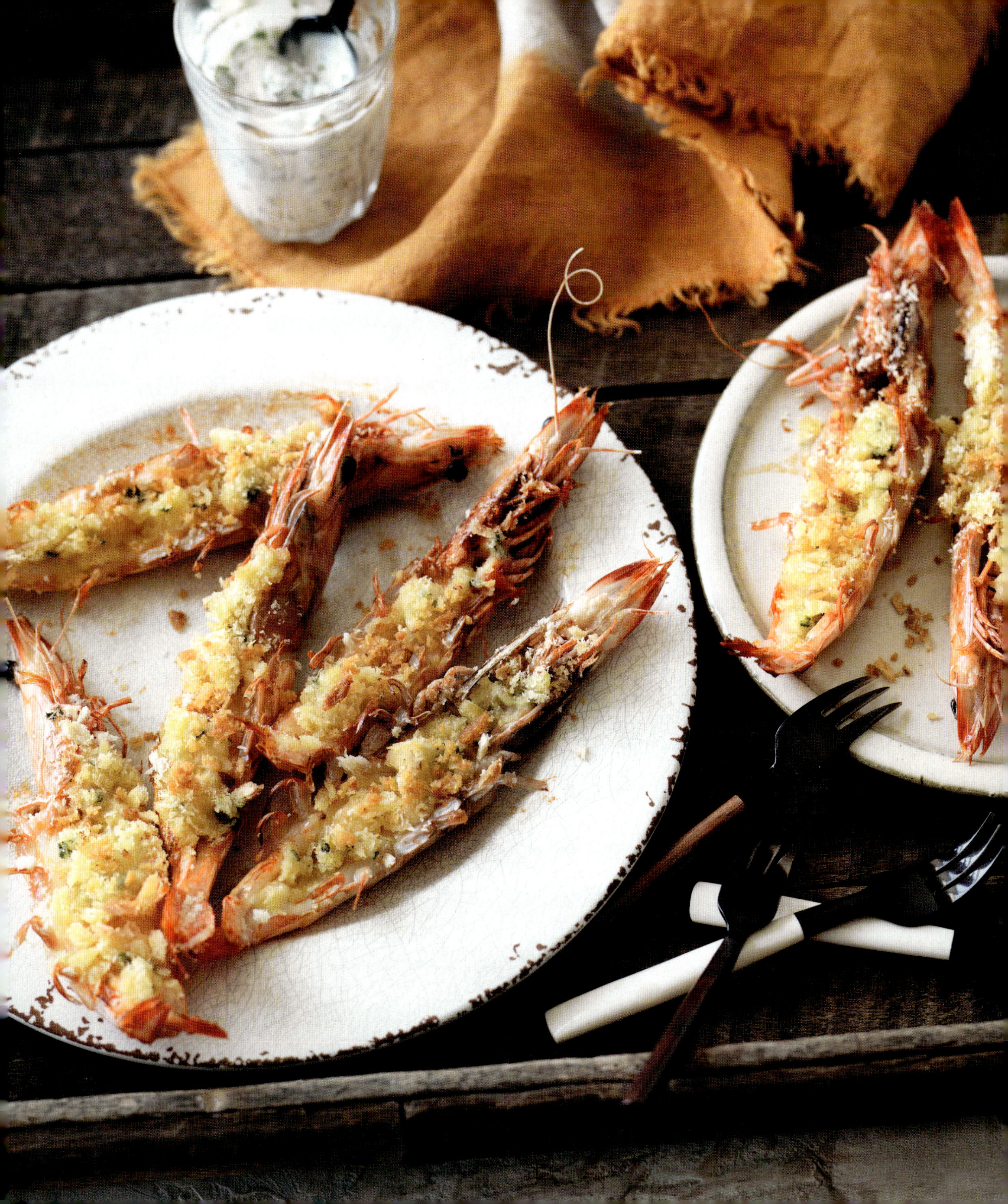

WATERMELON, CHERRY AND MINT ICE POPS (HQ)

I borrowed this amazing flavour combination from a good friend, Georgie, who has an ice pop company called Pure Pops. Make some of these this summer, and I promise you, it won't only be the little kids who will be impressed!

¾ cup caster sugar

large handful mint leaves

finely grated zest and juice of 1 lime

700g watermelon, peeled (500g flesh)

1 cup cherries, pitted

1. Combine the sugar with ¾ cup boiling water in a heatproof jug and whisk until sugar has dissolved. Add the mint and lime zest, and using a wooden spoon, gently push down to submerge the leaves in the liquid. Refrigerate for 1 hour or until completely cooled.

2. Meanwhile, process the watermelon, cherries and lime juice in a food processor until smooth. Strain through a fine sieve into a large jug, then pour the mint syrup though the sieve into the jug.

3. Pour the mixture into six ½ cup capacity ice block moulds. Cover with plastic wrap then insert an icy pole stick into the mould, through the plastic. Freeze for 5 hours or until firm.

Makes 6

If the ice block moulds won't stand upright on their own, use scrunched up aluminium foil like a nest to sit them in.

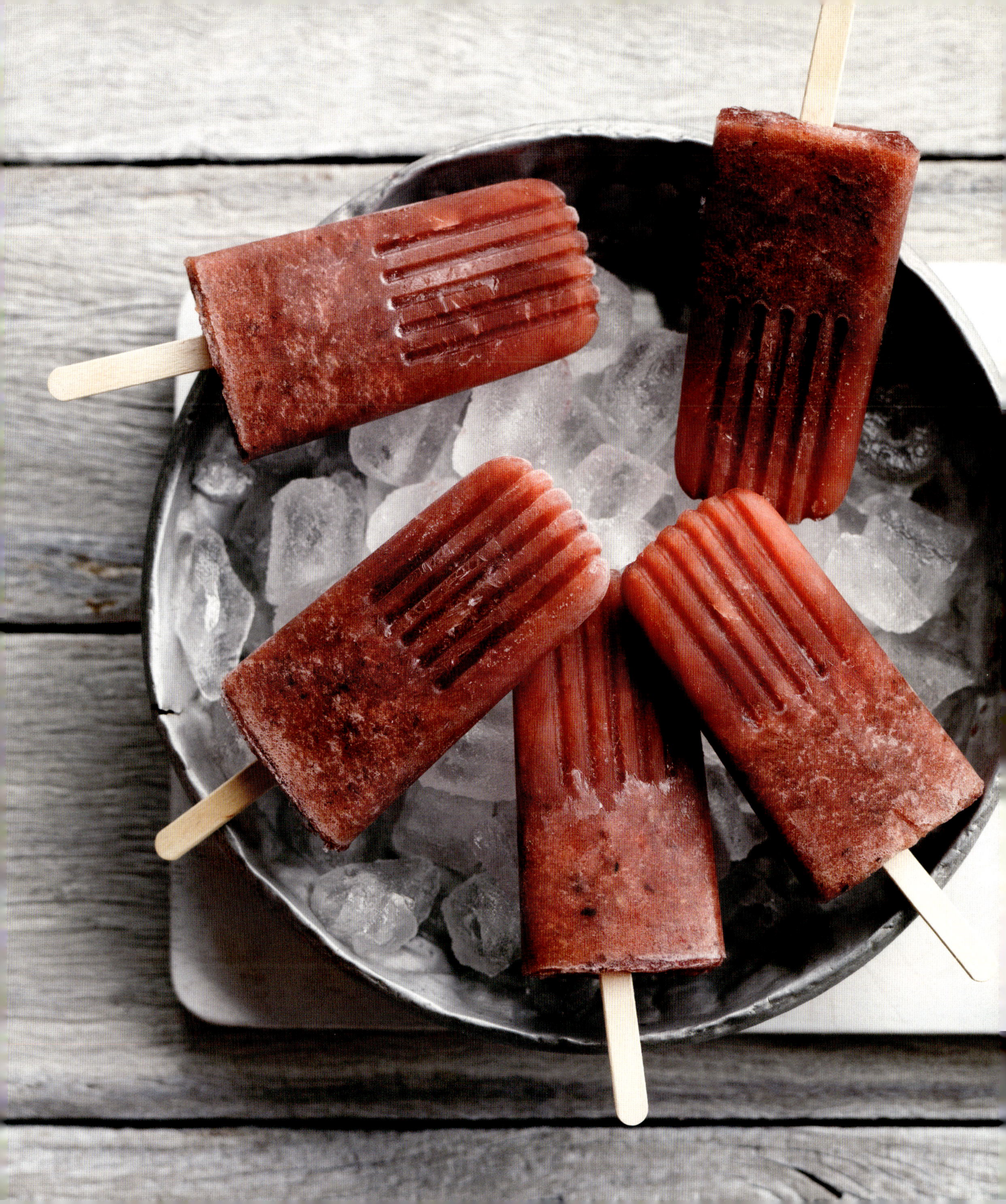

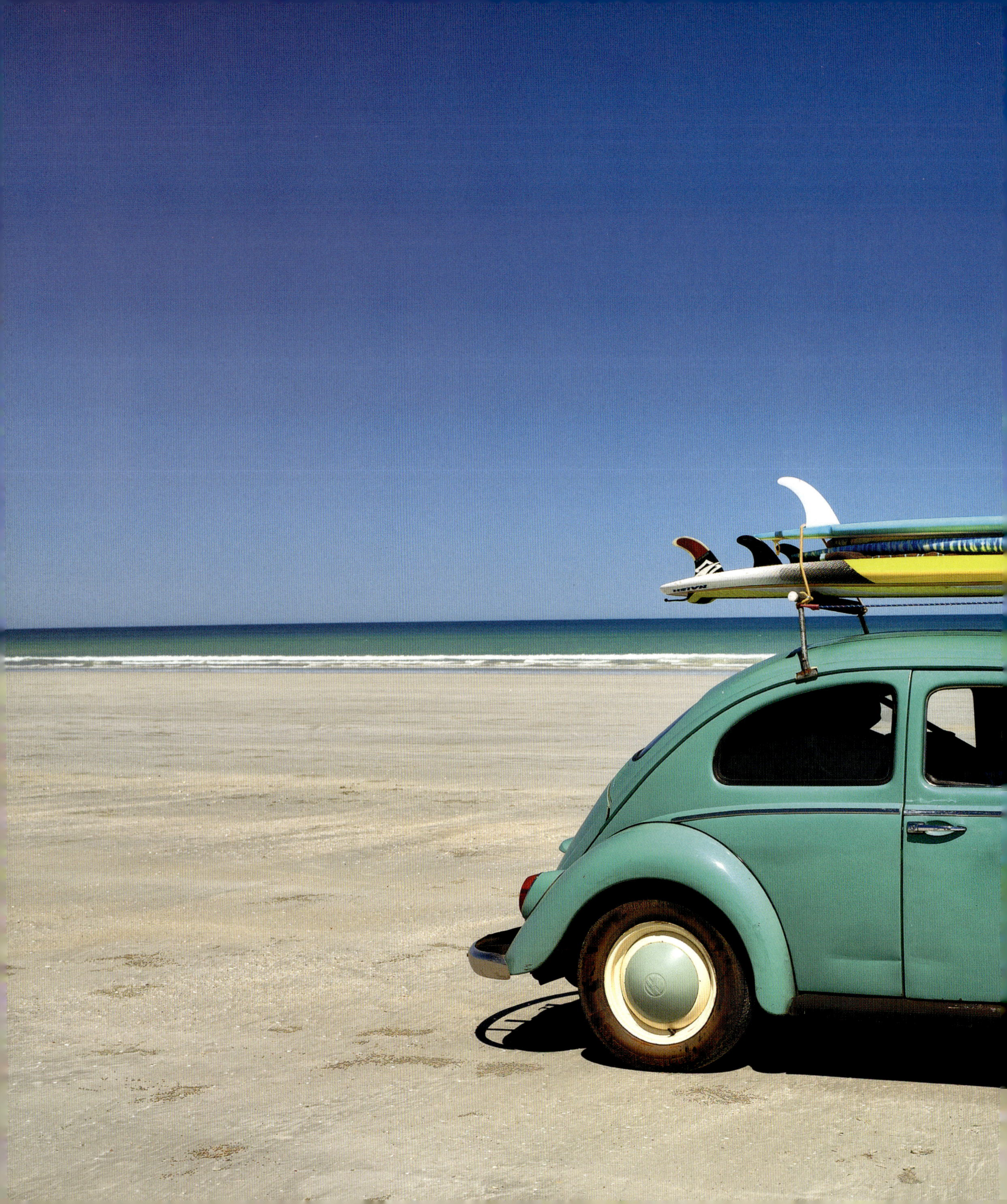

Broome

When I think of Broome, I think of blue water, white sand, pearls and camels – and that's pretty much what we got, plus much much more! What I didn't know about was the history, the culture and the mix of people who make up this fascinating Australian town.

Dan and I were desperate to hit Cable Beach first up, so it was time to see how Gigi would handle a bit of beach driving. Luckily we ran into Chris McLeod, an ex-RAAF cook, and his wife and kids who were heading out for a bit of beach fishing, so ditching the Bug we jumped in his 4-wheel drive and joined them.

Now, Dan and I are the worst people ever with a rod and reel, but there were no complaints – the sun was out, the air was warm and the water was that perfect turquoise you only ever see on postcards of tropical islands. I wrangled a little shovelnose shark, but otherwise I didn't have much luck. Fortunately, Chris had caught a really nice dhufish that morning. He showed us one of his favourite fish recipes, numus, which is like ceviche in that the flesh is sliced thinly and then cooked slightly in the acid of lemon or lime juice. Chris did this with chilli, coriander, red onion and kaffir lime leaf – super fresh, punchy flavors that Dan and I love, and are amazing to eat in the sun, straight off the beach where the fish was caught!

From ocean treats to one of the most delicious fruits of summer – the fragrant, intoxicating, sticky, sweet mango! We met up with Julie Weguelin, a local grower who is famous not only for her beautiful fruit picked straight from the tree but also the mango ice cream she makes up daily in batches from mango purée saved from the previous year's harvest. When we were in town the mangoes were still green, but they were perfect for our purposes – the delicious Green Mango Mud Crab Salad (page 95) and Green Mango Gado Gado Salad (page 100).

After a quick surf, it was time for some music. We were privileged to catch up with acclaimed musician and producer, Steve Pigram, who told us about Sun Pictures, the oldest open-air cinema in operation in Australia. It was originally an Asian emporium in Broome's old Chinatown until it became a picture theatre in 1913. Then Steve let Dan and I play along with him in a jam! Dan showed some serious skills with the ukulele. Me, I was stuck with the percussion instruments.

You can't visit Broome without a stop at one of the many pearling enterprises. We not only saw a pearl harvested straight from the shell, we also took the opportunity to whip up a quick and simple Japanese-style pearl meat dish right there on the shore (Jalepeño Ponzu Pearl Meat Ceviche on page 96).

We also had the honour of meeting a lady by the name of Pearl Hamaguchi, a beautiful person of Japanese, Chinese, Scottish and Indigenous heritage. She was happy to share her stories about the history of Broome, her Indigenous grandmother, the impact of World War Two on the Japanese people working the pearl leases, and what it was like growing up when the world was more turbulent, not just because of the war but in general for Indigenous Australians.

We completed our trip to Broome with a visit to Matso's Brewery and their latest venture, the Curry Hut, run by a couple of local Indian fellas, Hem Chandra Pande and his offsider, Vipin. They are as passionate about fresh food, local ingredients and making things by hand as Dan and me. Hem showed us how to make the most flavourful lamb kebabs I've ever eaten, and gave us a little rundown on the intricacies of the tandoor. We sat down together and shared an epic Indian feast, all washed down with Matso's famous ginger beer – and my favourite, the chilli beer!

HQ

The sun shines brightly on the seats at Sun Pictures ↓

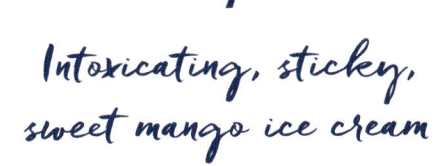

Intoxicating, sticky, sweet mango ice cream ↑

The lovely Pearl Hamaguchi ↑

PEARL MEAT SASHIMI WITH YUZU GINGER DRESSING (HQ)

Yuzu is a small citrus fruit used in Japanese and Korean cooking. It looks like a mandarin, although it can grow to be as large as a grapefruit. It is very aromatic. If it's not stocked in your local area, you can buy bottled juice from Asian supermarkets, Japanese speciality stores or online. Can't get it anywhere? Use lime juice.

300g sashimi-grade pearl meat, thinly sliced

1 teaspoon black sesame seeds, to serve, optional

micro coriander, to serve

YUZU GINGER DRESSING

2 teaspoons finely grated ginger

¼ cup light soy sauce

½ teaspoon finely grated horseradish

2 tablespoons yuzu juice

1 teaspoon caster sugar

1 teaspoon sesame oil

1. For the dressing, combine all the ingredients in a small bowl and refrigerate until serving time.
2. Arrange the pearl meat delicately on a plate, spoon over the dressing and garnish with micro coriander, and sesame seeds if you wish.

Serves 4 as a starter

If you can't get pearl meat, use a white-fleshed fish such as kingfish as we did here.

Use good quality jarred horseradish, or fresh wasabi if you have it.

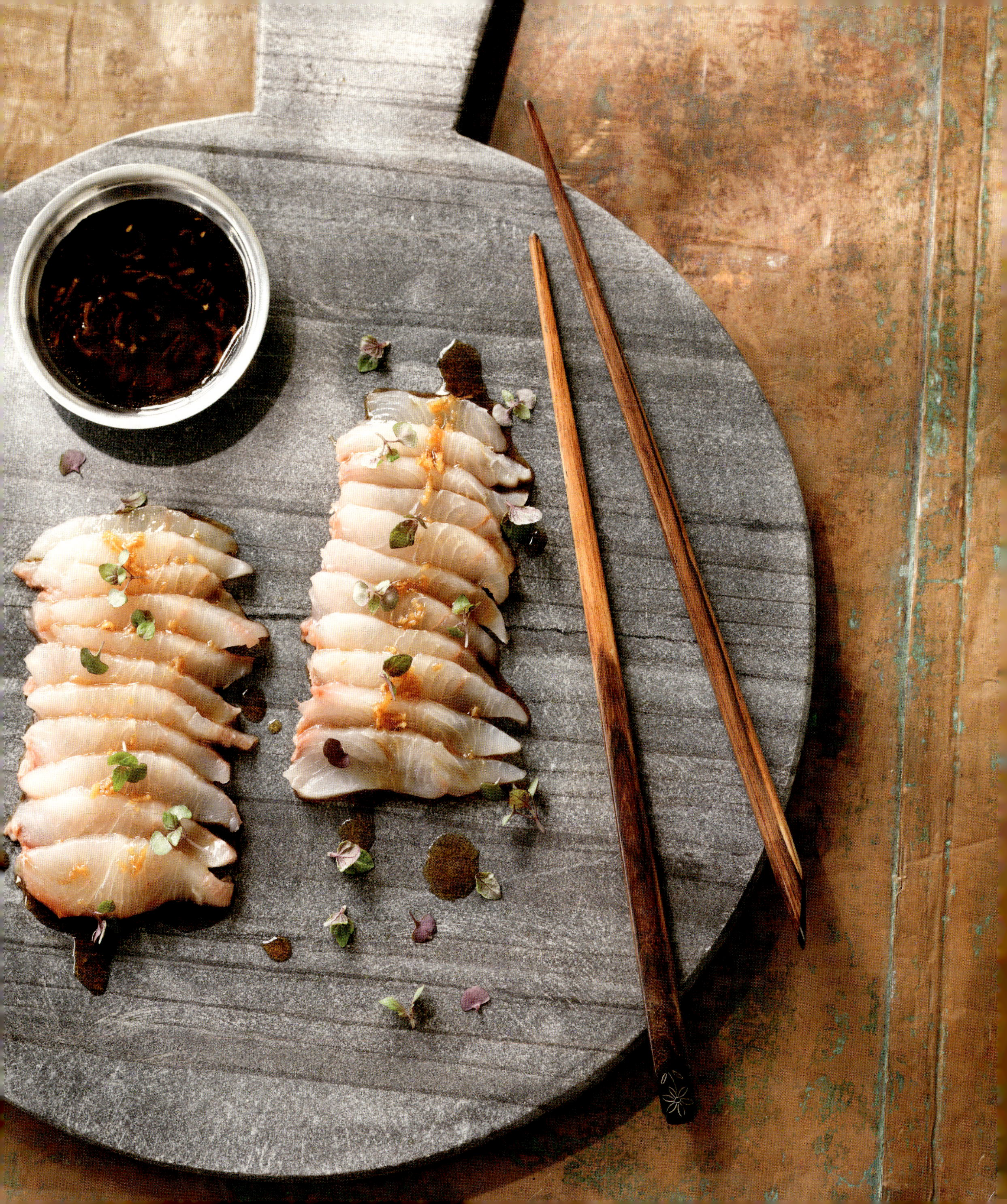

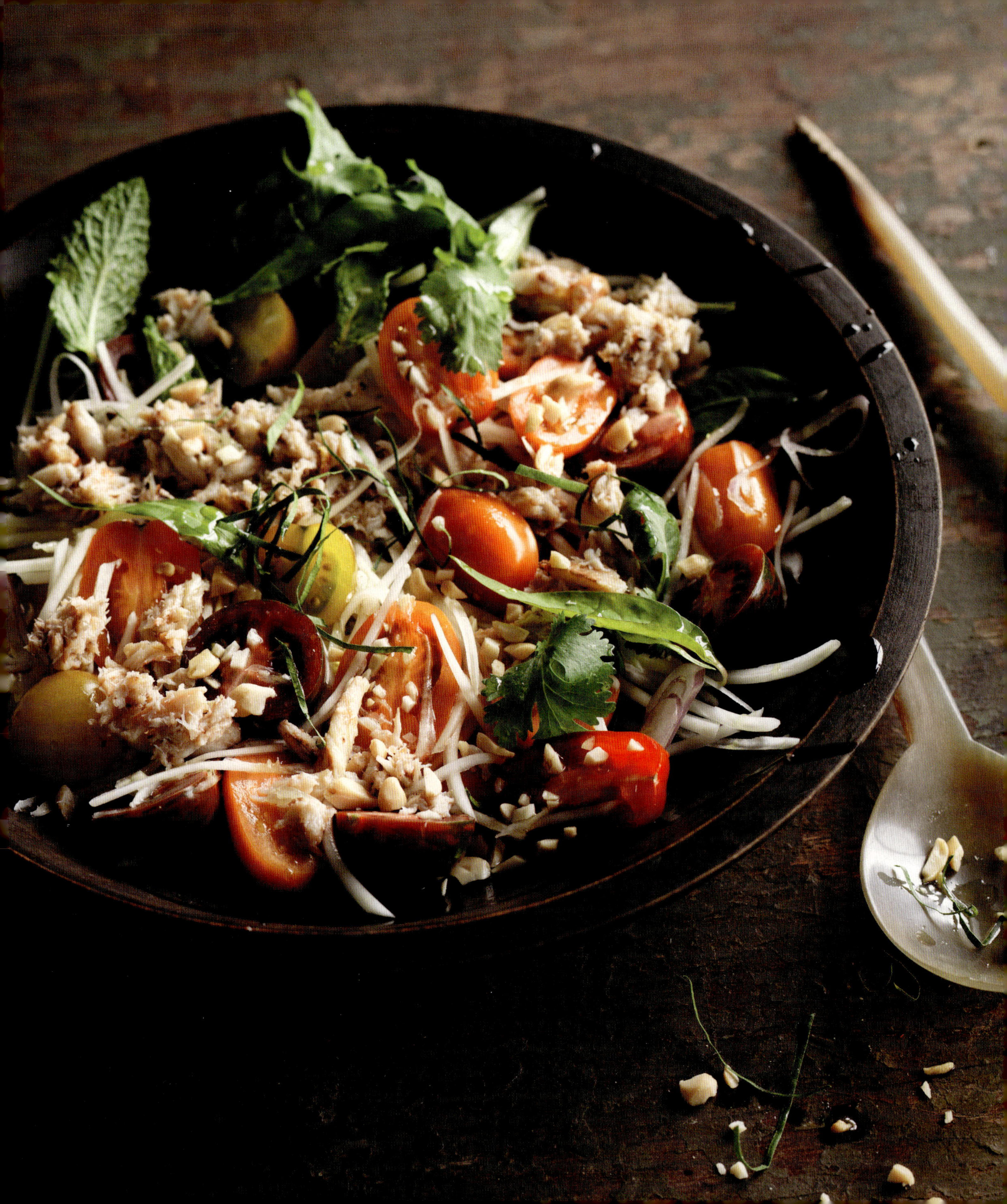

GREEN MANGO MUD CRAB SALAD (HQ)

2 green mangoes, peeled and grated

250g baby heirloom tomatoes, randomly chopped in chunks

1 eschalot, finely sliced

2 bird's eye chillies, finely sliced

finely grated zest 1 kaffir lime

¼ cup Vietnamese mint leaves, roughly chopped or torn

¼ cup mint leaves, roughly chopped or torn

¼ cup coriander leaves, roughly chopped or torn

1 whole cooked mud crab, meat picked

¼ cup peanuts, roughly chopped

2 kaffir lime leaves, finely sliced

DRESSING

2 tablespoons fish sauce

juice of 2 limes

1 tablespoons caster sugar

1 garlic clove, finely diced

1. Combine the grated green mango, tomatoes, eschalot, chilli and lime zest in a large (and I mean massive!) mortar, or a large bowl.
2. To make the dressing, combine the fish sauce, lime juice, sugar and garlic. You want a well balanced dressing, so be sure to taste and adjust if necessary.
3. Pour a little of the dressing over the mango and tomato mixture and use the pestle to gently bruise the tomatoes (or use the end of a rolling pin in a bowl).
4. Toss the salad with the herbs and mud crab. Serve dressed with the remaining dressing, topped with peanuts and kaffir lime leaf.

Serves 4

If you don't have kaffir lime, regular lime is fine.

Make the salad as hot as you like by adding more or less chilli.

Vietnamese mint can be found at greengrocers and Asian supermarkets. If you can't find any, then add regular mint.

BROOME | 95

JALAPEÑO PONZU PEARL MEAT CEVICHE

I am a massive fan of the clean Japanese flavours that have inspired me to come up with this happy little starter. You can easily obtain a bottle of ponzu, but just in case you'd like to make some from scratch I've given you the option. Kingfish is a good substutute for pearl meat.

½ jalapeño chilli, deseeded and sliced

1½ tablespoons lime juice

1 tablespoon lemon juice

3 coriander stalks, stems finely chopped, leaves set aside

2 teaspoons finely grated ginger

300g pearl meat, sliced thinly

PONZU SAUCE

¼ cup lime juice

1½ tablespoons soy sauce or tamari

1 tablespoon rice wine vinegar

2 teaspoons brown sugar or honey

pinch chilli flakes

1. For the ponzu sauce, whisk all the ingredients together. Set aside for a minimum of 30 minutes, for the flavours to marry.
2. Combine the jalapeño, lime and lemon juice, coriander stalks and ginger in a non-metallic bowl, and season with a pinch of salt. Add the pearl meat and turn to coat. Set aside for 2-3 minutes for the meat to 'cook' in the juices.
3. Drain the pearl meat and arrange onto a plate or board. Finish with a drizzle of ponzu sauce and the coriander leaves. Serve the remaining ponzu sauce on the side for dipping.

Serves 4

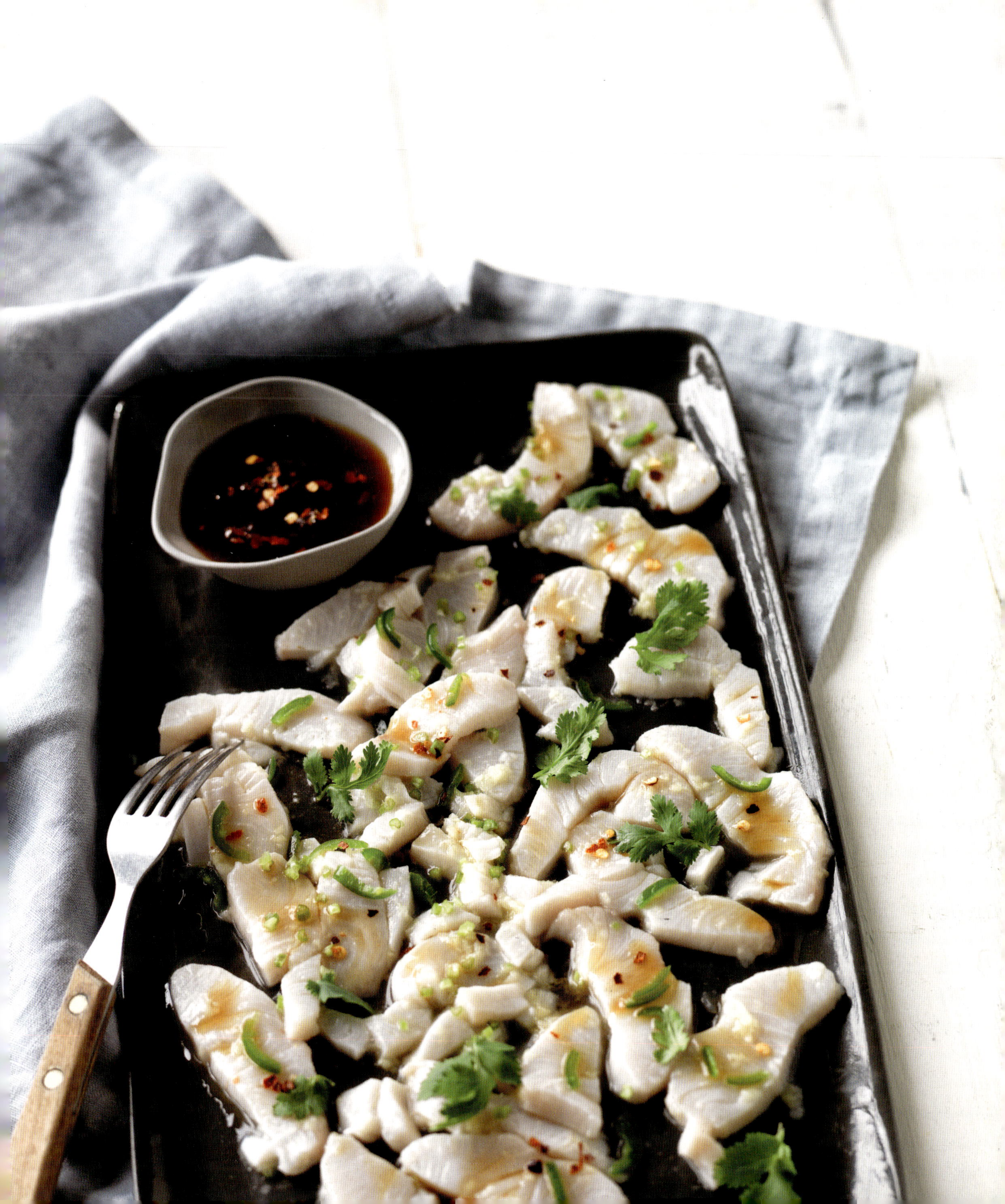

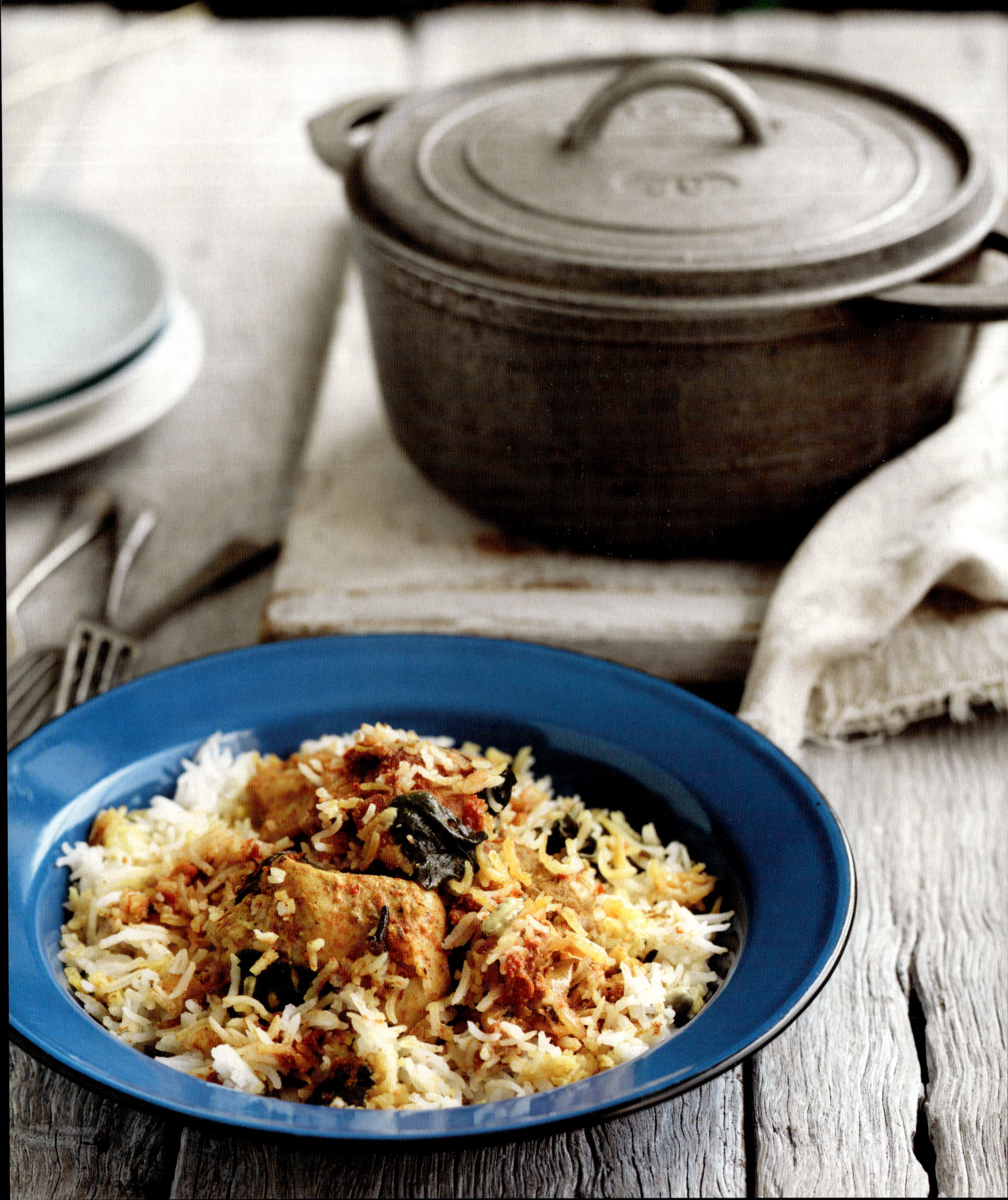

BROOME CHICKEN BIRYANI

Whenever it comes to Indian cooking, people are intimidated by the size of the ingredient list, but honestly – it's just spices! This is perfect for a one-pot meal for the family and it has a bit of theatre when you take it to the table. I love Indian food, and when I saw the chillies in Broome I couldn't wait to get cracking!

3 garlic cloves, roughly chopped

3cm knob ginger, roughly chopped

2 long red chillies, deseeded and roughly chopped

300ml natural yoghurt

1 tablespoon ground turmeric

1 tablespoon garam masala

2 teaspoons ground coriander

1 teaspoon ground cumin

small handful coriander leaves, finely chopped

700g skinless chicken thigh fillets, trimmed

juice of ½ lemon

pinch saffron

250ml coconut milk

1 tablespoon ghee or coconut oil

1 onion, sliced

2 cups basmati rice

4 cardamom pods

4 cloves

1 cinnamon stick

400g can diced tomatoes

½ cup chicken stock

1 cup baby spinach leaves

1. Preheat the oven to 180°C (160°C fan-forced). Use a mortar and pestle or small food processor to purée the garlic, ginger and chilli until a paste forms, then combine in a large bowl with the yoghurt, turmeric, garam masala, ground coriander, ground cumin and coriander leaves. Mix in the chicken and lemon juice, cover and marinate in the fridge for 30 minutes. Combine the saffron and coconut milk and set aside to soak.

2. Heat the ghee in a large ovenproof casserole dish over medium-high heat. Cook the onion for 5 minutes or until golden brown, then remove from the pan and drain on paper towel. Working in 2 batches, brown the chicken in the pan, turning to colour all over. Transfer to a plate.

3. Combine the rice and 2 cups of water in a medium saucepan. Add the cardamom pods, cloves and cinnamon stick. Cover and bring to the boil over high heat. Reduce the heat to low and cook for 6 minutes.

4. Put the onion back into the pan it was cooked in, along with the chicken and the tomatoes. Stir for a minute before adding the stock. Cook over medium heat for about 5 minutes until the sauce has reduced and thickened slightly. Reduce the heat to low and spread the sauce out evenly. Layer in the spinach, covering the surface. Next, layer on the partially cooked rice, being sure to make an even distribution.

5. Pour the saffron-infused coconut milk over the rice. Turn the heat to high and wait for the first beat of steam to come through. Once it does, put a tea towel over the top of the pan and cover with a lid. Pop it in the oven for 15 minutes to finish cooking. Take the entire pot to the table to serve.

Serves 4–6

GREEN MANGO GADO GADO

Besides the wicked colour, each element in this bright salad tells its own story. Rather than combining ingredients to make one taste, with this you enjoy different textures and pops of flavour with each bite.

1 large sweet potato (about 500g), peeled and cut into thin wedges

3 tablespoons olive oil

150g block firm tofu, cut into 2cm cubes

1 green mango, peeled and shredded

¼ red cabbage, cored and shredded

2 radishes, thinly sliced

3 hard boiled eggs, halved

bean sprouts and prawn crackers, to garnish

GADO FLAVOUR-MAKER SAUCE!

⅔ cup coconut milk

¼ cup unsalted roasted peanuts, or crunchy peanut butter

1½ tablespoons honey

2 teaspoons soy sauce or tamari

2 teaspoons tamarind puree

½ teaspoon sesame oil

1 long red chilli, deseeded and chopped

1 garlic clove, bruised

2 teaspoons lemon juice

1. To make the sauce pop all the ingredients (except the lemon juice) into a blender and blitz until combined (I love keeping some of the peanuts a bit chunky). Season to taste with lemon juice.

2. Preheat the oven to 200°C (180°C fan-forced) and line a baking tray with baking paper. Toss the sweet potato with 2 tablespoons of the oil and season with salt and pepper. Spread out evenly on the tray, then roast for 20–25 minutes or until golden brown and pierced easily with a knife.

3. Heat the remaining oil in a frying pan over medium-high heat. Cook the tofu on all sides for a few minutes until golden. Transfer to a plate and season with salt and pepper.

4. Pour half the sauce onto a platter. Arrange the green mango and remaining ingredients onto the platter. Garnish with bean sprouts and prawn crackers. Serve with remaining sauce on the side.

Serves 4-6

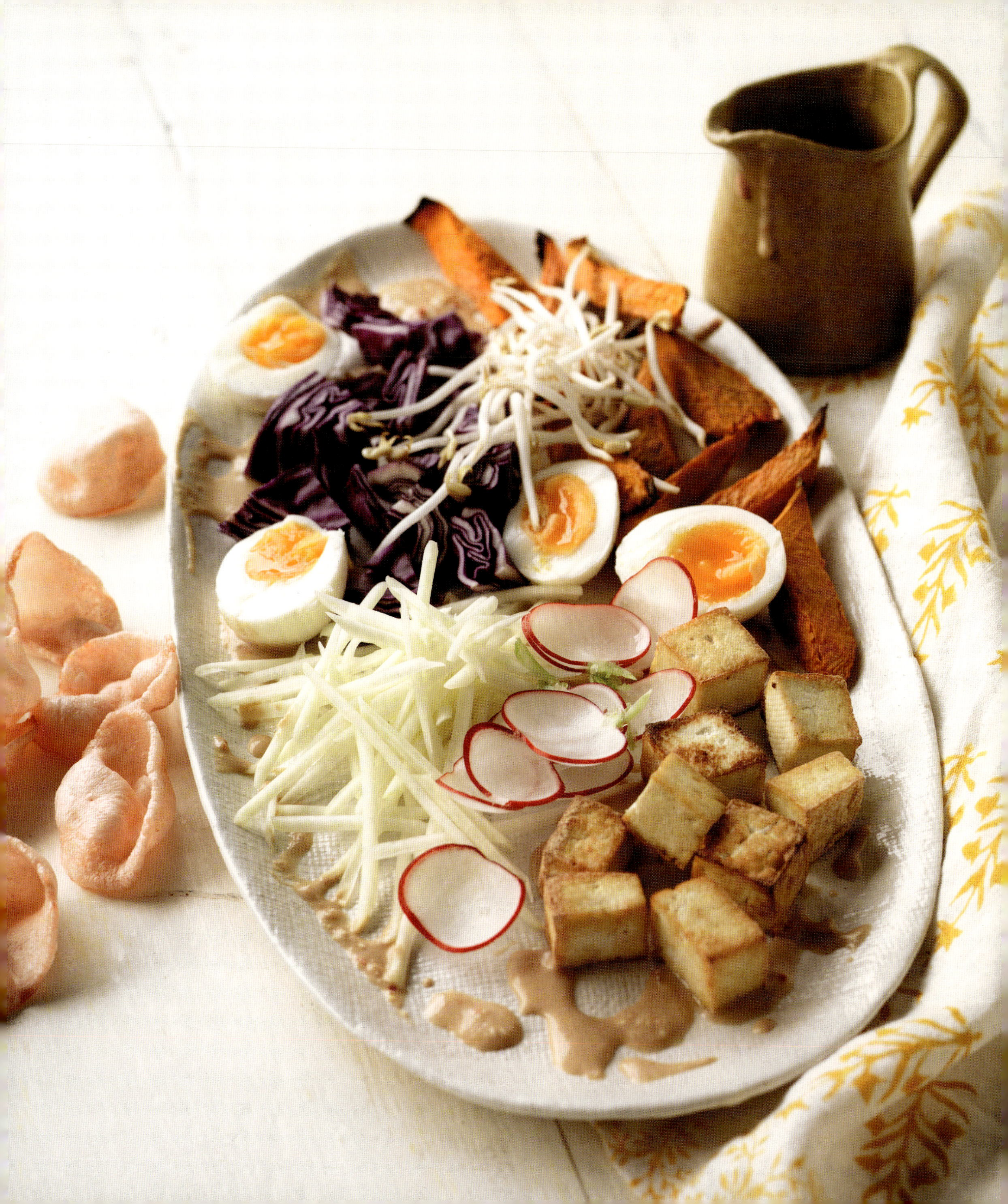

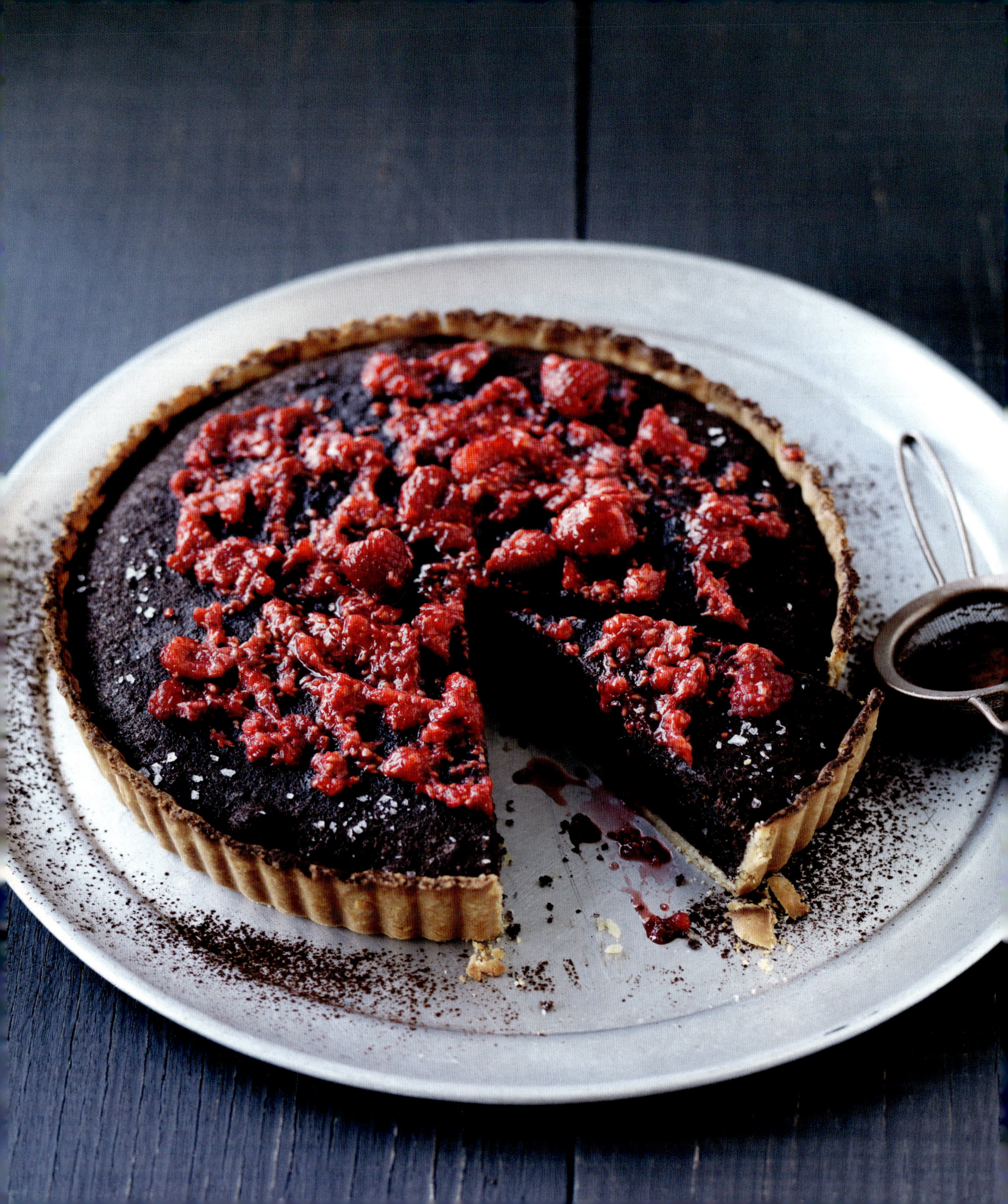

CHILLI CHOCOLATE TART (HQ)

Give me chocolate-flavoured anything and I'm a happy man. Throw in a little hint of chilli and I'm a happy and excited man! If you haven't tried this pairing before, you must give this tart a go. Be careful – if you are using Broome chillies, they are hot!

1⅔ cups plain flour, sifted

2 tablespoons pure icing sugar, sifted

125g unsalted butter, chilled and chopped

1 egg, lightly beaten

2 teaspoons vanilla paste

sea salt flakes, to serve

fresh raspberries and crème fraiche, to serve

FILLING

150g dark chocolate (70% cocoa), chopped

⅔ cup caster sugar

½ cup dark cocoa powder, plus extra to dust

1 teaspoon ground cinnamon

½ teaspoon ground chilli

250g hazelnut meal

200g unsalted butter, chilled and chopped

1 teaspoon finely grated orange zest

6 eggs

1. Process the flour, sugar, butter and a pinch of salt in a food processor in short bursts until mixture resembles breadcrumbs. Add the egg and vanilla and process, again in short bursts, until mixture just comes together. Gather the dough and form into a disc. Wrap in plastic wrap and refrigerate for 15 minutes.

2. Meanwhile, to make the filling, process the chocolate, sugar, cocoa, cinnamon, chilli and hazelnut meal in a food processor until finely ground. Add the butter and orange zest and process until combined. Add the eggs in two batches, processing until combined after each addition. Refrigerate until needed.

3. Roll the pastry out on a lightly floured surface until 5mm thick and use to line a deep 26cm loose-based fluted tart pan. Trim the pastry edges and rest in freezer for 30 minutes. Preheat the oven to 200°C (180°C fan-forced).

4. Spoon the filling into the tart shell and level the surface. Place the tart on a baking tray and bake for 45 minutes, or until the pastry is golden and the filling is firm to touch. Stand on a wire rack to cool.

5. Lift the tart from the pan. Dust the surface with extra cocoa powder and sprinkle with sea salt. Cut into wedges and serve with berries and crème fraiche.

Serves 8

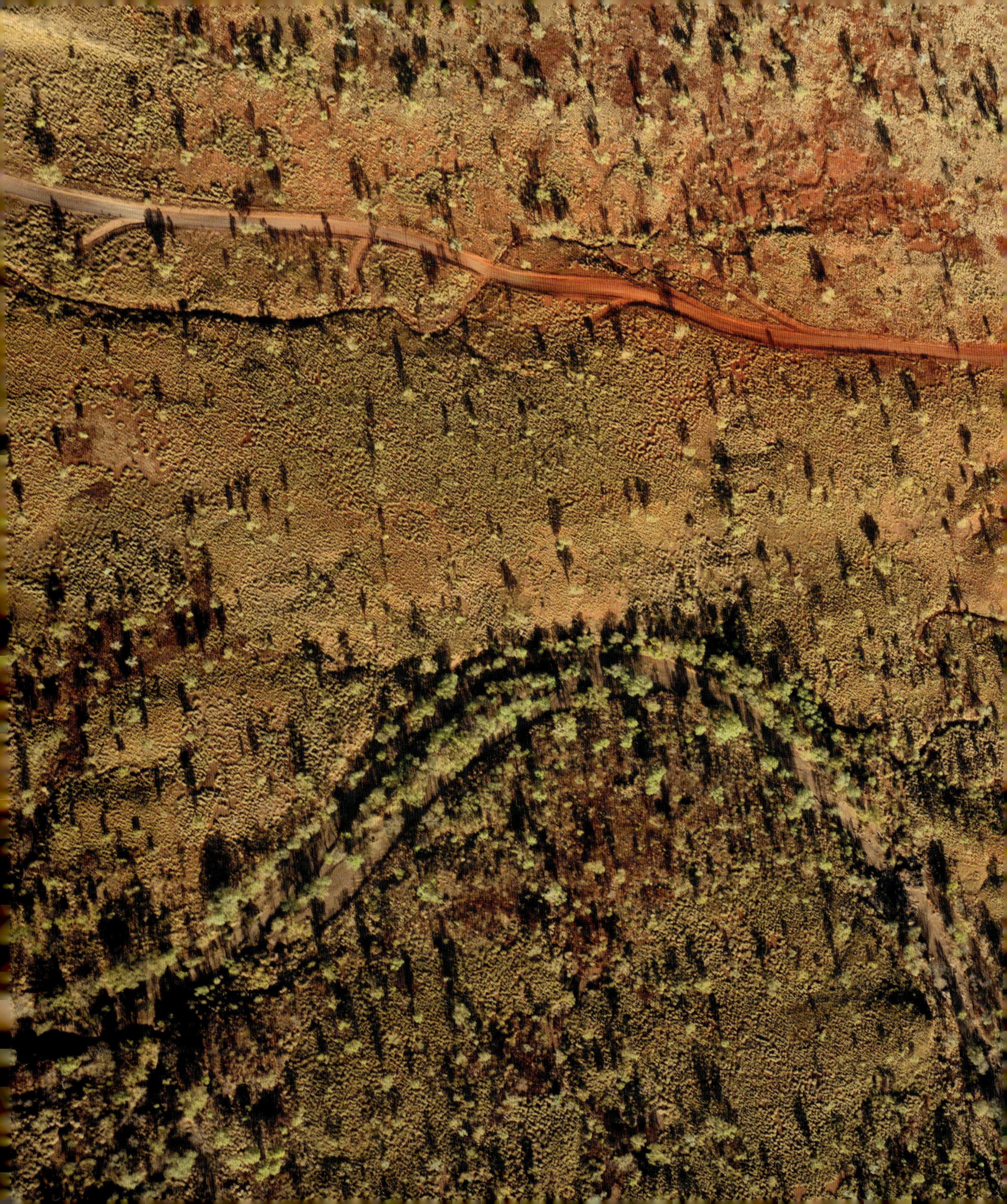

The INLAND NORTH

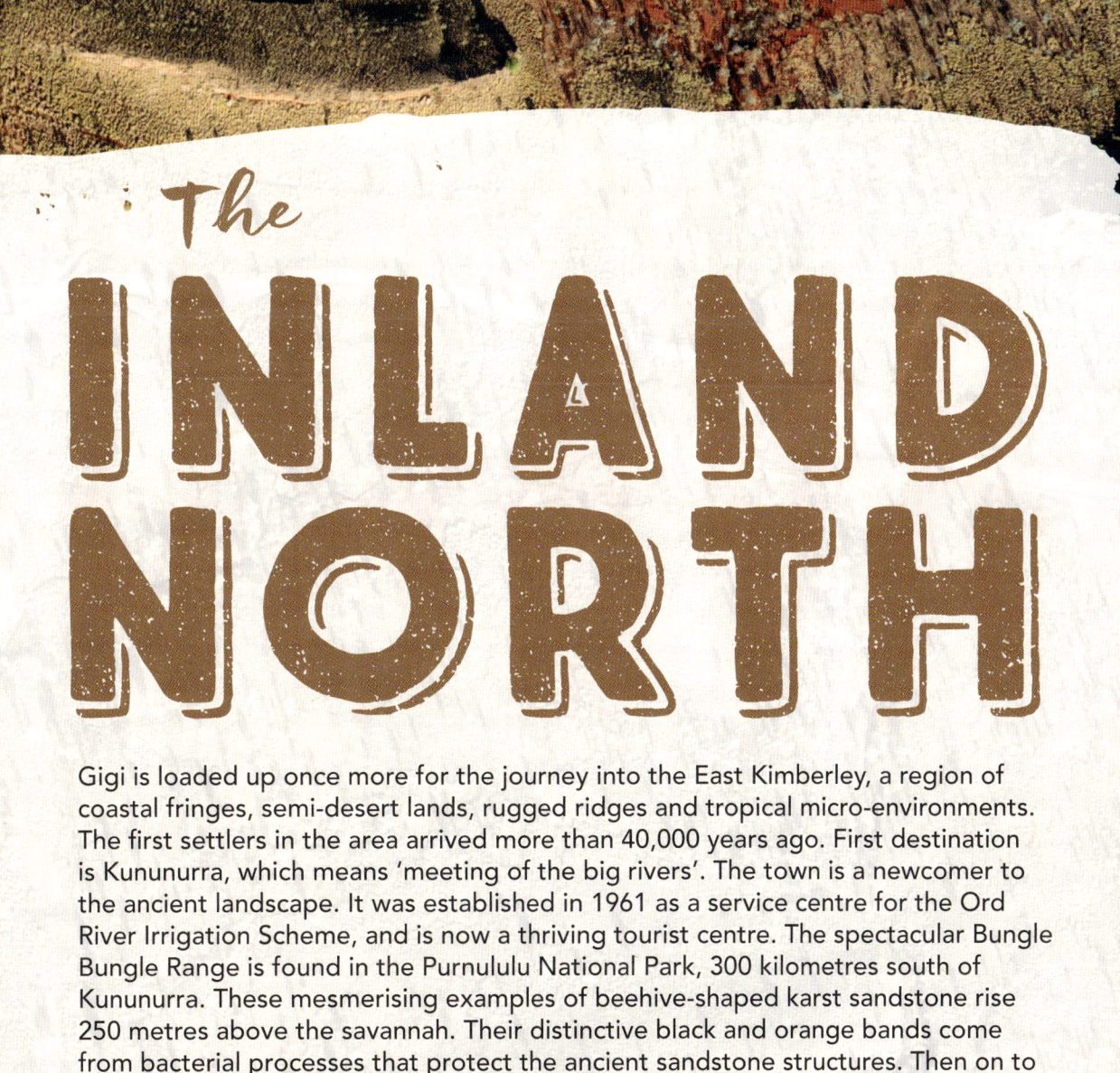

Gigi is loaded up once more for the journey into the East Kimberley, a region of coastal fringes, semi-desert lands, rugged ridges and tropical micro-environments. The first settlers in the area arrived more than 40,000 years ago. First destination is Kununurra, which means 'meeting of the big rivers'. The town is a newcomer to the ancient landscape. It was established in 1961 as a service centre for the Ord River Irrigation Scheme, and is now a thriving tourist centre. The spectacular Bungle Bungle Range is found in the Purnululu National Park, 300 kilometres south of Kununurra. These mesmerising examples of beehive-shaped karst sandstone rise 250 metres above the savannah. Their distinctive black and orange bands come from bacterial processes that protect the ancient sandstone structures. Then on to Katherine in the Northern Territory. This place marks the point where the traditional lands of the Jawoyn, Dagoman and Wardaman peoples converge. It has been an important meeting place for Indigenous people for thousands of years. Katherine is also a historic pioneering town where a growing number of new travellers now come together.

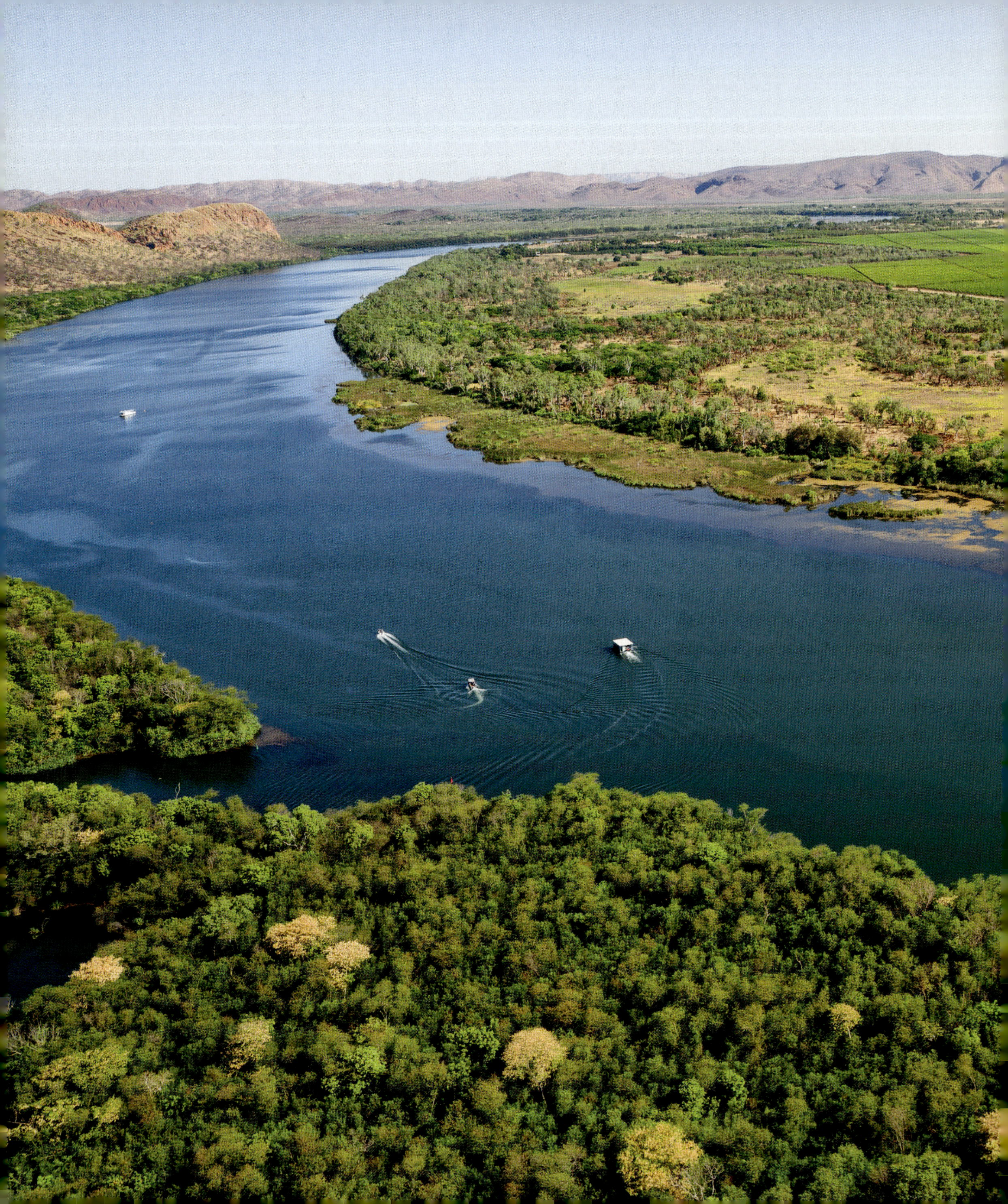

Kununurra

I had no idea what to expect from Kununurra as I hadn't heard much about it, but by the time we left I was looking at my calendar to see when I could go back. This is outback Australia, with no waves or beaches, but it has some of the most spectacular landscapes you'll ever see.

I believe in doing what we do in order to make a difference to people. This journey was not about making a name for ourselves, rather it was about inspiring people to find joy and meaning in the amazing array of fresh food and produce we are so lucky to grow in this country. The first stop in Kununurra was just that – visiting the Kununurra Girls Academy and talking to the students about health, wellbeing and the goodness of eating. One girl came up to me and said she will always now eat with plenty of colour on her plate. Result!

Kununurra was super special in that it's where we celebrated Hayden's birthday. He's not one to create a scene (he didn't tell anyone), so I decided to make one for him! After pretending the morning was an average day, I bought a cake and surprised him in the afternoon. It was one of those classic moments, seeing one your good mates happy and slightly shocked!

That same afternoon we were fortunate to go for a wicked surf, even though there aren't any beaches this far inland. Instead we went 'skirfing', which is a cross between surfing and wake boarding, where you ride the wake created by a boat. Picture red rock faces on the outer edges of a freshwater river with two hooligans skirfing behind … it was epic! To top it off, HQ and I saw freshwater crocs and enjoyed a breathtaking sunset on the ride back. Kununurra truly is one of the most beautiful places in Australia.

The plantations in these parts are known for a couple of crops, one of which I am fond of, and the other which I knew little about. Chia is an ingredient I use regularly, not just because of its health benefits but also because of its gelatinous, marshmallow-like texture and taste. But who knew how minimal the process is to get the seeds into that little packet you find at a farmers market?! It's as simple as removing the crop from the stem and blowing away the excess husk to reveal the seeds. The ancient Incas did this by hand, but now farmers use machines that are so finely calibrated that they lose a mere 4g of chia per hectare in wastage … pretty efficient if you ask me!

The other crop is sandalwood. The resin of the tree seems to be an ingredient in every perfume recipe around the world. Nowadays, farmers are also seeing the health benefits of sandalwood nuts, such as their anti-inflammatory effects and being a natural diuretic. Talk about a nut not getting enough credit! What I found interesting was that the sandalwood plant itself is a parasite and requires host plants around it to survive.

Kununurra is home to magnificent natural beauty, but one feature that I can't do justice to is the mountain range known as the Bungle Bungles. Hayden and I hopped in a tiny plane – I'm an anxious flyer, this had me on edge – and that two-and-a-half-hour journey had me blinking in amazement at the most phenomenal rivers, valleys and gorges. At one point the formation of cliffs resembled rough 60-foot waves right out at sea. Flying over Lake Argyle and seeing those immense karst rock structures with their black and orange bands was breathtaking, and the perspective offered by being 1000 feet up in the air made it look almost fake.

Repeat after me, 'I must go to Kununurra!'

DC

Harvesting chia seeds

Healthy and delicious sandalwood nuts

Skirfing was wicked!

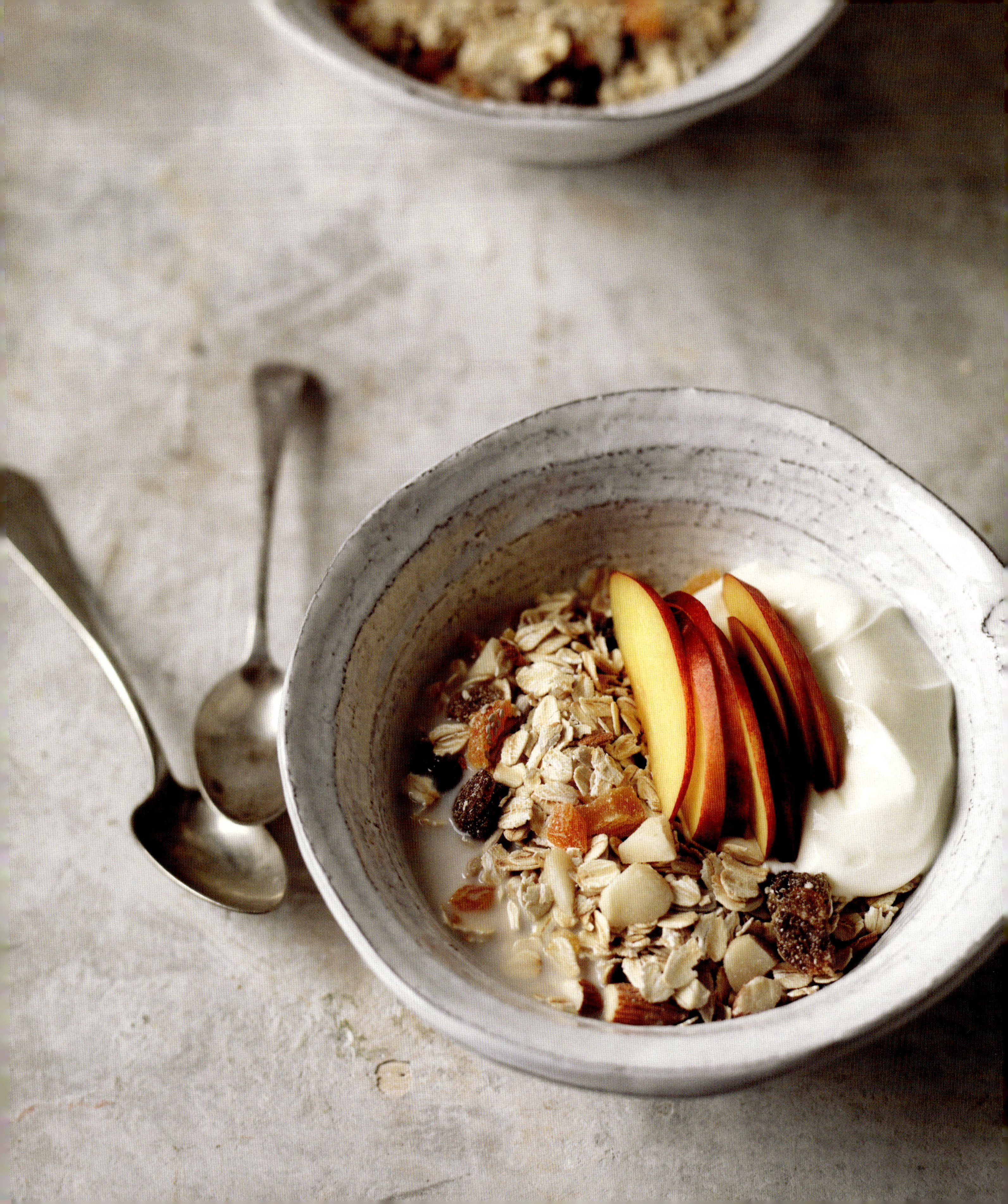

SANDALWOOD NUT CHIA MUESLI WITH YOGHURT AND SEASONAL FRUIT (HQ)

350g rolled oats

120g sultanas

80g sandalwood nuts, roughly chopped

70g macadamias, roughly chopped

75g sunflower seeds

60g dried apricots, chopped

50g chia seeds

30g coconut flakes

milk, natural yoghurt and fresh fruit in season, to serve

1. Place all the ingredients (except yoghurt and fruit) into a large bowl and mix until evenly combined. Place into a large airtight jar or container for storage.
2. Serve a good scoop with yoghurt and your favorite seasonal fruits.
3. Store leftover muesli in an airtight container in the fridge to keep it at its best.

Makes 6 cups

> Sandalwood nuts are a healthy Australian native nut. Ask about them at your health food shop, or jump online to find a stockist. If you can't get them, use 2 cups pecans.

> If you can't find sandalwood nuts, use almonds.

MANGO CHIA LASSI (HQ)

If you've been to India, you'll know how cooling lassi can be on a hot, hot day. In 'Kunners' the weather is just as hot, the people are just as friendly and the mangoes are just as abundant, and so lassi is just as refreshing. Make sure to drink this up quickly before the chia turns it into a thickshake!

1 large fresh mango, flesh chopped
1 cup natural yoghurt
1½ teaspoons chia seeds
1 cup ice cubes

1. Put all the ingredients into a blender and add a pinch of salt. Blend together until smooth and frothy. Pour into glasses and enjoy!

Serves 2

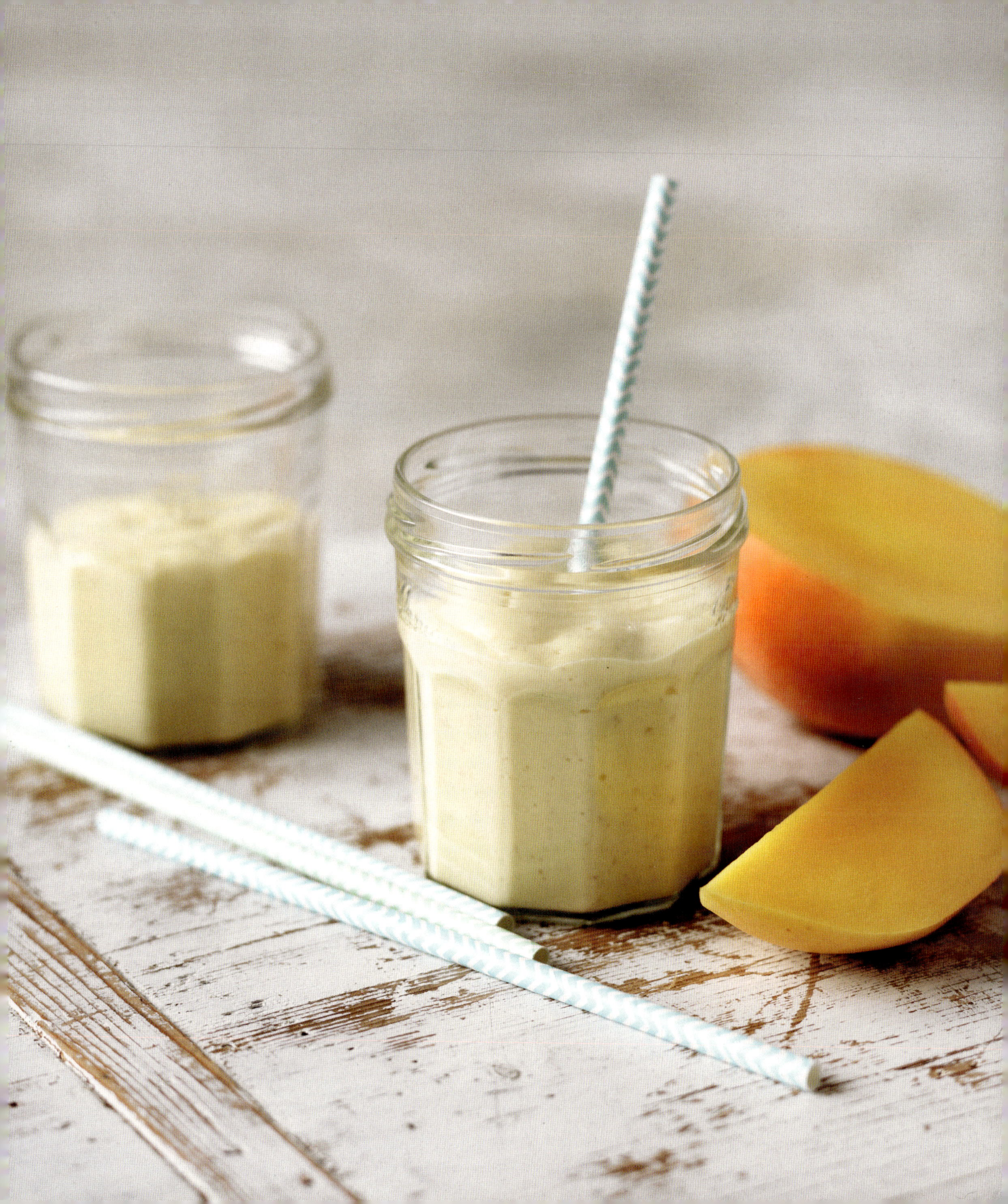

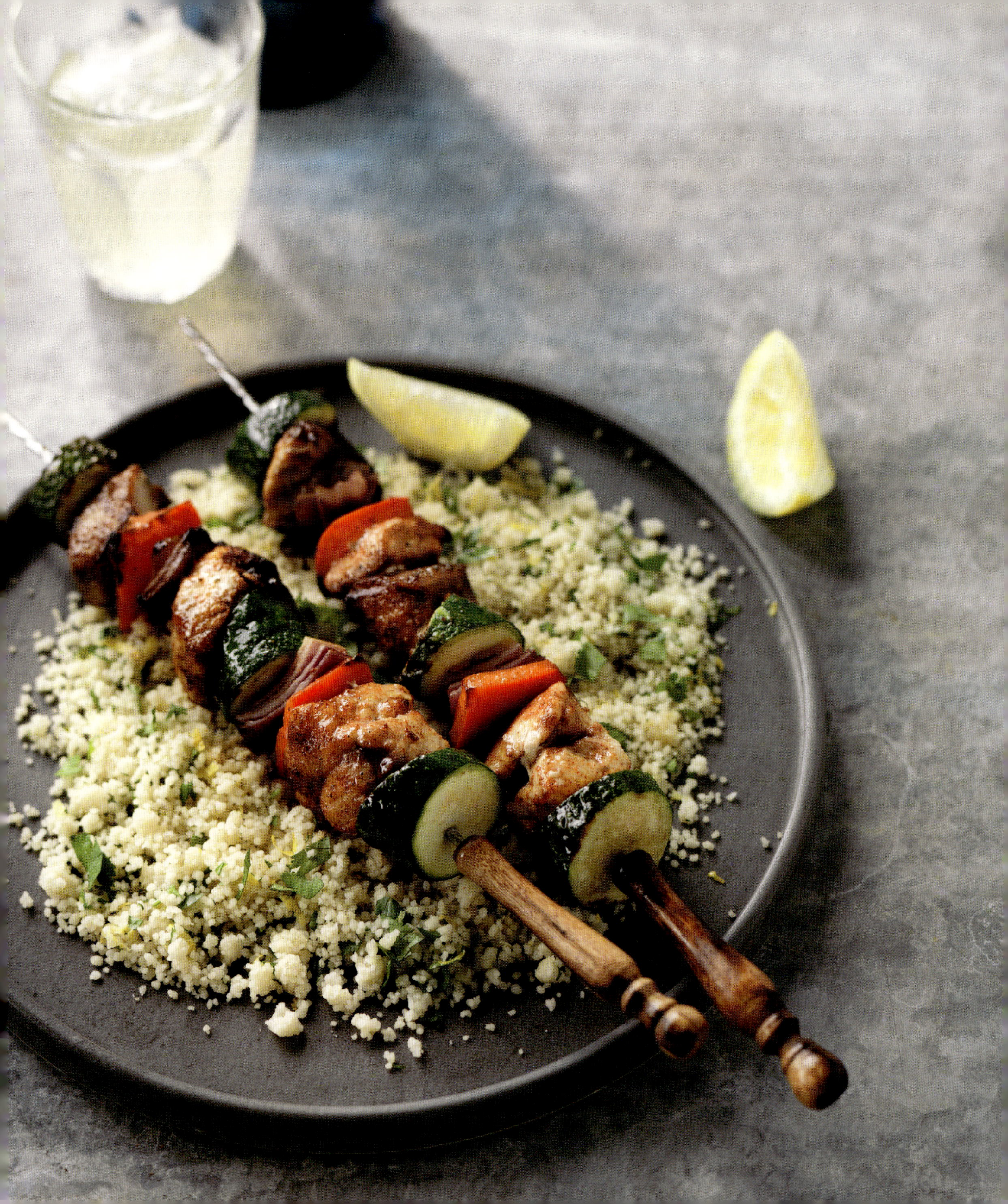

MOROCCAN BARRA SKEWERS WITH COUSCOUS

When you're making skewers like this, it's a good idea to first separate the ingredients into piles so you end up with an even quantity of ingredients on each one. If you're using wooden skewers, soak them in water for about 20 minutes first, so they don't burn while cooking.

2 teaspoons smoked paprika

2 teaspoons ground cumin

2 teaspoons ground coriander

½ teaspoon chilli powder

500g barramundi, cut into 2.5cm chunks

1 zucchini, cut into wedges

1 large red capsicum, cut into squares

1 red onion, cut into wedges

1 tablespoon rice bran oil

lemon wedges, to serve

COUSCOUS

1 cup couscous

2 tablespoons olive oil

½ cup coriander leaves, roughly chopped (reserving some for garnish)

finely grated zest of 1 lemon

1 tablespoon lemon juice

1. Preheat a BBQ grill or flat plate to medium-high heat. Combine the spices in a large bowl and season with salt. Add the barra chunks and toss to coat. Thread pieces of barra, zucchini, capsicum and onion onto 8 skewers. Brush with oil.

2. Cook the skewers for about 2 minutes each side (so 8 minutes in total), until tender and cooked through.

3. Meanwhile, bring 1¼ cups water to the boil in a medium saucepan. Add the couscous, cover tightly and turn off the heat. Stand for 5 minutes to absorb the water. Uncover, drizzle with 1 tablespoon of the oil and fluff up the grains with a fork.

4. Transfer couscous to a large bowl and cool slightly. Add the coriander, lemon zest and juice, and remaining oil. Season with salt and pepper and toss to combine.

5. Serve skewers on a bed of couscous on a large platter, topped with a sprinkling of coriander and with lemon wedges on the side.

Serves 4

Any firm, white-fleshed fish, such as snapper or kingfish, will work well here.

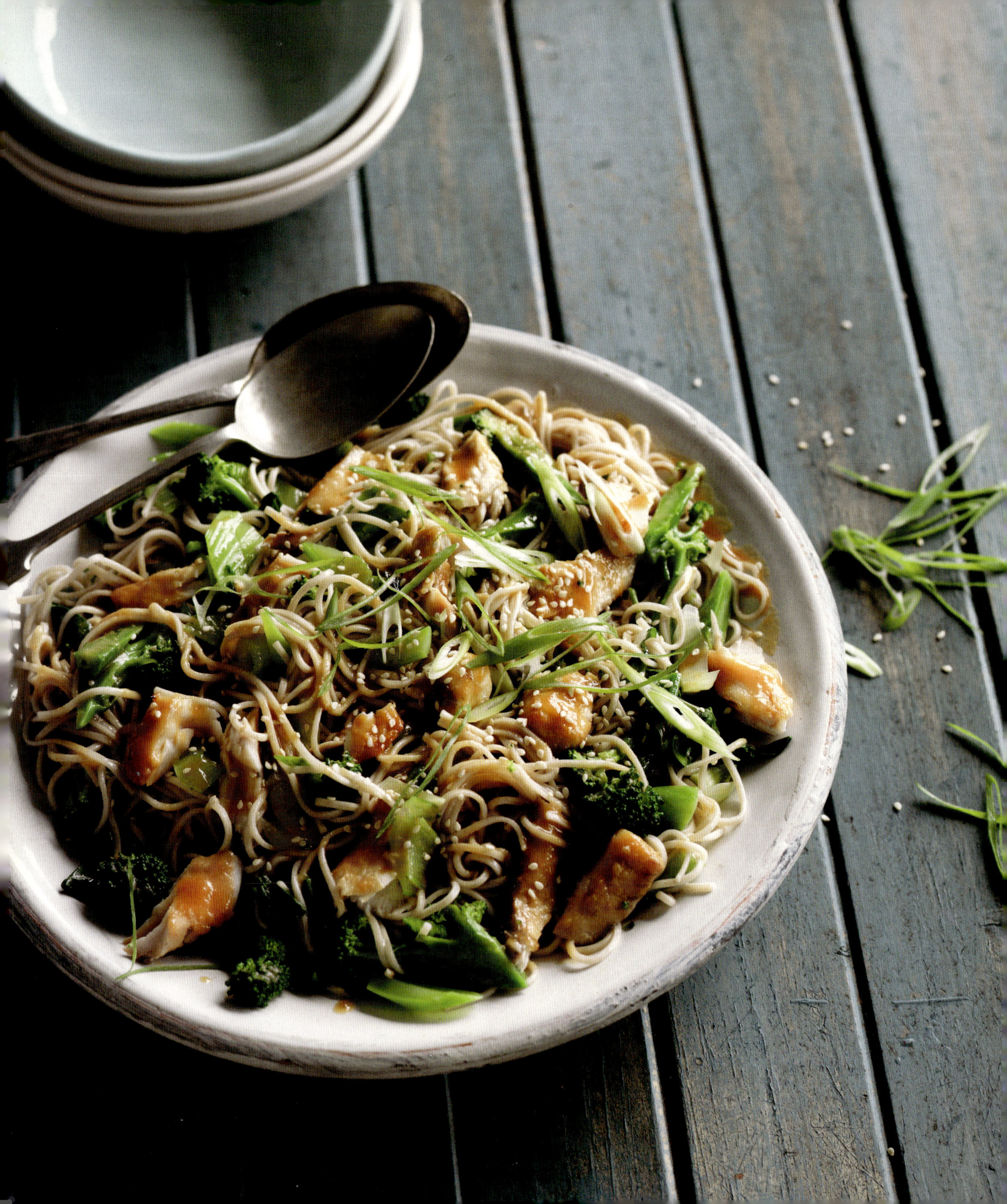

FAMILY MISO BARRA WITH SOBA NOODLES (DC)

I like to think of this one as the Japanese version of a family spaghetti dish. You all sit at the table, grab some tongs and get your noodle-like twirl on. Then everybody is super happy, slurping away on some seriously authentic flavours, not to mention the amazing bite on that well-cooked barramundi!

2 tablespoons white miso paste

¼ cup mirin

2 tablespoons rice wine vinegar

1 tablespoon tamari or soy sauce

1 tablespoon honey

1 teaspoon sesame oil

4 barramundi fillets, cut in half lengthways

2 teaspoons finely grated ginger

1 garlic clove, crushed

1 teaspoon salt

200g soba noodles

1 bunch broccolini, roughly chopped

1 small bunch baby bok choy, thinly sliced

toasted sesame seeds, to garnish

sliced green shallot, to garnish (optional)

1. Whisk the miso, mirin, rice wine vinegar, tamari, honey and sesame oil in a small bowl until the miso dissolves. Place the barramundi in a shallow dish and pour the miso mixture over to coat. Marinate for a minimum of 30 minutes, in the fridge.

2. Preheat the oven to 180°C (160°C fan-forced) and line a baking tray with baking paper. Lift barra out of the marinade and place onto the baking tray. Reserve the excess marinade. Bake for 12 minutes or until a fork is warm to touch once inserted into the thickest part of the fish and the flesh is flaky.

3. Combine the ginger, garlic and salt in a medium saucepan with 6 cups of water. Bring to the boil and add the soba noodles. Cook for 4 minutes then use a slotted spoon or tongs to transfer to a colander. Rinse under cold running water and set aside to drain.

4. Add the broccolini to the cooking liquid. Cook for 2 minutes before adding the bok choy to cook for a further minute. Drain well and toss with the noodles. Meanwhile, put the reserved marinade into a small saucepan and bring to the boil. Boil for 1 minute, then remove from the heat and cool.

5. To serve, spread the noodle mixture out onto a large serving plate. Break up the barra and mix through. Drizzle with the sauce and sprinkle with sesame seeds and green shallot.

Serves 4

COCONUT CHIA PUDDING

Spiced granola adds texture to this deliciously soft pudding. You can turn your oven into a dehydrator by turning the temperature to its lowest and placing a spoon in the door to allow air and moisture to escape. Cook the granola for a further 40 minutes than stated in the recipe if you want it extra crunchy. This recipe makes about 6 cups of granola.

1 cup coconut milk
1 cup unsweetened almond milk
¼ cup roughly chopped fresh dates
1 cinnamon stick
½ cup chia seeds
Gluten Free Spiced Granola, to serve (recipe below)
125g strawberries, roughly chopped

GLUTEN FREE SPICED GRANOLA

2 cups quinoa, rinsed and well drained
1½ cups raw mixed nuts
¼ cup desiccated coconut
2 teaspoons ground allspice
¼ cup tahini
¼ cup honey

1. To make the granola, preheat the oven to 140°C (120°C fan-forced) and line a large baking tray with baking paper. Combine the quinoa, nuts, coconut and allspice in a large bowl. Stir the tahini and honey together in a small bowl, then add to the quinoa mixture. Mix through until evenly combined. Spread evenly onto the tray and cook for 30 minutes or until crunchy and golden. Stir occasionally during cooking, making sure to be gentle, as you want it to clump into crunchy clusters. Cool completely, then store in an airtight container.

2. For the pud, combine the coconut and almond milks, dates and cinnamon stick in a medium saucepan. Place over medium-low heat, cover and bring to the boil. Remove from the heat and set aside to cool so the flavours infuse.

3. Remove the cinnamon stick (rinse, dry and keep for future use). Pour the mixture into a bowl and stir in the chia seeds. Cover and put in the fridge overnight.

4. In the morning, layer the pud into bowls (or jars, if you want to be trendy) with some granola and the strawberries.

Serves 4

Replace the quinoa with buckwheat or activated buckinis, if you prefer.

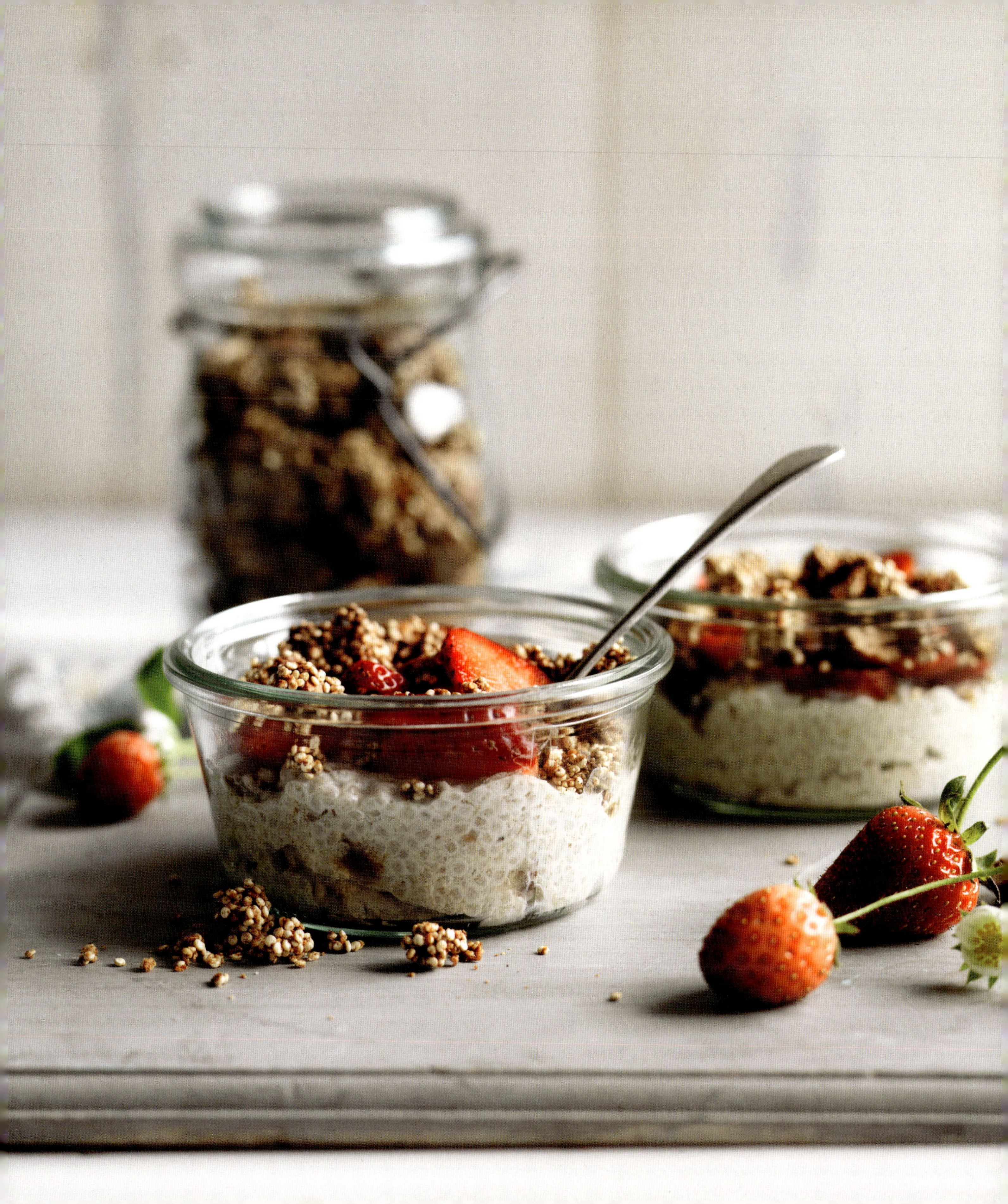

BLUEBERRY RAW CHEESECAKE WITH SANDALWOOD CRUST ⓓⓒ

My number one rule when it comes to food is that it must taste delicious! If you can make it clean and colourful as well, that's an added bonus. This little wonder is both super delicious and loaded with nutrients. Although it has a solid fridge life, it never lasts that long at home!

FILLING

2 cups raw cashews

½ cup coconut milk

1 tablespoon honey

1 tablespoon coconut oil

CRUST

1 cup pecans

1 cup sandalwood nuts

1 tablespoon honey

120g fresh dates, pitted

1 tablespoon coconut oil, melted (plus extra to grease)

TOPPING

250g fresh blueberries, plus extra to serve

2 teaspoons honey

2 teaspoons coconut oil

1. To make the filling, soak the cashews in water for 4 hours. Drain, reserving ½ cup of the water.

2. Meanwhile, for the crust, line the base of a 22cm springform cake tin with baking paper, and grease the sides with coconut oil.

3. Put all the crust ingredients into a food processor. Pulse until the nuts are well chopped and the mixture sticks together when you squeeze it between your fingers. Press into the base of the tin and use the back of a spoon to spread evenly. Place in the freezer for 2 hours to set.

4. To finish the filling, combine soaked cashews, half the reserved water and the remaining ingredients in a blender and blend until smooth. You may need to add a little more of the water as you should be able to pour it out in a thick but steady stream.

5. Remove the cake tin from the freezer and pour the filling over the base. Use the back of a spoon to spread evenly and smooth the surface, then place in the fridge to set for 30 minutes.

6. For the topping, place all the ingredients into a blender and blend until smooth. Pour the topping over the filling and use the back of a spoon one more time to spread evenly. Place in the freezer for 1 hour before transferring to the fridge. Serve topped with extra fresh blueberries … as you can never have too many!

Serves 12

> You can use frozen blueberries, but you will need to thaw them well before blending.

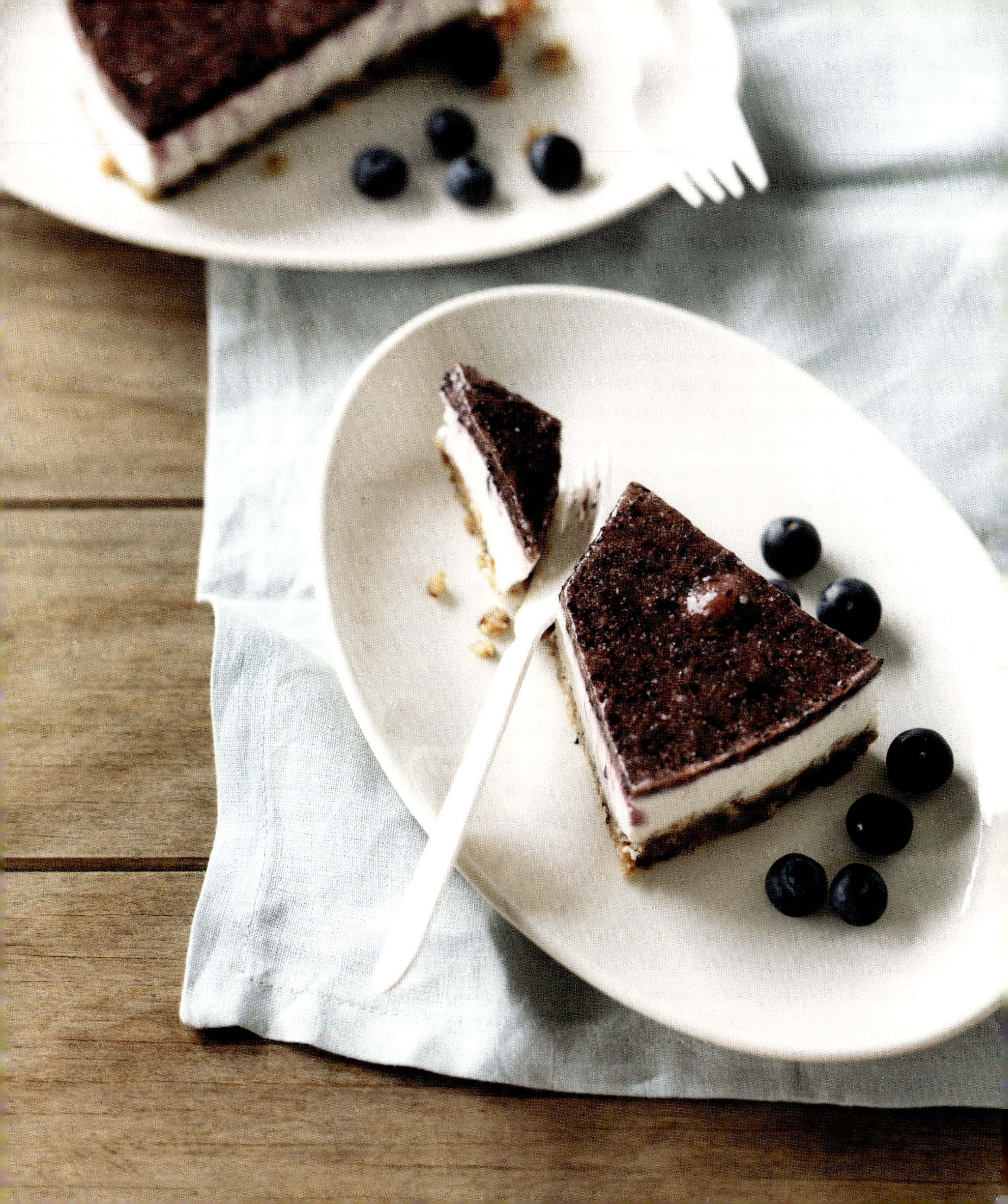

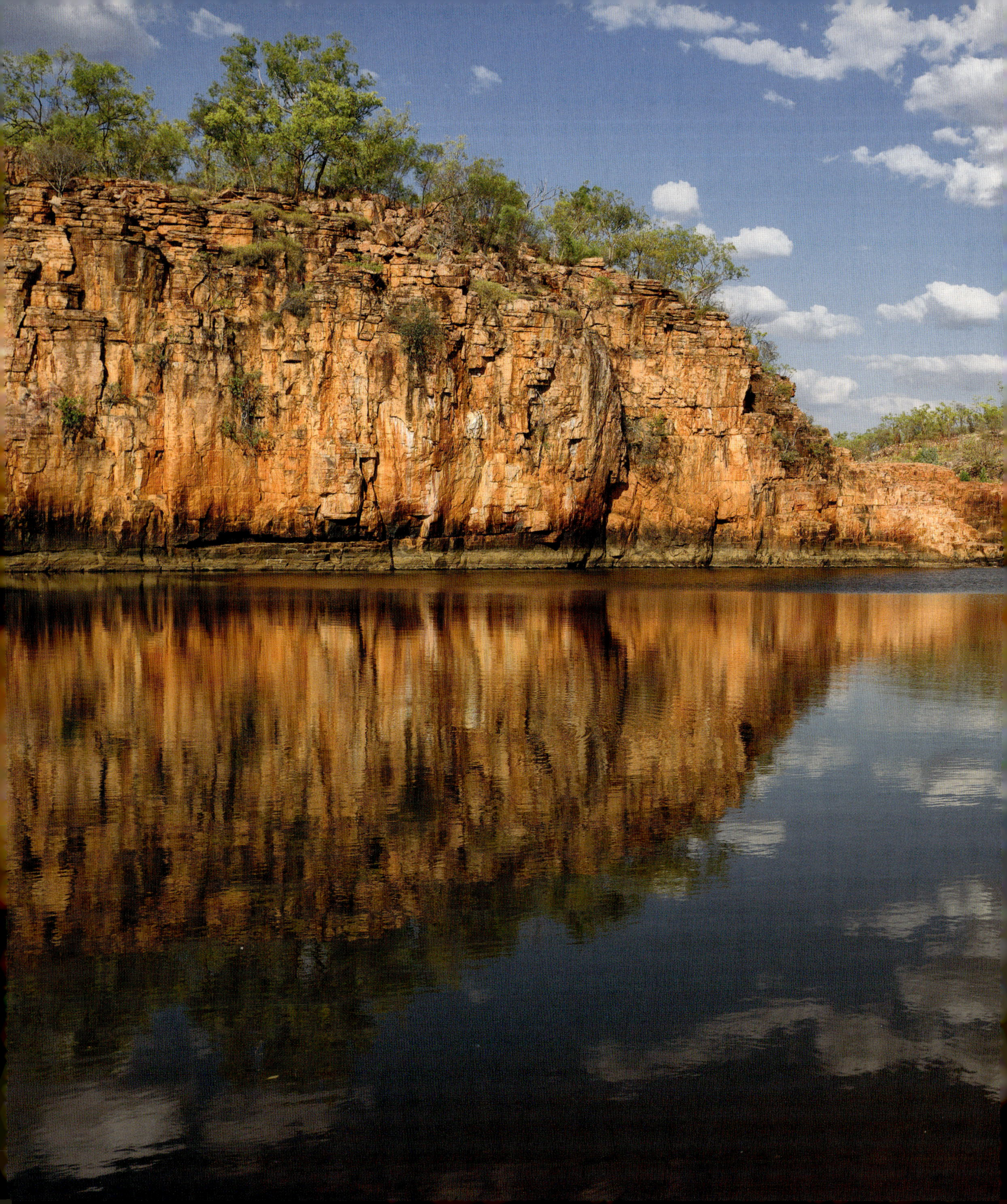

Katherine

Driving through the red dirt landscapes of the north-west of Western Australia was an incredible experience. Our blue car stood out like nobody's business in contrast to our surroundings, not only because we were packing surfboards hundreds of kilometres from the coast! As Dan and I travelled closer to the border of the Northern Territory, the landscape began to change – we were surrounded by more escarpments and gorges. When we saw the sign welcoming us, we jumped out for a quick snap and a foot race to see who would be first over the border, as neither of us had been to the Territory before.

We arrived in Beswick, an Indigenous community about 90 minutes south-east of Katherine (well, in Gigi it takes about that long!). We were there to meet Tom E. Lewis, a celebrated Australian actor, artist and musician who made his film debut back in 1978 as Jimmy in The Chant of Jimmy Blacksmith. He's been in loads of films, including The Proposition by Nick Cave. He told us that in 2016 he will be playing King Lear at the Barbican in London.

Spending a day with Tommy and his family at Beswick was one of the most special experiences of our trip. Not only did we hear his extraordinary story (and I got a few pointers on my didj playing!) but we also spent time with his family. We dug in the bush with his aunties for 'sugar bag', a native underground beehive filled with the most delectable honey. They were so cheeky and funny, bickering over the sugar bag, trying to steal it from each other's buckets and slapping each other's hands. Then we made some delicious local-style damper by bashing to a pulp the seed from dut dum (water lilies) and wrapping it in bark and cooking it over the fire. All the while we were encouraged by laughing, excitable young kids. I think they especially loved our little blue Bug!

To wrap up our amazing visit, Tommy took us to his secret spot, a waterfall cascading into a freshwater swimming hole surrounded by vibrant red rock and beautiful white sand – which was covered in croc tracks! There were so many it was like a kid had dragged a spade through the sand. After a day of sitting around in 40-degree heat, we were ready for a swim. Tommy told us it was safe, so we waded in and swam around. He tried to get us to go under the waterfall, but we weren't venturing any further in with all the crocs!

Dan and I were keen to go for a fish in Katherine, so we grabbed our rods and headed to the river. Again we had no luck, but we did run into two locals, Manuel Pamkal and Ben Lewis, who were setting some traps for freshwater prawns. We pulled in a few nets with them and managed to catch some. Running into cool characters is what this trip was all about.

Manuel wanted to show us two young blokes how to make fire with a fire stick. It was the first time Dan and I had ever done this and it was a real treat to learn from him. Plus, it got the fire roaring and ready to cook up the prawns, and the sneaky catfish we'd caught! It was a really relaxing setting. The sun was setting and we were sitting in the dirt with bare feet. The ground-baked fish tasted amazing, the sort of food you make on a camping trip with mates.

During our visit to Katherine, DC and I made possibly two of my most favourite recipes in the whole trip – my Sicilian Honey Fish with Macadamias (page 132), and his amazing Barramundi Family Coconut Curry (page 131), a big sharing bowl of curry goodness!

HQ

Manuel and his fire sticks

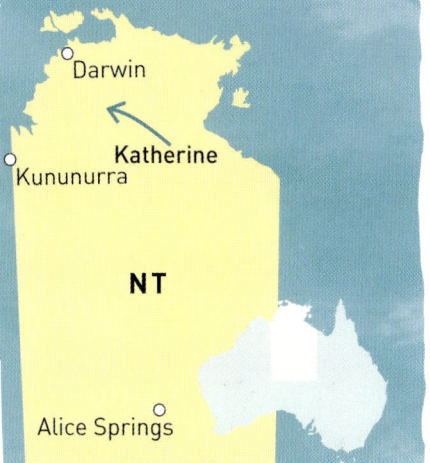

Honey fish cooking in the pan

Darwin
Katherine
Kununurra
NT
Alice Springs

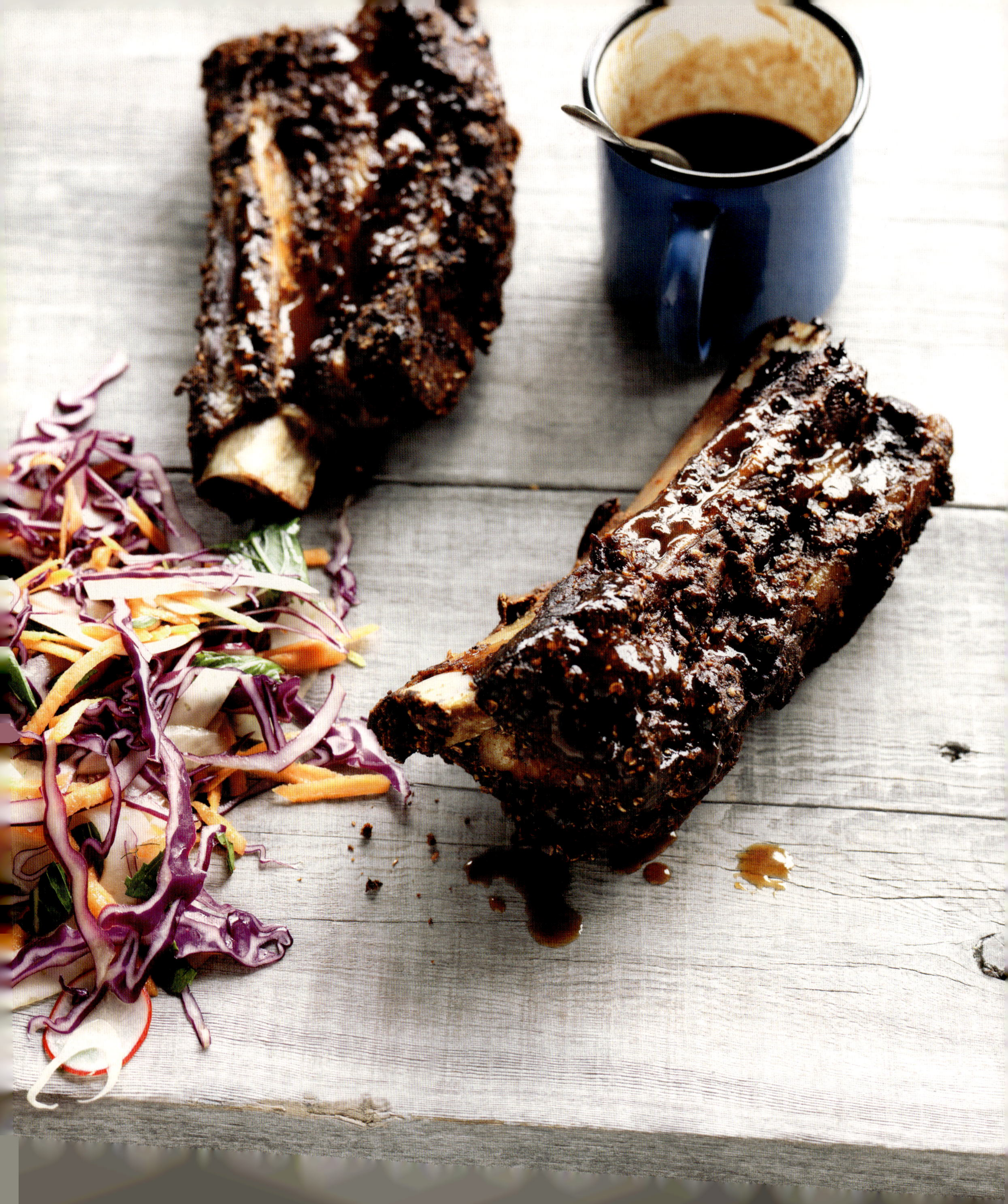

SMOKED BUFFALO RIBS (HQ)

I didn't realise there were so many buffalo up in the Territory, but we saw a whole heap, particularly at dusk. Some of our new Indigenous friends said they make a great meal that can feed a whole community. I've done something less traditional with my approach to cooking ribs and I've gone for the trend of smoked meat. It works really well!

2kg buffalo ribs, bone in (see Note)

2 cups hickory wood chips

2 cups bought BBQ sauce, thinned slightly with water

RUB

¼ cup smoked paprika

2 tablespoons ground coriander

2 tablespoons ground cumin

2 tablespoons salt

1 tablespoon garlic powder

1 tablespoon freshly ground pepper

1 tablespoon chipotle chilli sauce

2 teaspoons mustard powder

1. Combine all the ingredients for the rub in a large bowl. Add the ribs and rub all over, coating all the meat. If time permits, allow them to sit in the rub overnight in the fridge.

2. Preheat a covered BBQ to about 120°C. Turn off the centre burners. Place woods chips in a smoker box and place over a hot section on one side of the BBQ. Place a foil container of water on the other side.

3. Put the ribs into a large roasting pan and place into the centre of the BBQ (where there is no direct heat). Close the lid and cook for 4 hours, making sure to maintain the temperature. Baste the ribs regularly with the BBQ sauce.

4. Once the ribs are cooked, remove from the pan and cook on a BBQ grill plate over high heat to give some nice colour and finish the ribs off. Set aside on a tray, loosely covered with foil, to rest for 15 minutes. Serve with your favourite salad.

Serves 6

Use 2kg beef short ribs if you can't get buffalo ribs.

HONEY SRIRACHA ROAST CHOOK (HQ)

1.5kg chicken

1 tablespoon Sriracha chilli sauce

1 tablespoon fish sauce

1 tablespoon lime juice

1 tablespoon vegetable oil

2 teaspoons honey

½ cup coriander leaves, roughly chopped

1 long red chilli, sliced on angle

1 green shallot, sliced on angle

steamed jasmine rice, to serve

1 lime, cut in wedges, to serve

1. Preheat the oven to 180°C (160°C fan-forced). Place the chicken skin side up in a roasting pan. Combine the sauces, juice, oil and honey, and brush all over the chicken skin.

2. Roast for 50 minutes, or until the juices run clear when you pierce a skewer into the thickest part of the thigh.

3. Transfer to a large board, drizzle with pan juices and top with coriander, chilli and shallot. Serve with rice and lime wedges.

Serves 4

Sriracha is a Thai hot chilli sauce that you can buy in most supermarkets.

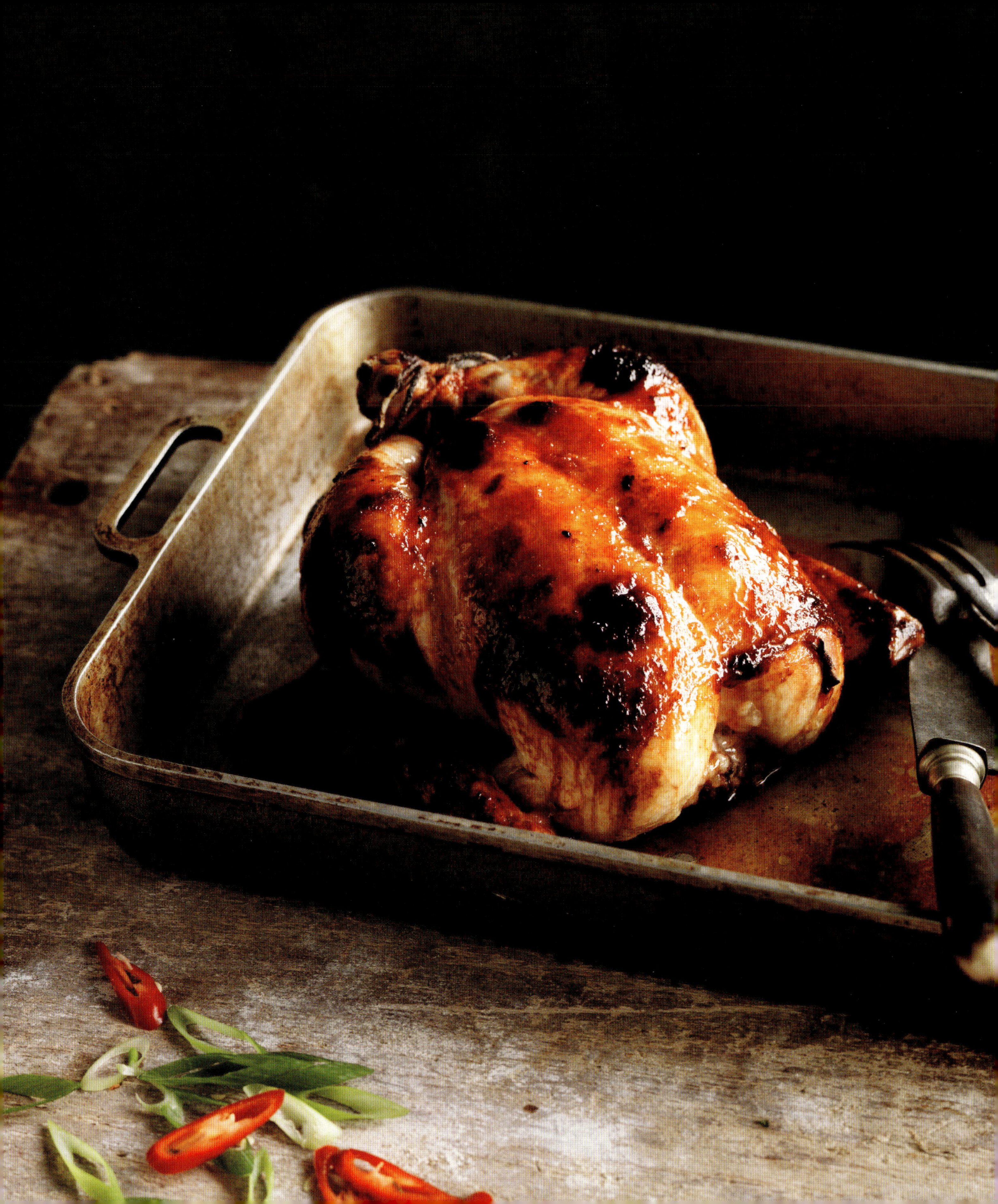

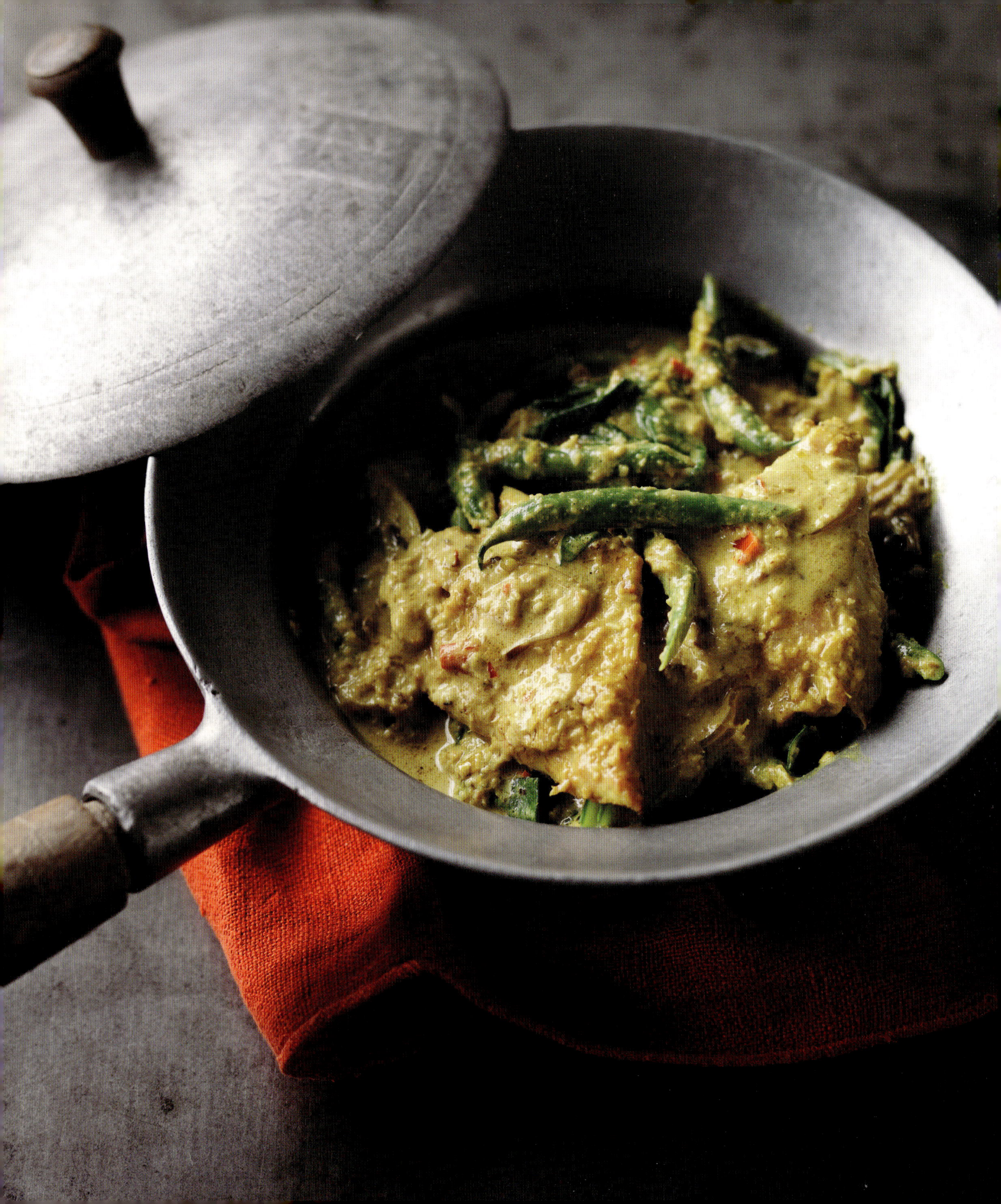

BARRAMUNDI FAMILY COCONUT CURRY

2 tablespoons olive or coconut oil

1 eschalot, finely chopped

¼ cup desiccated coconut

2 tablespoons curry paste (recipe below)

2 teaspoons ground turmeric

1 cup coconut milk

1 cup fish stock

2 teaspoons fish sauce

2 teaspoons honey

2 teaspoons lemon juice

50g green beans, trimmed and sliced on an angle

4 barramundi fillets, halved lengthways

1 bunch choy sum, trimmed and roughly chopped

coriander sprigs and steamed rice, to serve

CURRY PASTE

1 lemongrass stalk, white part only, finely chopped

1 long red chilli, finely chopped

3cm knob ginger, chopped

2 garlic cloves, chopped

2 teaspoons shrimp paste

1 tablespoon olive oil

5 coriander stalks, finely chopped

1. To make the curry paste, use a mortar and pestle or small food processor to grind the lemongrass, chilli, ginger and garlic with a pinch of salt. Add the shrimp paste and continue to grind until combined. Add the oil to thin it out and help it come together. Finish off by combining with the coriander stalks.

2. Heat the oil in a deep frying pan over medium-high heat. Cook the eschalot for 3–5 minutes or until golden brown. Add the coconut and cook for a further 1–2 minutes or until you achieve a nutty aroma.

3. Stir in the curry paste for 2 minutes, or until fragrant, before adding turmeric, coconut milk and stock. Bring to a simmer and add the fish sauce, honey and lemon juice. Sprinkle in the green beans, cover and cook for 2 minutes.

4. Lift the lid and add the barramundi fillets. Reduce the heat to medium and cook, covered, for 6–8 minutes, adding the choy sum for the last 3 minutes of cooking. Finish by tearing up coriander and sprinkling on top. Serve in bowls with steamed rice.

Serves 4

Freeze leftover curry paste to use another time.

SICILIAN HONEY FISH WITH MACADAMIAS

This dish is not authentically Sicilian, but I know they do a similar thing there. What they don't have is fresh barra, sweet bush honey or buttery macadamia nuts to add the special crunch! Try this interesting combo inspired by excellent produce in the Northern Territory. You'll love it!

¾ cup macadamias
25g butter
2 tablespoons rice bran oil
¼ cup oregano leaves
2 teaspoons lemon juice
2 tablespoons honey
¼ cup fish stock
4 x 200g firm white fish fillets
2 tablespoons balsamic vinegar
2 tablespoons extra virgin olive oil
4 cups (loosely packed) mixed baby salad leaves
¼ cup finely grated Parmesan cheese

1. Preheat the oven to 180°C (160°C fan-forced). Spread the macadamias onto an oven tray and roast for about 7 minutes or until golden. Cool, then coarsely crush.

2. Melt the butter and half the oil in a saucepan over medium heat. Add the oregano leaves, taking care as the oil will spit. Cook for 1–2 minutes, then add the lemon juice, honey and fish stock. Simmer for 5 minutes until reduced and slightly thickened. Season with salt and pepper and stir through the macadamias.

3. Meanwhile, heat the remaining oil in a large non-stick frying pan over medium-high heat. Cook the fish (in batches if needed) for 3 minutes on each side, or until cooked through and golden. Remove and keep warm.

4. Whisk the balsamic and olive oil together and season with salt and pepper. Toss with salad leaves and top with grated Parmesan.

5. To serve, place a piece of fish on each plate and spoon over some of the sauce. Serve with salad.

Serves 4

Use thick fillets such as barramundi or blue-eye here.

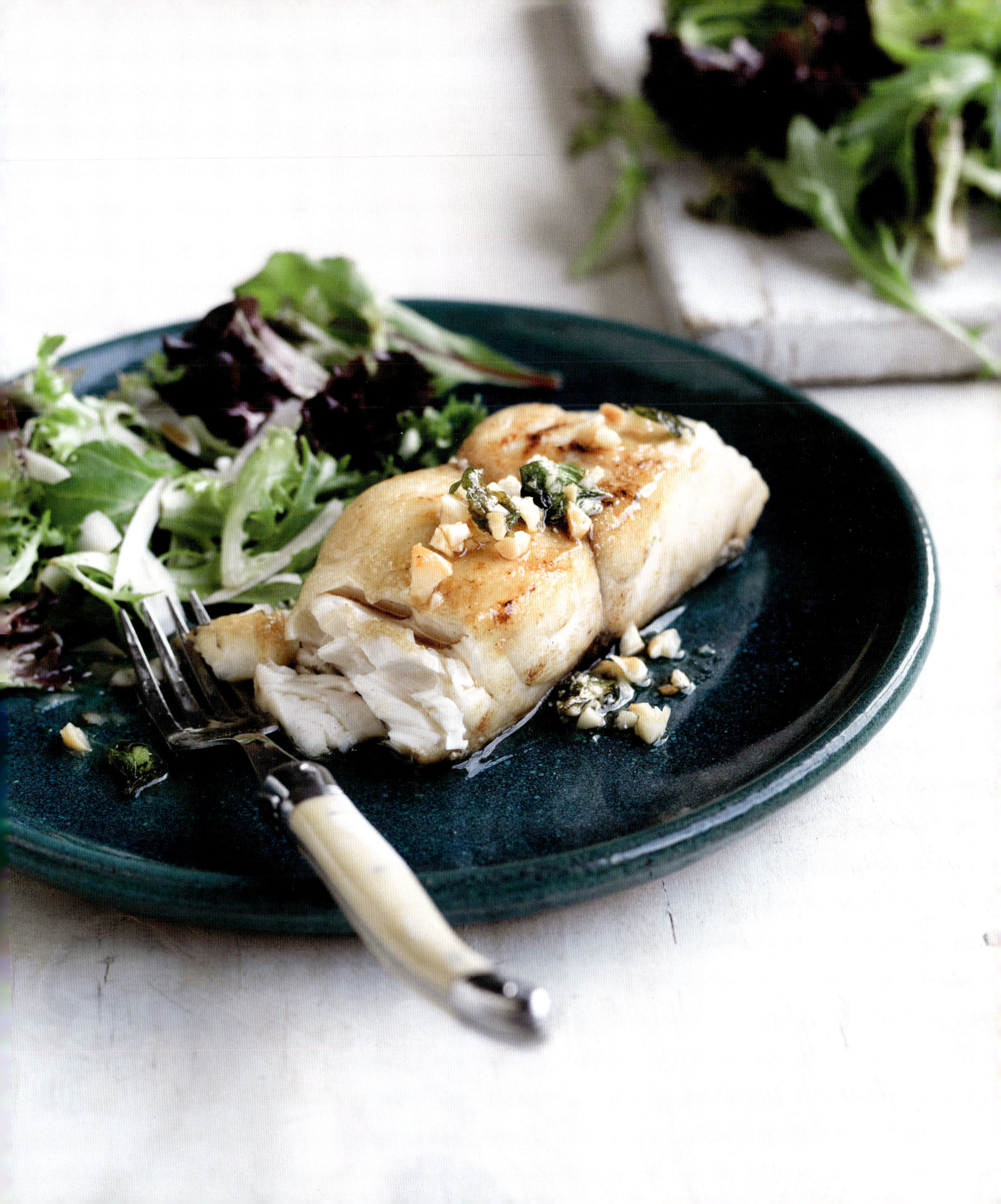

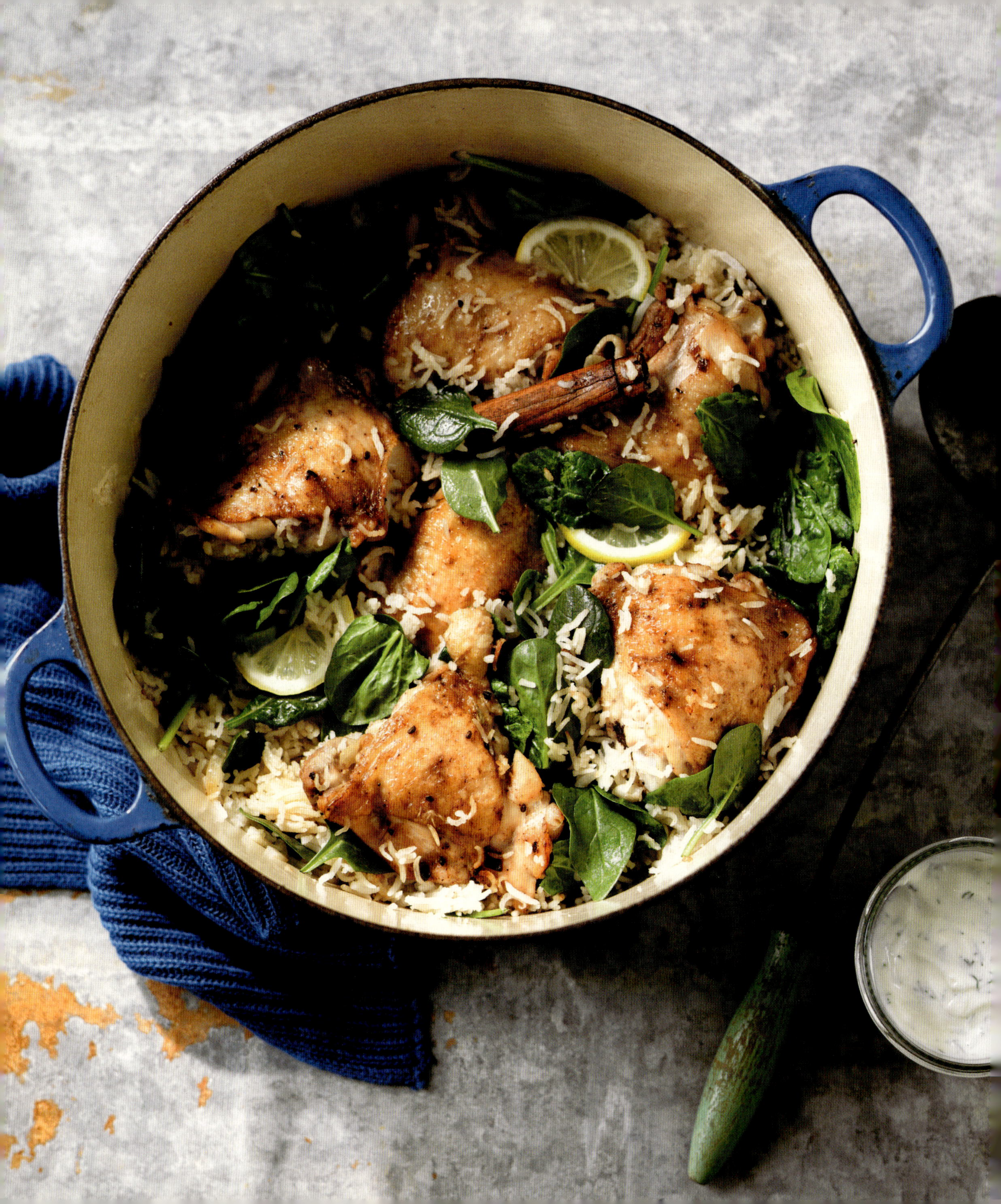

CARAMELISED ONE-PAN CHICKEN OF AWESOMENESS! (DC)

Cardamom and cloves are spices so aromatically pleasing they are found in many food cultures across the world. Middle Eastern cooking excites me right now, and how could I not pair this super easy crowd-pleaser with amazing fresh natural yoghurt?

8 cardamom pods

6 cloves

1 teaspoon chilli powder

1kg chicken thighs, skin on

¼ cup olive oil

1 onion, sliced

2 garlic cloves, crushed

1½ cups basmati rice

3 cups chicken stock

1 cinnamon stick

1 lemon, halved and sliced

2 cups baby spinach leaves

½ cup natural yoghurt

1 tablespoon chopped dill leaves

1. Dry roast the cardamom pods and cloves in a small frying pan over medium heat for about 2 minutes or until aromatic. Cool slightly, then use a mortar and pestle to roughly crush. Remove the pods and finely grind the cardamom seeds with the cloves. Mix in the chilli powder and a pinch of salt and pepper.

2. Place the chicken into a shallow dish and sprinkle with the spice mixture. Drizzle with 1 tablespoon of the oil and massage through until evenly coated. Cover and marinate in the fridge for a minimum of 30 minutes.

3. Heat 1 tablespoon of the oil in a deep heavy-based frying over medium-high heat. Cook the onion for 5–7 minutes or until golden brown. Remove and set aside. Add the remaining tablespoon of oil to the pan, and add the chicken, skin side down. Cook until golden and crispy, then turn over to seal the flesh side, roughly 3–4 minutes in total. Transfer to a plate.

4. Return the onions to the pan and spread evenly over the base. Sprinkle the rice in an even layer over the onion. Arrange the chicken skin side up on the rice and pour the stock around, avoiding the chicken skin. Pop in the cinnamon stick, cover tightly and bring to the boil. Reduce the temperature to low and cook for 30 minutes.

5. Uncover briefly and add the lemon and spinach. Season with salt and pepper, cover and cook for a further 10 minutes.

6. Use a fork to fluff up the rice and fold the spinach and lemon through. To serve, combine the yoghurt and dill in a bowl and spoon over the top.

Serves 4

BANANA CAKE WITH NATIVE HONEY RICOTTA

I rarely use refined sugar in my recipes, but after sampling the honey in Katherine I was compelled to splurge on this amazing gold! You can make this cake gluten free if you substitute gluten free flour or almond meal, and add gluten free baking powder.

180g butter, chopped, at room temperature
2 cups good quality honey
3 eggs
3 cups self-raising flour
1 teaspoon ground cardamom
2 ripe bananas, mashed
1 cup natural yoghurt
1 banana, extra, sliced on an angle
2 cups ricotta
finely grated zest of half a lemon

1. Preheat the oven to 170°C (150°C fan-forced). Grease a 25cm springform cake tin and line the base with baking paper.

2. Use electric beaters to beat the butter and 1½ cups of the honey until light and creamy. Add the eggs one at a time, beating well after each addition.

3. Sift together the flour, cardamom and a pinch of salt. Using a spatula, fold into the butter mixture, then fold in the banana and yoghurt.

4. Pour into the prepared tin and arrange the banana slices on top. Bake for 1 hour and 10 minutes or until a skewer comes out clean. Cool in the tin for 10 minutes, then release the sides and slide onto a wire rack to cool.

5. Combine the ricotta with the remaining honey and lemon zest in a bowl and serve on the side.

Serves 12

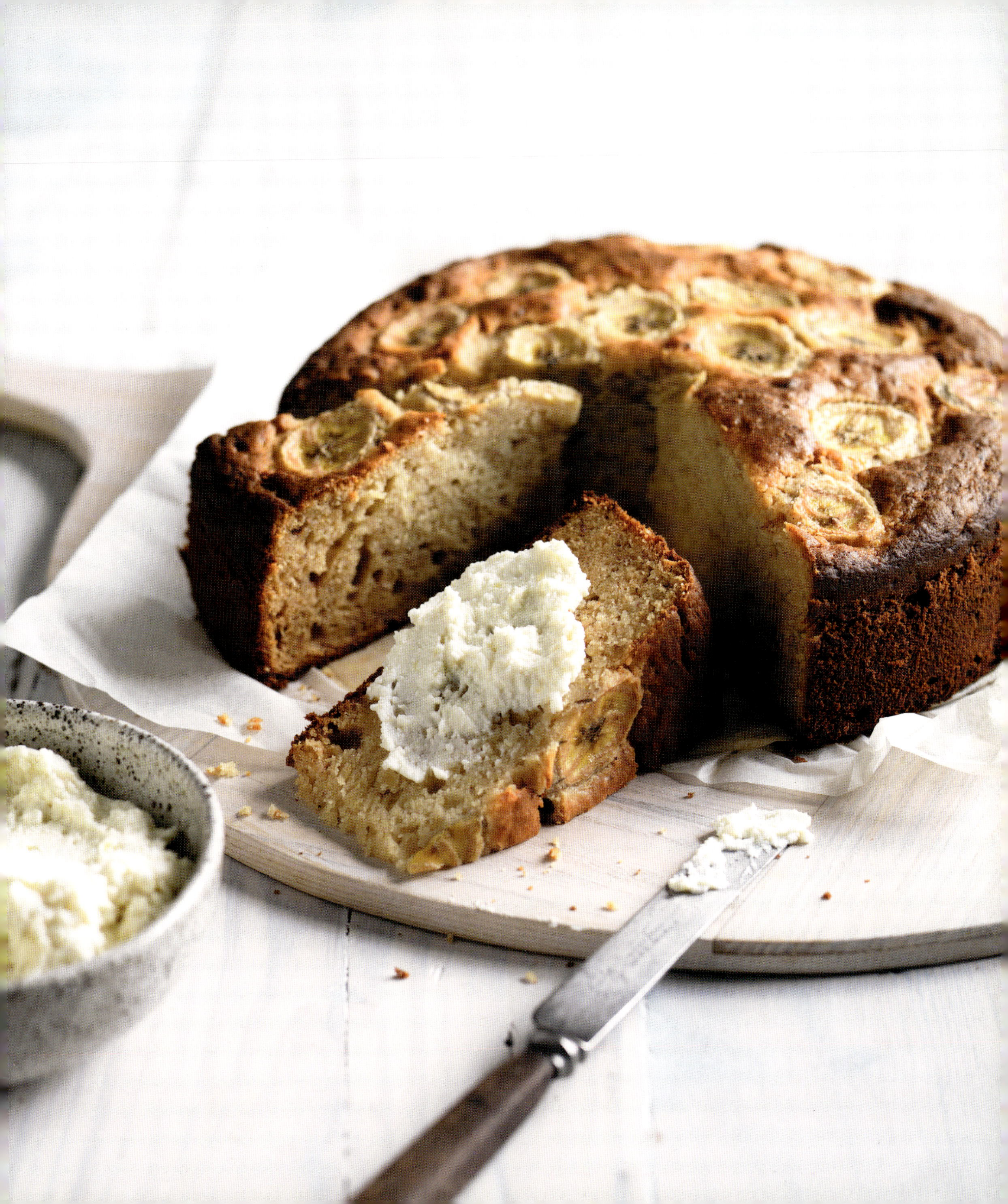

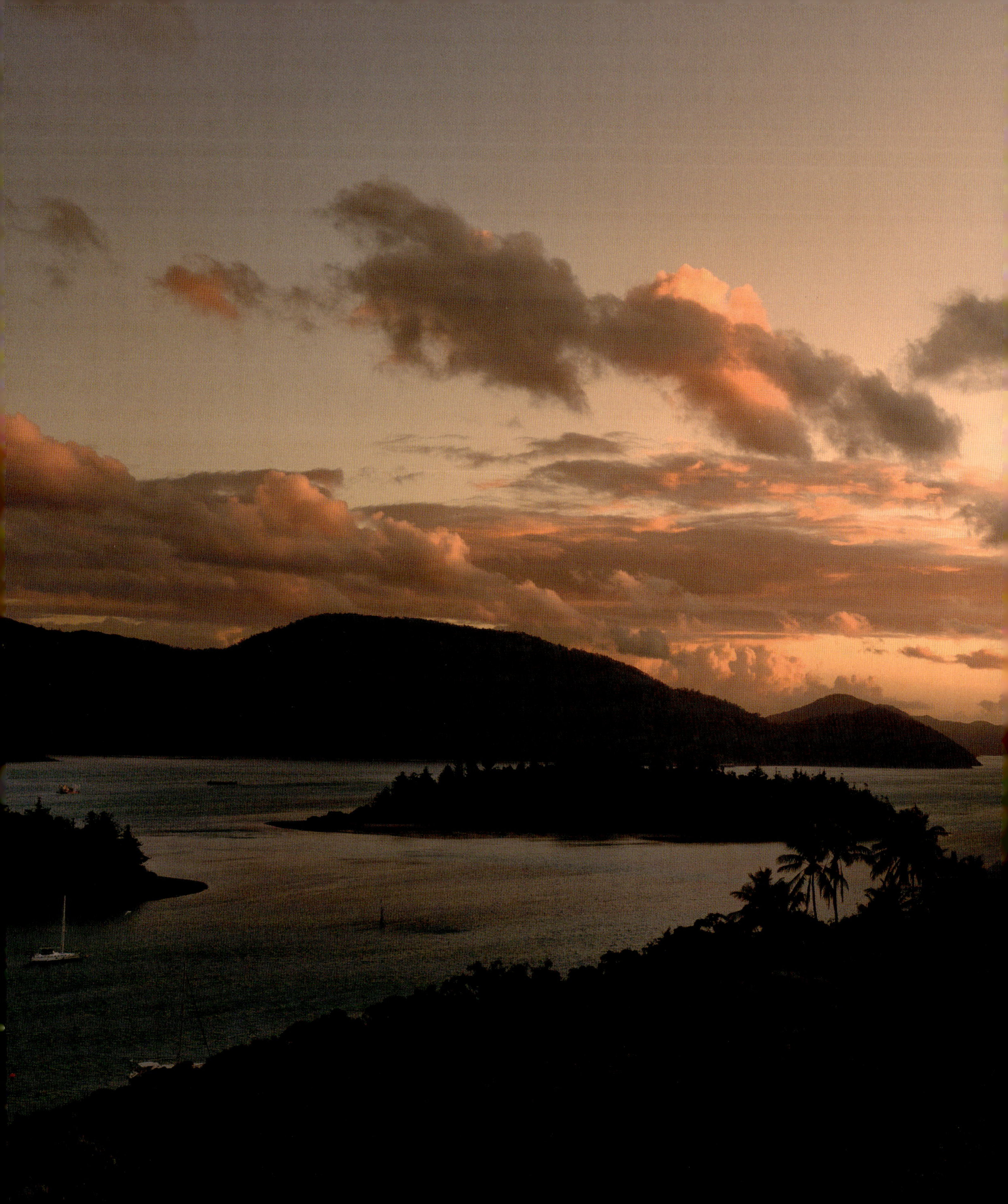

The TROPICAL NORTH

Back on the road and heading far north into the tropics. First stop is Cairns, a vibrant coastal city on the eastern side of Cape York Peninsula between the Coral Sea and the Great Dividing Range. It's the only place in the world where two World Heritage sites meet, the Great Barrier Reef and the Daintree Rainforest. It enjoys an average of 300 days a year of balmy sunshine. From Cairns, Gigi turns south to Townsville on the shores of Cleveland Bay where the placid Ross River flows calmly through the bustling city. Next to the glorious Whitsundays, 74 islands basking in the heart of the Great Barrier Reef in the Coral Sea. Many islands are uninhabited and feature dense forests, bushwalking trails and wide, pristine beaches. There are no crashing waves or deadly undertows, so the waters are perfect for sailing. The only sight more beautiful than sunset in the Whitsundays is sunrise in the Whitsundays. The journey continues south to subtropical Bundaberg, nestled 15 kilometres inland amid sugar cane fields and banana plantations. The molasses from the sugar goes to make the city's most famous export, Bundaberg Rum. Its odd name is perhaps a hybrid of 'bunda', the Kabi Indigneous word meaning 'important man', and 'berg', the German term denoting a mountain.

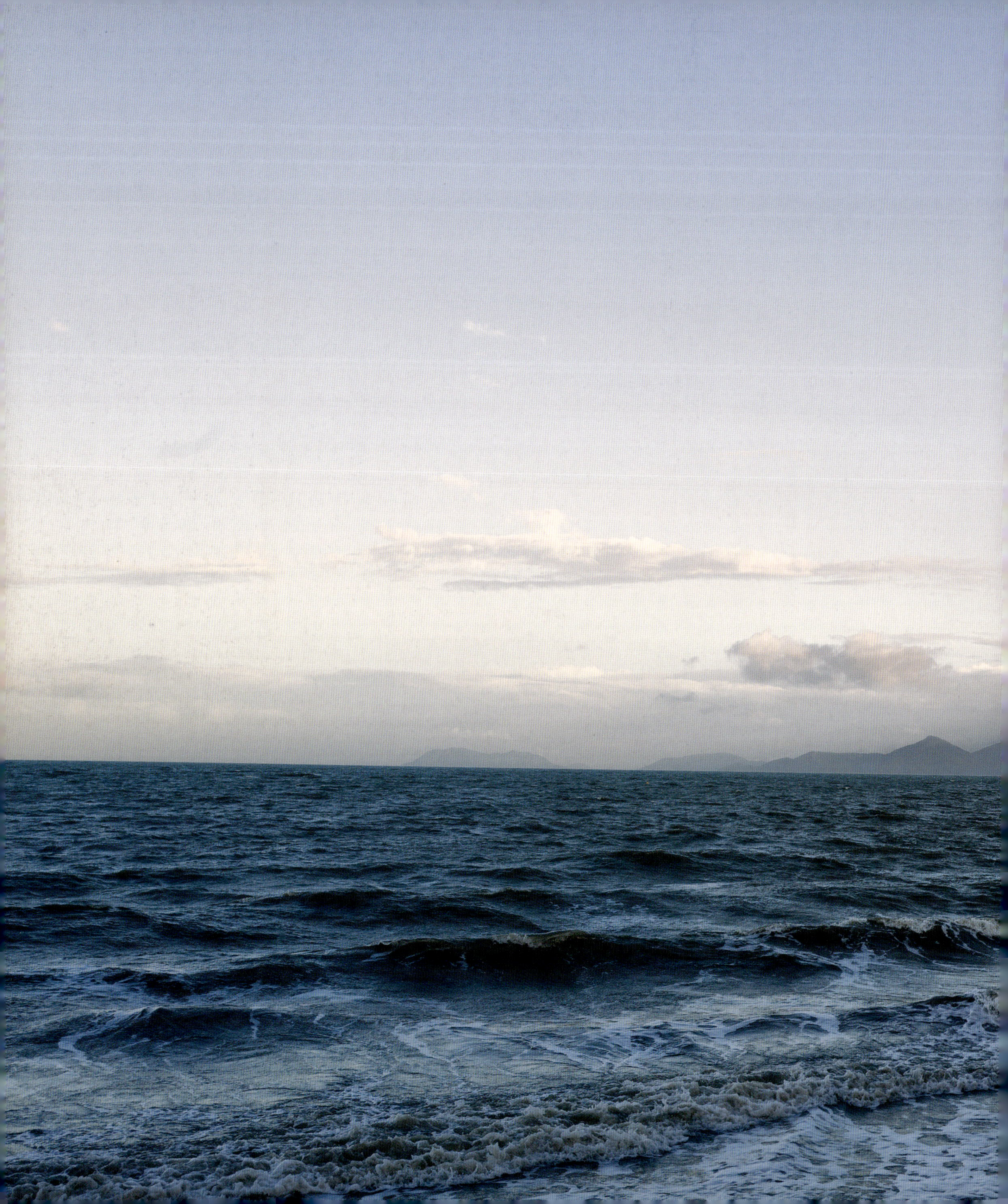

Cairns & Townsville

This journey into North Queensland was a particularly special one for me. I hadn't been to this part of the country for 12 years, and that's a long time in most people's lives, but it's even longer when it comes to revisiting the home of your extended family and grandmother.

We started out in the most wicked fashion on the SkyRail Rainforest Cableway from Cairns to Kuranda. We climbed the walls of the Barron Gorge in a gondola – much different from those found in Venice – and as we looked back through the cable car we could see coffee plantations and suburban Cairns behind us, right out to the ocean. HQ and I found that, with all the flying across the country we'd been doing, the things that once made us a little anxious now excited us.

When we jumped off the gondola, we were off to the Kuranda Honey House, a famous local store. Trish Green, the owner, has an impressive understanding of beekeeping. I am a massive fan of honey and when Trish offered us a first-hand experience of handling bees, we had to say yes. The fun began when Quinny and I jumped into our beehive suits. Picture a couple of guys in white onesies with fully enclosed face nets … yeah, buddy! We couldn't help but pull out some robot dance moves and pretend we were starship troopers from *Star Wars*! I was surprised the bees were so relaxed when we helped ourselves to some of their fresh harvest after all their hard work. One of the most interesting facts that Trish taught us is that female bees do all the work, and the purpose of the male is to mate with the queen bee. Once they mate, they die. Imagine that for a life …

Something else she explained to us was that it's where the bees pollinate that gives honey its distinctive flavour. Some get their pollen from flowering avocado trees, which leads to creamy avocado flavour in the honey; others from the rainforest, resulting in a beautiful floral note.

Driving through Ingham and arriving at the house of my maternal grandmother, Nunna, happened so quickly. I did vaguely remember the streets from when I was here last – and I definitely remembered the sugar cane train! Rocking up to Nunna's house was really special. We hadn't seen each other for 8 years, and when Nunna walked down the stairs she had a tear in her eye. I gave her the biggest hug, and didn't want to let her go. That emotional moment made me realise that I have to see her more often.

For the next few hours Hayden and I cooked up ravioli from scratch and Nunna took control of the sugo, a traditional rich Italian tomato sauce. I learned so much about her this time; we have heaps in common. She loves to do everything by taste and feel, such as the sugo she was making, and when it comes to food she has the same spark as me. What topped it off was having Mum and Dad there for the dinner that night, too. They brought a famous family photo of me as a three-year-old playing dress-ups in my chef outfit. We all had a good laugh and chatted the night away – pure family time. It was great to share that with Hayden.

Our final stop was the Reef HQ Aquarium in Townsville, the national education centre for the Great Barrier Reef. I never thought I would say it, but patting and holding a leopard shark is like holding a Labrador. It just wanted to stick around and grab a tickle! We also visited the turtle hospital and we were blown away by the care given to rehabilitating sick and injured marine turtles. Since opening in 2009, the hospital has released 70 of these lovely animals back into the Great Barrier Reef Marine Park. We share this world with such wonderful creatures.

DC

Check these out!
Gourmet mushrooms

Cairns
Townsville
QLD
Brisbane

Visiting the turtle hospital

Nunna

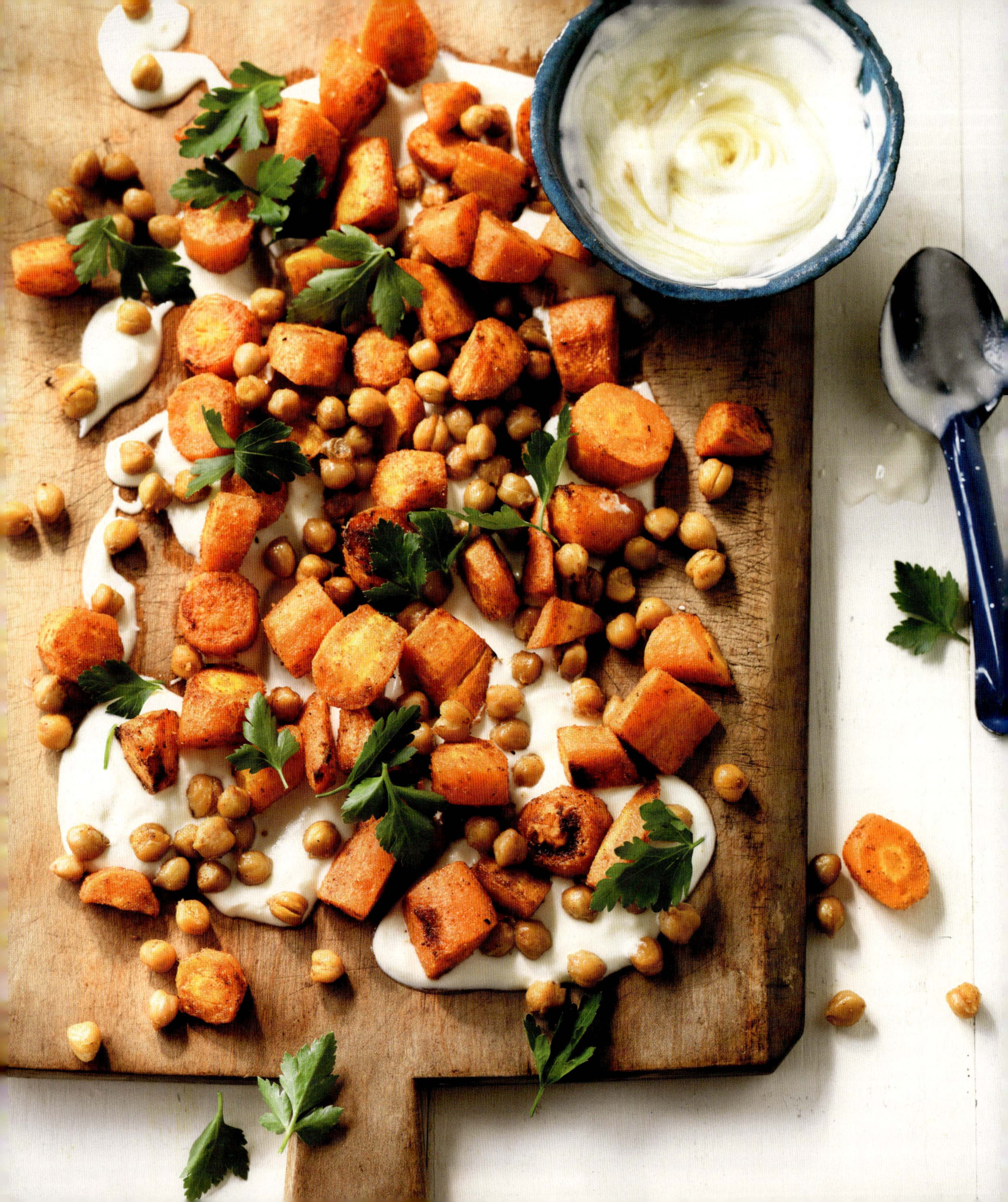

SPICED CARROTS AND CHICKPEAS ON HONEY YOGHURT ⓓⓒ

I am super guilty of serving things on boards because (1) it saves washing up; and (2) it is much cooler! I mean, what's better than placing a board on the table for your family and mates to tuck into? Have a go at this famous starter and you'll know what I mean!

8 carrots (about 600g), topped and chopped into uneven chips

2½ tablespoons olive oil

2 teaspoons ground cumin

2 teaspoons ground coriander

½ teaspoon cayenne pepper

400g can chickpeas, rinsed and drained

1½ cups natural yoghurt

2 tablespoons honey

fresh herbs, to garnish

1. Preheat the oven to 200°C (180°C fan-forced) and pop a roasting pan into the oven. Toss the carrots and olive oil in a bowl. Sprinkle with cumin, coriander and cayenne pepper and season with salt and pepper. Give it a toss before adding the chickpeas and mixing through.

2. Remove the pan from the oven and tip in the carrots and chickpeas. Roast for 20–25 minutes, tossing once or twice during cooking, until slightly crisp on the edges.

3. Combine the yoghurt, honey and a pinch of salt together in a bowl. Spoon half onto a board making big and small dollops (let your imagination do its thing). Place the carrots and chickpeas rustically on top and spoon over the remaining yoghurt mixture. Top with fresh herbs for a bit of colour.

Serves 6–8 as a starter or a side

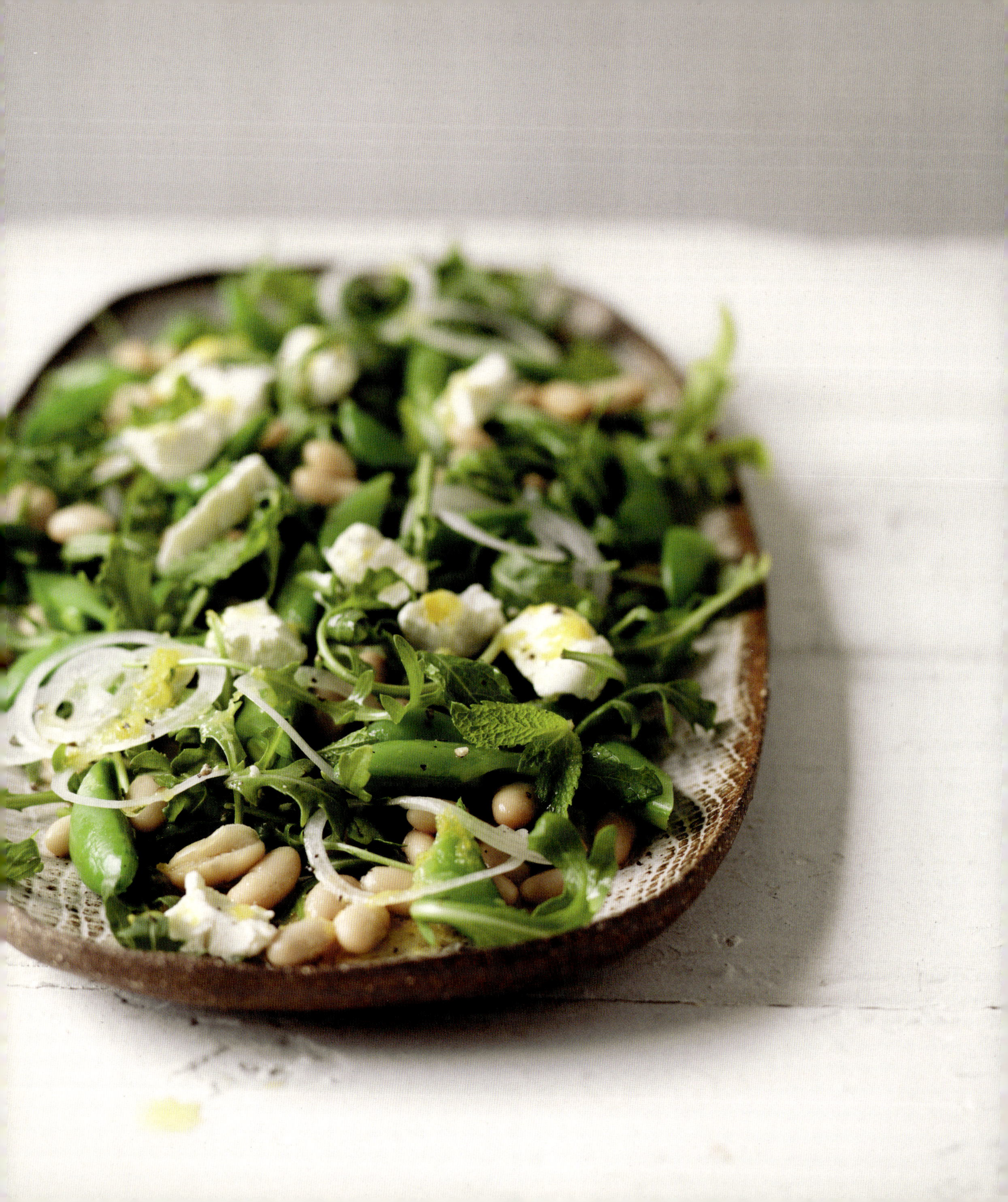

PEA, MINT AND WHITE BEAN SALAD WITH GOAT'S CHEESE (HQ)

150g sugar snap peas, trimmed

400g can white beans, rinsed and drained

½ cup mint leaves

1 cup baby rocket

½ small white onion, cut into thin rings

100g goat's cheese

finely grated zest and juice of 1 lemon

¼ cup extra virgin olive oil

1. Place the peas into a heatproof bowl and cover with boiling water. Stand for 1 minute, then drain well and plunge into a bowl of iced water. Let cool, then drain and pat dry with paper towels.
2. Gently toss together the white beans, peas, mint, rocket and onion. Crumble the goat's cheese over and dress with the combined lemon zest, juice and extra virgin olive oil.

Serves 4

FIELD OF MUSHROOMS ON SOURDOUGH (DC)

This is one of the tastiest breakfasts you will ever wrap your lips around! I never liked mushrooms growing up, but now I can't get enough of their earthy, umami character. The best thing about this dish is you can cook the mushrooms in a batch so you have them on tap. Just reheat and get your toast ready!

4 garlic cloves, unpeeled

¼ cup olive oil

2 onions, sliced

400g field mushrooms, thickly sliced (or other favourite mushies)

75g butter, chopped

5 thyme sprigs

juice of 1 lemon

8 slices sourdough bread

1 tablespoon olive oil, extra

75g feta

1. Preheat the oven to 180°C (160°C fan-forced). Lay a piece of foil out on a bench and place the garlic on top. Drizzle with 1 tablespoon of the olive oil and season with salt. Wrap the foil around to enclose the garlic, and pop in the oven for 20 minutes or until soft and caramelised.

2. Heat the remaining oil in a large frying pan over medium-high heat and cook the onion for 5 minutes or until golden brown. Squeeze out the soft roasted garlic flesh and stir into the onion for 1 minute. Add the mushrooms and allow to sweat for 10 minutes. You are looking to get rid of most of the moisture.

3. Add the butter, thyme and lemon juice and season with salt and pepper. Cover and cook for a further 5 minutes over low heat so the flavours infuse.

4. Toast the sourdough, drizzle olive oil over and spoon on the mushroom mix. Crumble the feta on top and tuck in!

Serves 4

Take it to another level by rubbing the bread with a cut raw garlic clove and drizzling with oil before toasting in the oven.

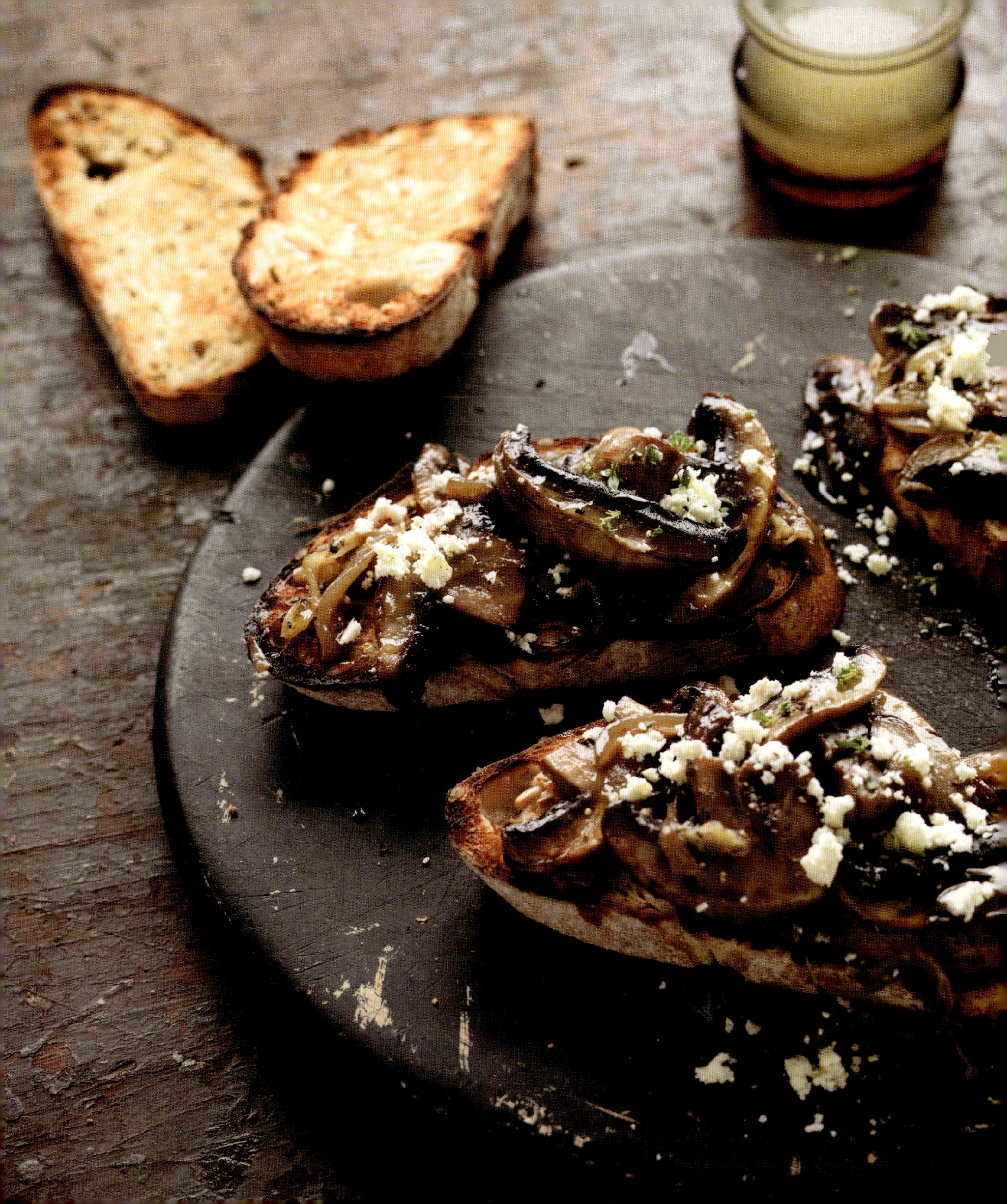

CREAMY GARLIC MUSHROOM LINGUINE

Use any combination of mushrooms for this delicious winner, or just one or two types if you prefer. I like pine mushrooms when they're in season.

400g dried linguine

40g butter

1 tablespoon olive oil

2 garlic cloves, crushed

1 teaspoon thyme leaves

400g assorted mushrooms, sliced

½ cup flat-leaf parsley, chopped (reserving some for garnish)

⅔ cup thickened cream

finely grated zest ½ lemon (reserving some for garnish)

1. Cook the linguine in a large pot of rapidly boiling salted water according to packet instructions, or until al dente. Drain well.

2. Meanwhile, heat a large heavy-based frying pan over medium heat and add the butter and oil. As it begins to sizzle, add the garlic, thyme and mushrooms.

3. Sauté the mushrooms for about 4 minutes until they begin to soften and colour slightly. Season with salt and pepper, then add parsley and stir in the cream.

4. Bring cream to the boil and then reduce the heat and simmer for a minute or so to reduce slightly. Add the pasta and lemon zest, and toss to coat in the sauce.

5. Serve in a large bowl or on a platter and garnish with reserved parsley and lemon zest.

Serves 4

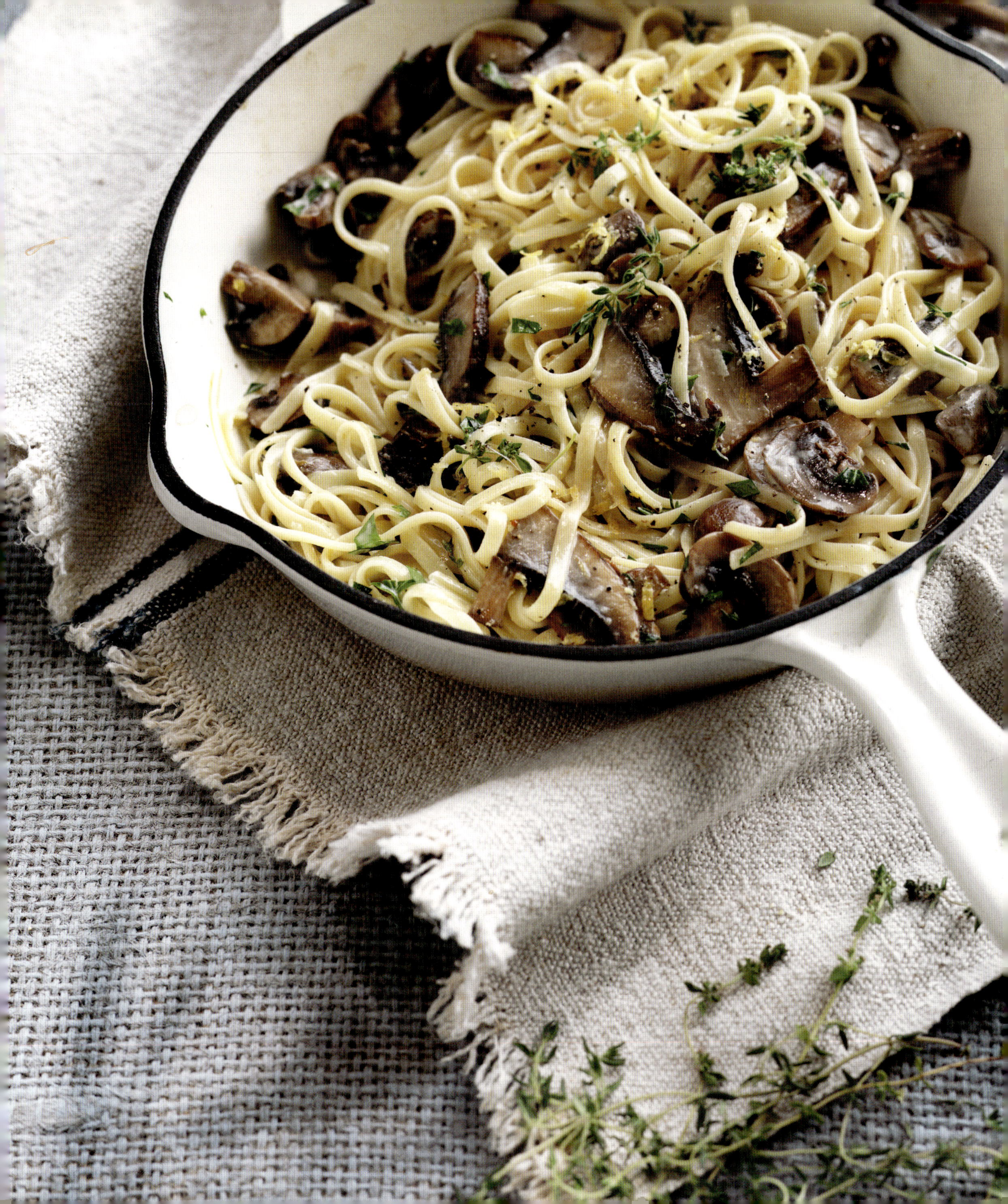

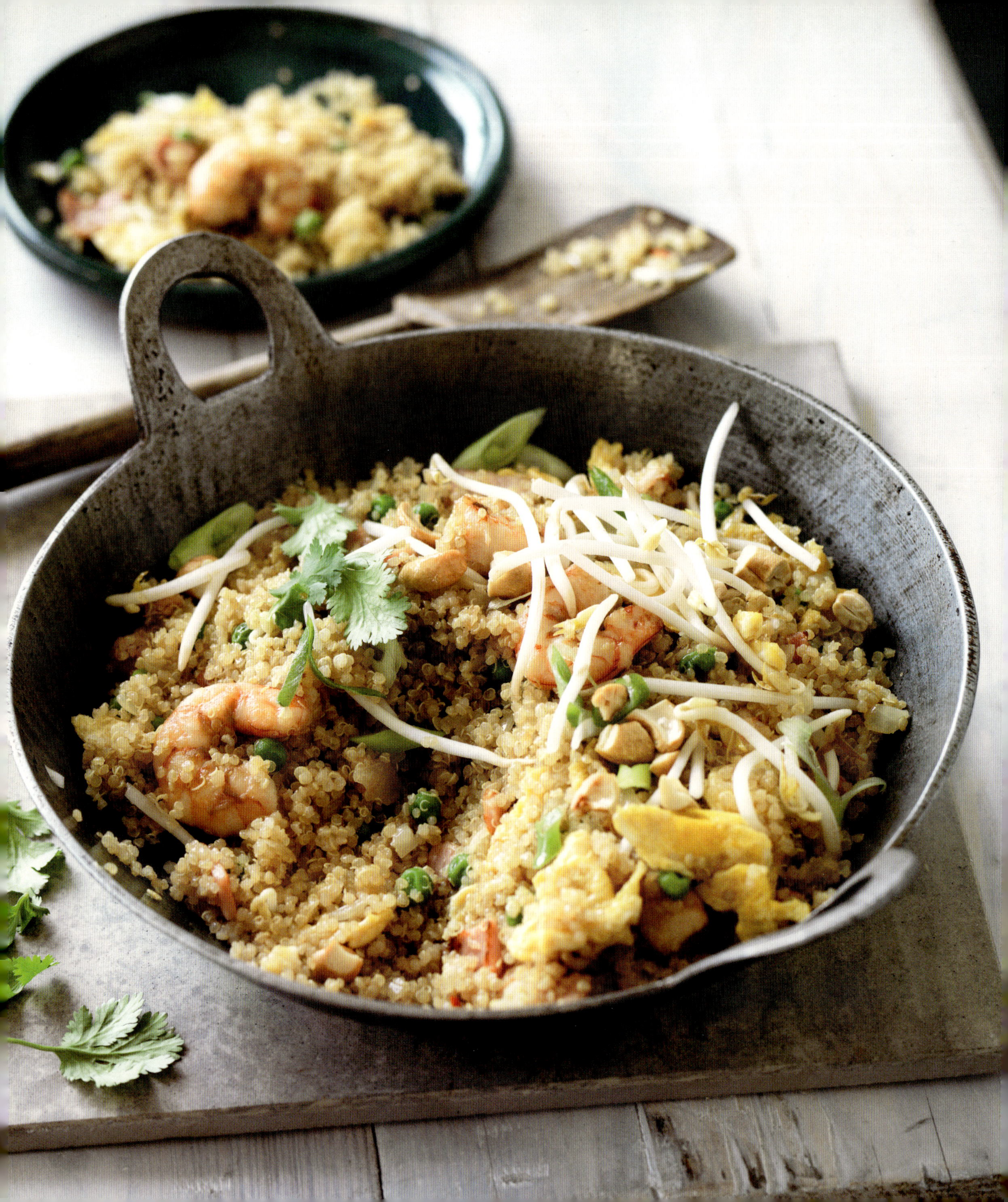

PRAWN FRIED QUINOA

1 cup quinoa, rinsed

1 tablespoon sesame oil

3 rashers lean bacon, roughly chopped

1 onion, sliced

1 garlic clove, finely chopped

1 teaspoon finely grated ginger

1 long red chilli, deseeded and finely chopped

600g green prawns, peeled and deveined

¾ cup frozen peas

2 eggs, lightly beaten

1 cup bean sprouts

2 tablespoons tamari or soy sauce

¼ cup chopped unsalted roasted cashews

2 green shallots, chopped

coriander sprigs, to serve

1. Put the quinoa into a medium saucepan and cover with 2 cups of water. Cover and bring to the boil. Reduce the heat to low and simmer, covered, for 10–12 minutes or until the quinoa has absorbed all the water and is tender.

2. Heat 2 teaspoons of the oil in a large wok over medium-high heat and brown the bacon for 3 minutes. Lift out with a slotted spoon and drain on paper towels. Add the onion to the wok and stir-fry for 3 minutes, then add the garlic, ginger and chilli. Stir-fry for another minute.

3. Add the prawns and stir-fry until they change colour, then fold in the quinoa and peas. Don't stir too much or the quinoa will become stodgy. Return the bacon back to the wok, then push the lot to one side. Pour the eggs into the exposed area and cook, turning the egg to cook quickly and break up into pieces.

4. Gently fold the bean sprouts and tamari through. Serve topped with cashews, green shallot and coriander.

Serves 4

DURBAN STYLE PRAWN CURRY ⓗⓠ

I have been very lucky to travel to some of the most spectacular parts of the world, one such place being South Africa. It's much like Australia in its climate, beaches and love for food. This dish pays tribute to the glorious cooking I've enjoyed there.

1 tablespoon coriander seeds

1 teaspoon fenugreek seeds

2 teaspoons fennel seeds

1 cinnamon stick

3 cloves

1½ teaspoons ground turmeric

½ teaspoon chilli powder

1½ tablespoons coconut oil

5 cardamom pods, bruised

2 teaspoons yellow mustard seeds

20 fresh curry leaves

2 whole dried chillies

2 onions, chopped

3 garlic cloves, crushed

3cm knob ginger, finely grated

1.2kg green prawns, peeled and deveined

2 x 400ml cans coconut milk

½ cup coriander leaves, roughly chopped

1 lime, cut into wedges

steamed basmati rice and Indian-style breads, to serve

1. Combine the coriander, fenugreek and fennel seeds in a dry frying pan with the cinnamon stick and cloves. Toast over medium heat for 1–2 minutes until fragrant. Use a mortar and pestle or spice grinder to grind to a powder. Stir in the turmeric and chilli powder and set aside.

2. Heat the coconut oil in a large pot or wok over medium-high heat. Add the cardamom and mustard seeds and cook until the spices begin to pop. Add the curry leaves, dried chilli, onion, garlic and ginger. Sauté for five minutes until things begin to get nice and fragrant and the onion develops a good golden colour.

3. Add the prawns and spice mixture and stir to coat well. Cook for 2 minutes until fragrant. Stir in the coconut milk, bring to a simmer and cook for a few minutes, until the prawns just turn orange. Season with salt to taste.

4. Serve in a large bowl garnished with coriander and lime wedges and accompanied by steamed rice and Indian breads.

Serves 4

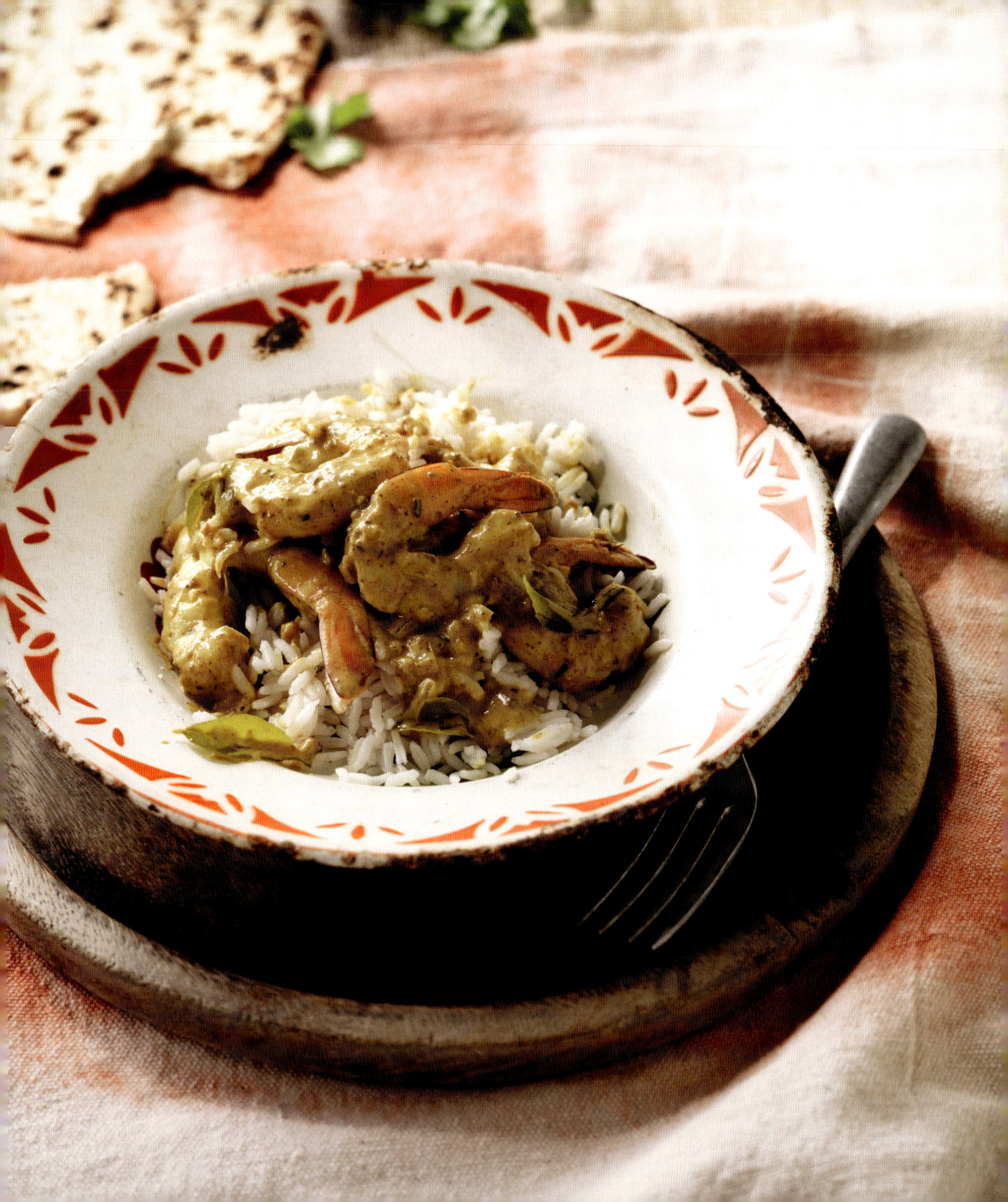

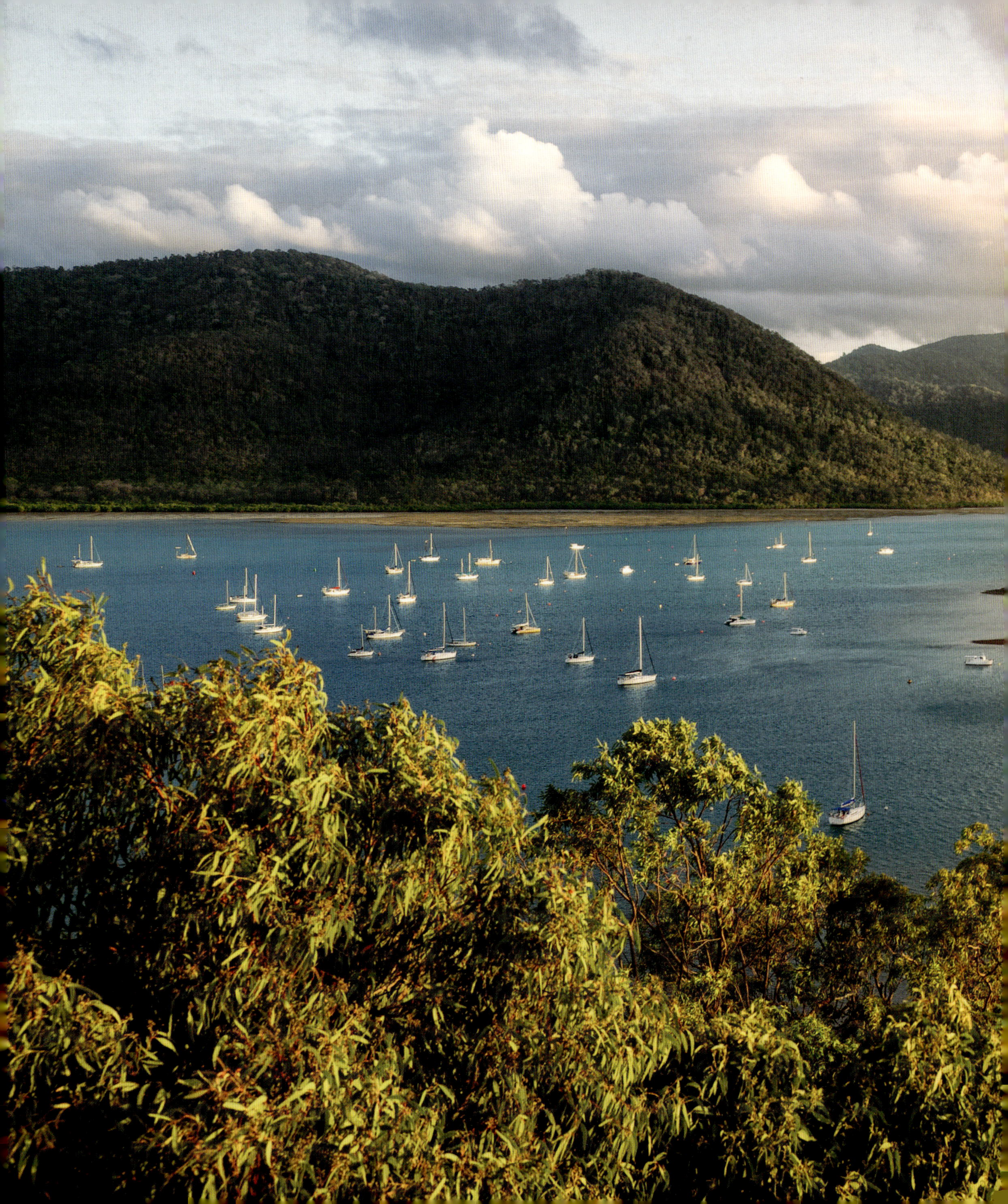

The Whitsundays

Deep blue waters, white sand beaches, coral reefs and pine covered mountainous islands – it's my type of paradise (maybe throw in some waves for good measure!). This is what the Whitsundays is all about: a water-lover's playground, a place to escape and relax, and that is exactly what DC and I proposed to do. We met paddle boarder Jaclyn Watson and her friend Sandy Hapgood, who invited us to jump aboard one of Sandy's boats to explore these beautiful islands.

The Whitsundays are the perfect place for a sail, even for two rookies like Dan and me, with 74 islands and many secluded bays and inlets. Under the guidance of our skipper, Sandy, we were put straight to work. Our first stop was on the north-eastern side of the famous Hayman Island where we hopped from the boat in the tender to go for a snorkel in the wondrous colourful reef. The highlight for me was seeing a massive Maori wrasse, one of the largest coral reef fish in Australia.

After a few hours in and out of the water and sharing some lunch, it was time to head to our safe harbour for the night, the Nara Inlet. There, at the Ngaro cultural site, we saw the remarkable cave paintings made by the Ngaro people dating back nearly 9,000 years. You would expect paintings of that great age to have deteriorated, but it's not the case. They were as vivid as if they had just been painted yesterday, relaying essential information, such as the best places to fish, how to climb the mountain and how to escape rising tides.

The following day we were underway again, this time to Hill Inlet to do a little stand-up paddle boarding and to soak up the surrounding beauty. We topped this off with Dan's amazing dinner: Harissa Bream with Flatbread and Homemade Labneh (page 166) – sooo tasty! It just goes to show that you don't need to be in a well-equipped kitchen to create amazing food. A little cooker on the back of a boat with fresh ingredients will do!

The next morning we took off in the tender nice and early to catch the sunrise over world famous Whitehaven Beach. This wasn't without complication! First up, we couldn't land on the back beach as the tide was too low. Then, when we made our way around the point to the beach, the wind and swell was too large for us to land there. A missed opportunity, but still lots of fun.

Heading back to reality and away from the beautiful fresh air and breeze of the ocean is always hard, but luckily we were surrounded by amazing people who love to share their passions and their stories and who want Dan and I to fall in love with their favourite places, just like they have.

Now that we were competent sailors, Dan and I took the helm and headed back to the port in Airlie Beach, ready for our next landward adventure.

HQ

Our type of paradise!

The tranquil waters of the Coral Sea

MORETON BAY BUG ROLLS

The lobster roll is a US classic that both Churchy and I love. Here I've given it a little Aussie twist with barbecued Moreton Bay bugs. This is the ideal lunch to eat on a boat in the Whitsundays, as Dan discovered when I made one for him!

2 garlic cloves, crushed

50g butter, melted

4 Moreton Bay bugs, split in half, cleaned

4 soft long rolls, split through the top

potato chips, to serve

SAUCE

½ cup whole egg mayonnaise

¼ cup finely diced celery

2 tablespoons finely diced red onion

¼ cup chervil, finely chopped

1 tablespoon Sriracha hot sauce

3 teaspoons lemon juice

1. To make the sauce, combine all the ingredients in a small bowl and season with salt and pepper to taste.

2. Preheat a BBQ grill or flat plate over medium-high heat. Combine the garlic and butter in a small bowl and season with pepper. Place the bugs onto the BBQ and spoon some of the garlic butter over the meat. Cook, turning frequently and basting with more garlic butter, for 4–5 minutes or until the bug meat is cooked.

3. Set the bugs aside until cool enough to handle, then pull the meat from the shells. Roughly chop the meat, and add to the sauce. Serve in the rolls, with potato chips (and a cold beer!).

Serves 4

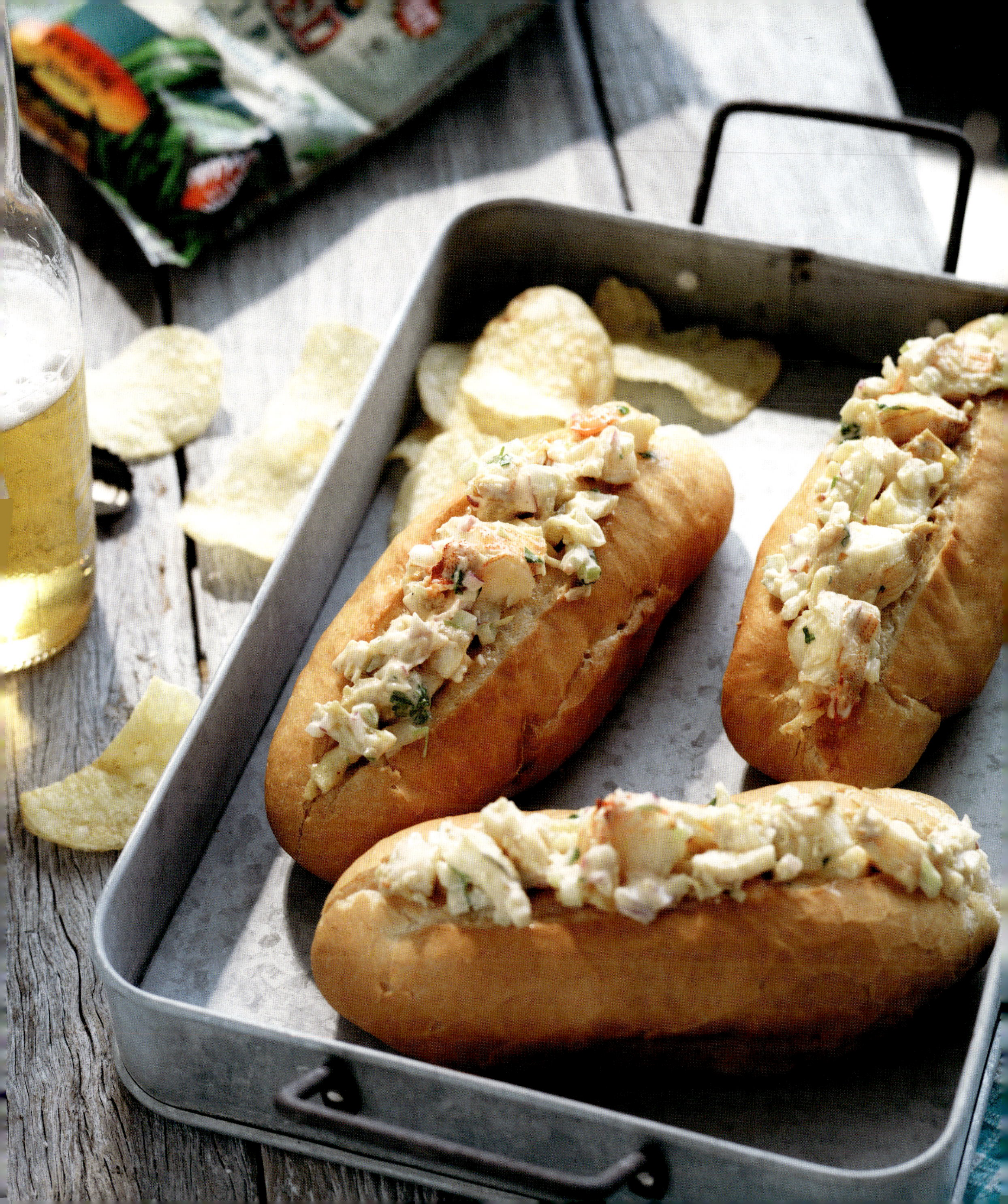

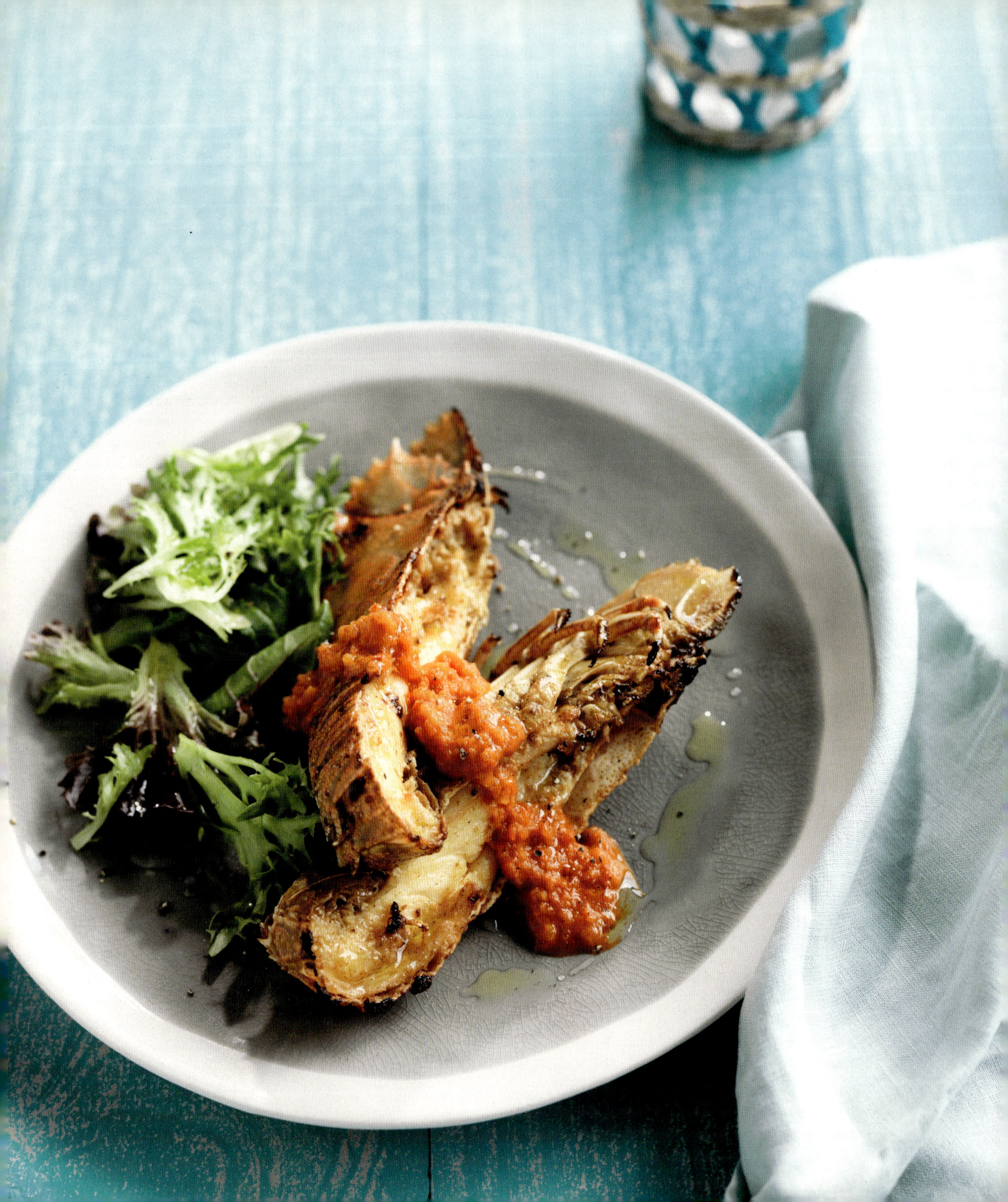

BUGS WITH CREOLE SAUCE

1 red capsicum

1 tablespoon olive oil

1 onion, sliced

1 garlic clove, finely chopped

1 tablespoon tomato paste

½ teaspoon cracked black pepper

⅓ cup fish stock or water

2 tablespoons red wine vinegar

2 teaspoons Worcestershire sauce

Tabasco sauce, to taste

pinch sugar

handful flat-leaf parsley, finely chopped

handful chervil or fresh coriander, finely chopped

20g butter

1 teaspoon lemon juice

4 Moreton Bay bugs, halved and cleaned

1. If you have a gas stove roast the capsicum on all sides by holding it with tongs in the flame until the skin is all dark and wrinkly. Alternatively, cook in a 200°C/180°C fan-forced oven 15–20 minutes or until the skin is shrivelled and wrinkly. Place the capsicum in a bowl and cover with plastic wrap. Set aside for 10 minutes.

2. Slip the skin from the capsicum and remove the core, seeds and all the white membrane. Finely chop the flesh and set aside.

3. Meanwhile, heat the oil in a medium saucepan over medium-low heat. Add the onions and cook until translucent. Add the garlic and cook until golden. Stir in the tomato paste, then the capsicum and pepper before adding the stock. Cover and bring to a simmer. Cook for 8–10 minutes until thickened slightly. Add the vinegar, Worcestershire sauce and Tabasco and sugar. Put into a blender and pulse until smooth. Stir through the herbs and season with salt.

4. Melt the butter in a frying pan over medium high heat. When it bubbles and starts to colour, stir in the lemon juice. Add the bugs, flesh side down, and cook for 2–3 minutes or until golden. Flip the bugs over and take the pan off the heat. Transfer the bugs, flesh side up, to serving plates and spoon the sauce over.

Serves 4

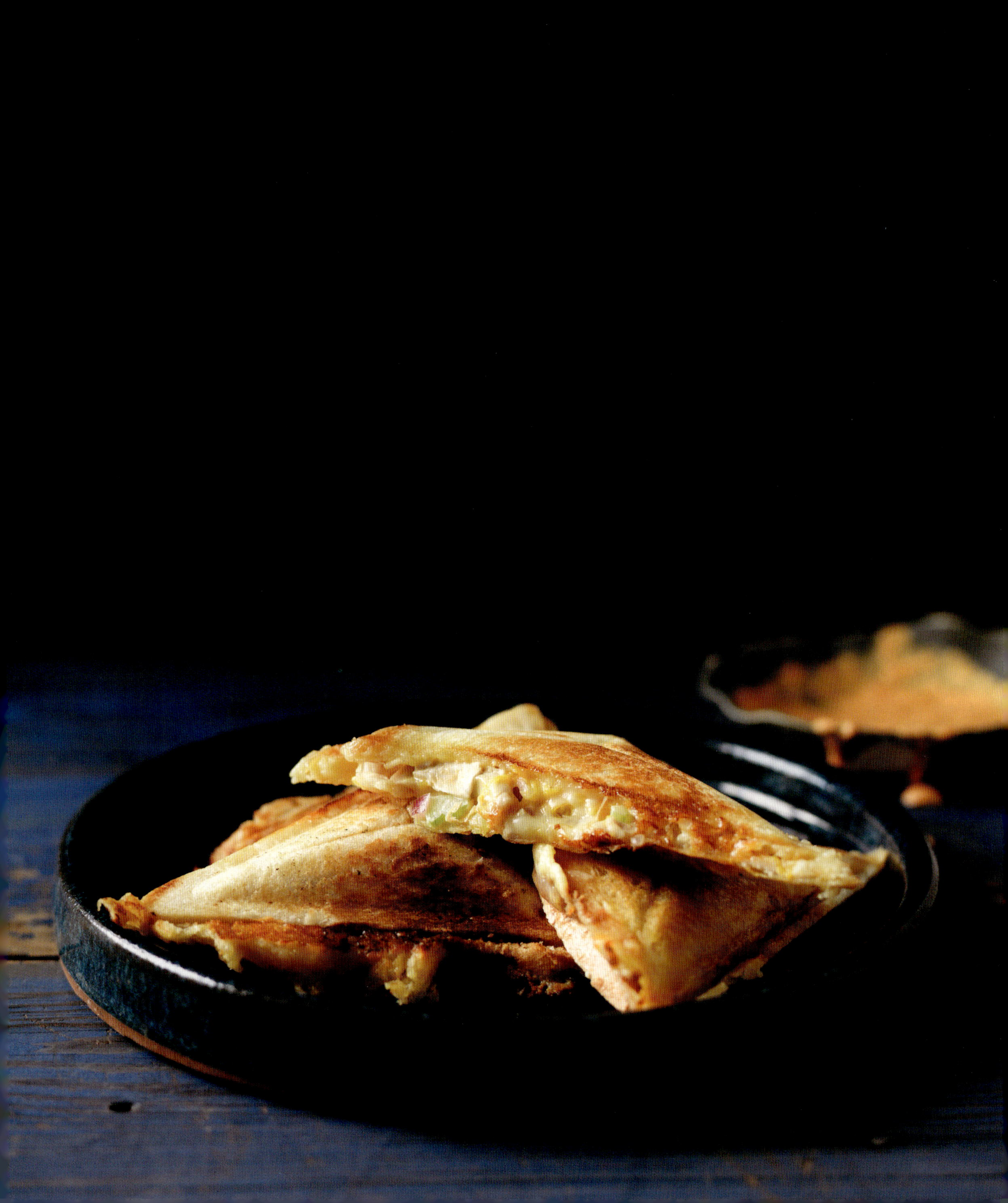

CHICKEN AND CHEESE JAFFLES WITH SPICY CAPSICUM SAUCE (HQ)

Aussie kids have fond memories of jaffles, from burnt mouths to campfire cook-ups. If you have never experienced this melted hot goodness, then give it a go. Plus, the dipping sauce is unreal!

2 cups chopped cooked chicken

¼ cup whole egg mayonnaise

1 small carrot, grated

1 celery stick, finely sliced

½ small red onion, finely diced

8 slices white bread

60g soft butter

8 slices tasty cheese

CAPSICUM SAUCE

150g drained chargrilled red capsicum

1 garlic clove, crushed

⅓ cup sour cream

1 teaspoon chilli powder

1 tablespoon olive oil

2 teaspoons lemon juice

1. To make the capsicum sauce, combine all the ingredients in a food processor and process until smooth. Season with salt and pepper and transfer to a small bowl.

2. Heat a jaffle iron or sandwich toaster. Combine the chicken, mayo, carrot, celery and onion in a bowl, and season with salt and pepper.

3. Spread the bread with butter, then place half the bread slices, butter side down, on a board. Top each one with a slice of cheese, ¼ of the chicken mixture, then another slice of cheese. Put the remaining bread slices on top, butter side up.

4. Lift a sandwich onto the jaffle maker and cook for a few minutes, until the bread is golden brown. Repeat with remaining sandwiches. Serve with the sauce for dipping.

Serves 4

You can buy chargrilled capsicum in a jar or from the deli counter at the supermarket.

HARISSA BREAM WITH FLATBREAD AND HOMEMADE LABNEH

Making your own labneh is seriously wicked. Keep some stocked in the fridge, ready for plenty of tasty options. Leftover harissa paste will keep for up to 1 week in the fridge.

2 tablespoons harissa paste (recipe below)

2 teaspoons ground coriander

1 teaspoon ground cumin

4 bream fillets

2 tablespoons olive oil

1 onion, finely chopped

1 teaspoon ground allspice

1 tablespoon honey

lemon juice, to taste

microherbs and flatbread, to serve

LABNEH

500g natural yoghurt

50ml olive oil

1 teaspoon salt

HARISSA PASTE

1 red capsicum

2 long red chillies

2 teaspoons cumin seeds

1 tablespoon olive oil

1 onion, roughly chopped

3 garlic cloves, roughly chopped

1 tablespoon tomato paste

juice of ½ lemon

1. To make the labneh, mix the ingredients together in a bowl. Line another bowl with muslin cloth. Spoon the yoghurt mixture into the cloth. Bring the sides of the cloth together and tie to secure. Hang over a bowl in the fridge for 24–48 hours (the longer you leave it, the more liquid will drain and the firmer it will become). Unwrap the labneh and transfer to an airtight container.

2. For the harissa paste, preheat the oven to 250°C (230°C fan-forced) and line a baking tray with baking paper. Place the capsicum and chilli onto the tray and roast for 20–25 minutes, until soft. Transfer to a plate, cover with plastic wrap and set aside for 15 minutes to steam. Deseed and remove skin from both and roughly chop the flesh.

3. Toast the cumin seeds in a dry frying pan over medium heat for about 1 minute or until fragrant. Set aside. Heat the oil in the frying pan over medium-high heat. Cook the onion for about 5 minutes or until golden brown. Add the garlic and cook for 1 more minute. Combine all the ingredients with a pinch of salt in a blender and blitz until smooth.

4. Combine 1 tablespoon of the harissa paste, the ground coriander, cumin and a pinch of salt. Spread all over the fish, cover and marinate in the fridge for a minimum of 1 hour or up to 3 hours.

5. Heat the oil in a frying pan over medium-high heat. Cook the bream for 1 minute on each side until lightly golden. Remove and set aside. Add the onion to the pan and cook until golden.

6. Stir in the remaining 1 tablespoon of harissa paste, the allspice and honey. Season with salt and pepper, then return the fish to the pan and use a spoon to baste with the sauce. Cover and cook for 4 minutes or until cooked through. Season with a squeeze of lemon juice and sprinkle with microherbs. Serve the fish with the sauce, flatbread and labneh.

Serves 4

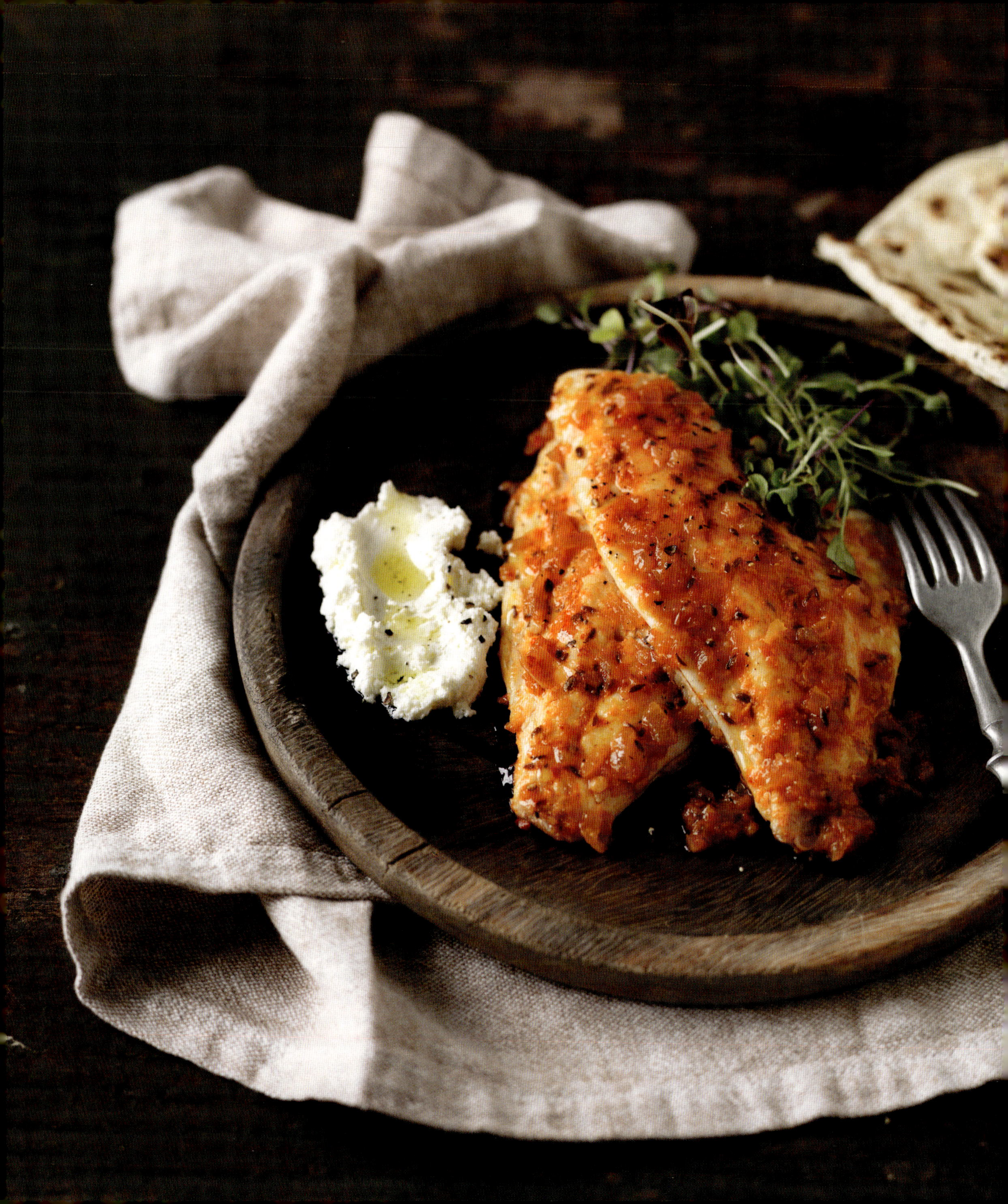

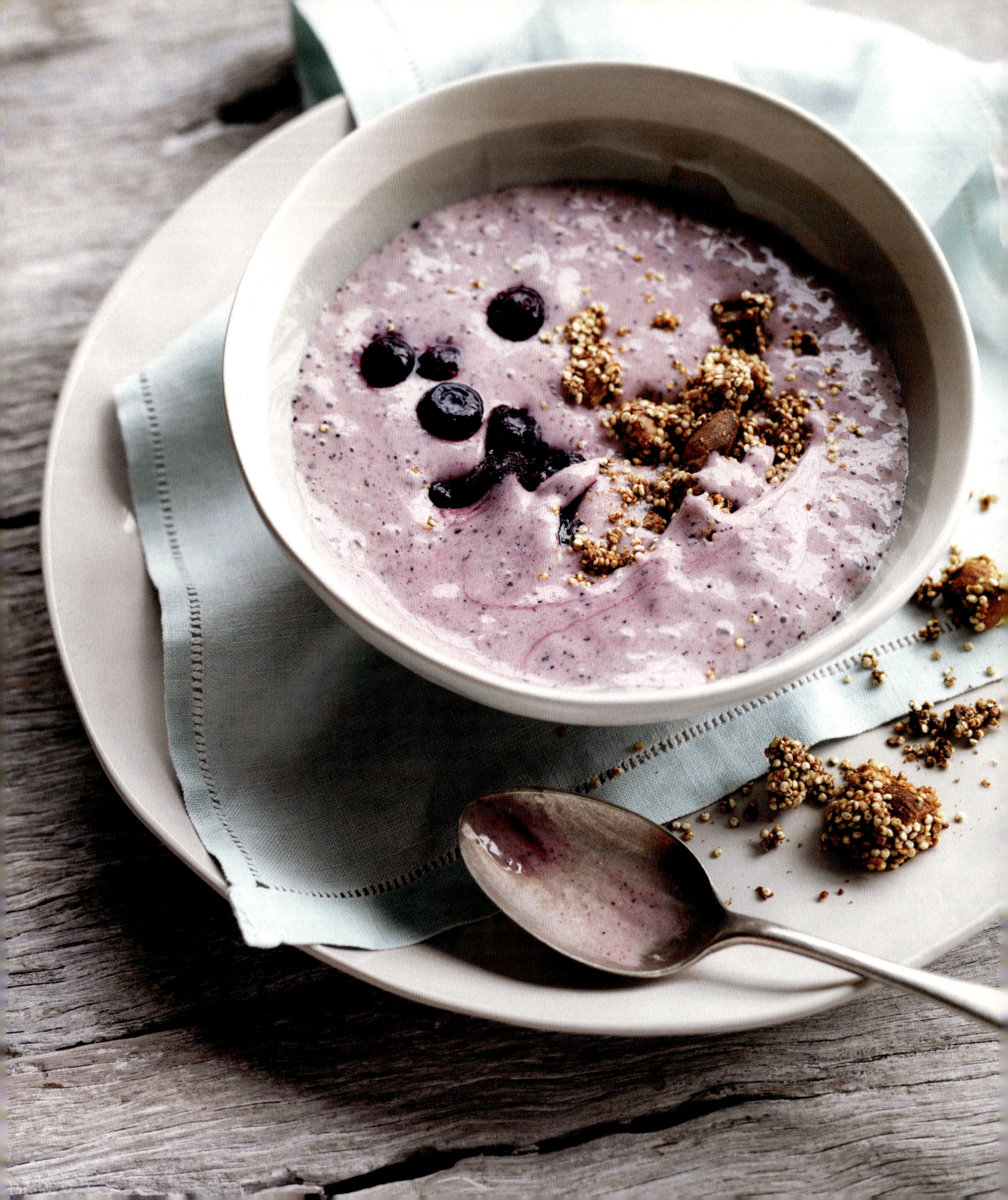

ACHACHA BOWL

I love coming across ingredients I've never heard of before. It gets me excited about how much there is in this world to eat! Achacha is a small fruit with orange skin and white flesh that has a sweet and tangy flavour. It's from Bolivia but has much in common with tropical fruits such as mangosteen or lychee. It's in season in December and January, and you can look for it at growers or organic markets. Freeze the pulp for further use if you find any. Blueberries are a great substitute.

½ cup almond milk

1 banana, frozen

½ cup frozen blueberries

½ cup achacha pulp, frozen

2 teaspoons almond butter

1 scoop vanilla protein powder (optional)

Gluten Free Spiced Granola, to serve (see page 118)

extra frozen blueberries, to serve

1. Combine the milk, banana, blueberries, achacha, almond butter and protein powder in a blender. Process until thick and smooth. You can add more almond milk if need be (it should finish like a slightly thin sorbet).
2. Pour into a bowl and serve topped with granola and blueberries.

Serves 1

ACHACHA SANGRIA (HQ)

2 achacha fruit

750ml bottle fruity chardonnay, chilled

500ml sparkling water, chilled

¼ cup triple sec

¼ cup sugar (or to taste)

mint sprigs and ice cubes, to serve

1. To open the achacha, pierce the skin at the equator with your thumbnail. Pinch the fruit on either side of the cut, and it will pop open. Eat the fruit. Cut the skin into strips, combine with 1 cup of plain water and stand overnight to infuse.
2. Strain the skins from the water. Combine with the remaining ingredients in a large jug, and stir to dissolve the sugar. Serve over ice.

Makes about 6 cups

See page 169 for info about achacha.

If you can't find achacha, use passionfruit pulp, pushed through a sieve. Add a few seeds back in if you like.

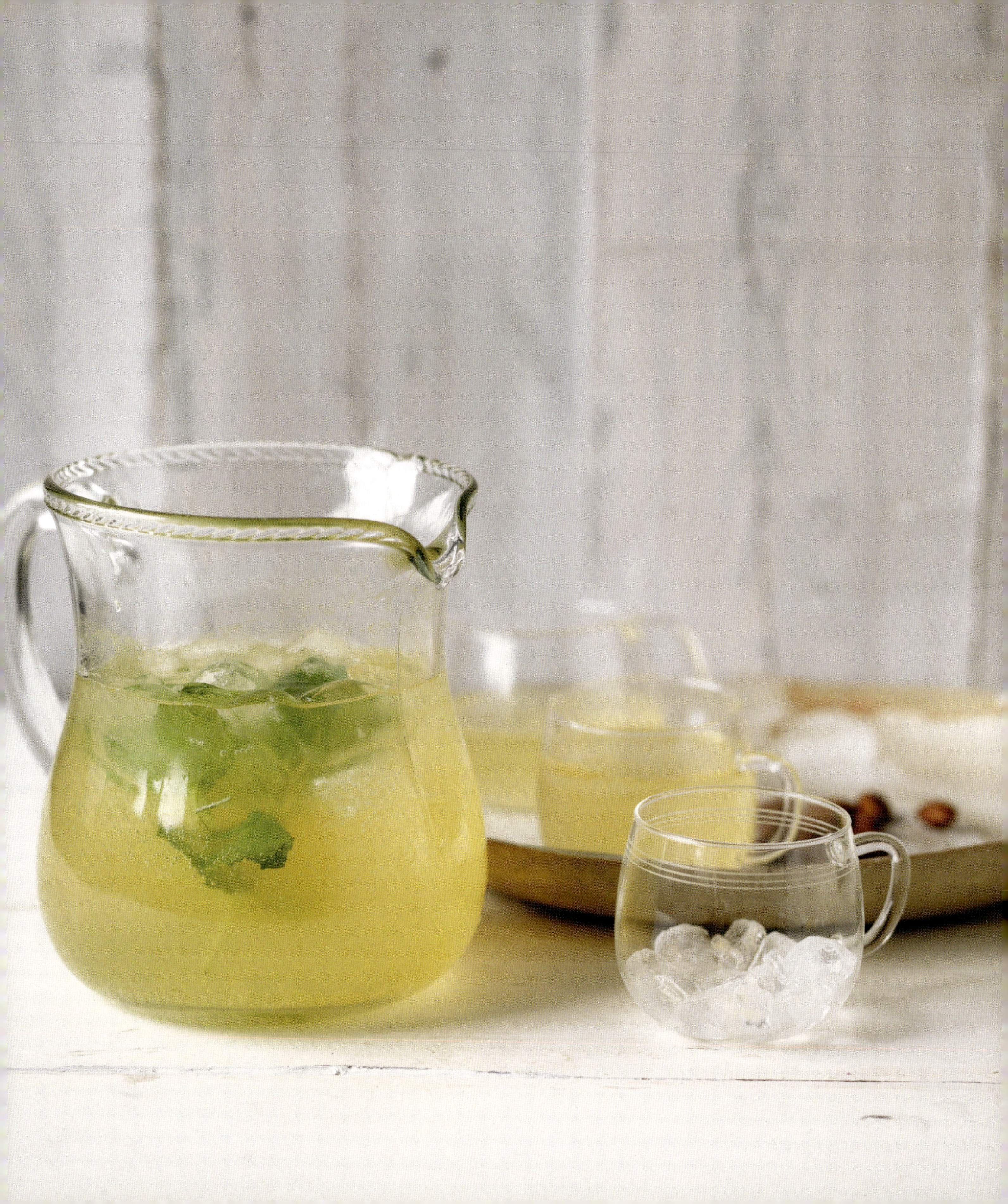

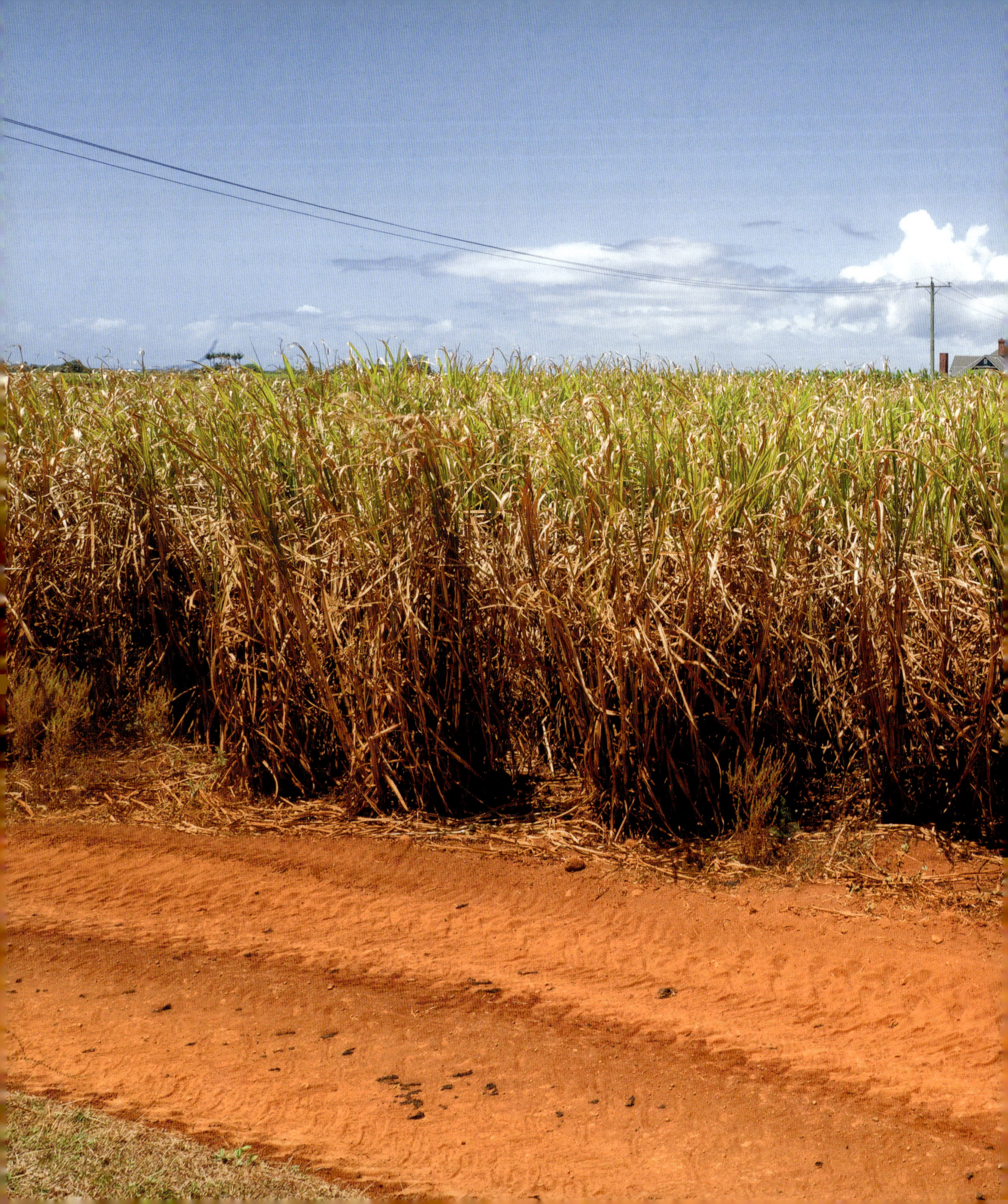

Bundaberg

Bundaberg. What a town! Naturally, the first thing that comes to mind is the relationship this spot has with a particular brand of rum, but there's far more to this place than that. I thought Bundaberg was further inland, but it's only five minutes from the coast and this made it very special. You feel like you're in the middle of country Australia with epic singlets, charming locals and the warm feeling that everyone knows everyone – and you're only a jog from a wave. The best of both worlds!

I am a massive advocate of following your passion and breathing enjoyment into every day. So when HQ and I joined some young boys at a surf school at Bargara Beach, we both knew that giving them some tips was going to be a really tough day in the office! Hayden worked as a professional lifeguard for nearly 10 years, and both of us have practically lived our entire lives at the beach or out on the water. Enjoying the laughter and satisfaction of those grommets was wicked.

Bundaberg is home to Springhaven Meadows, a seriously awesome banana plantation owned by a lovely couple called Gavin and Jacinta Jowett. They have 30,000 acres of banana farmland, but the biggest kicker is that they have begun to produce banana flour. It's gluten free and can be used as a quality substitute when baking or cooking anything that requires flour. I loved hearing everything about it! The bananas readily soak up moisture, so for each cup of regular flour you need only one-third of a cup of banana flour. Gavin and Jacinta take the flesh from the freshly picked green bananas when they're a starchy carbohydrate and before it becomes sweet, and then dehydrate it and pound it into flour. In the beginning, all they had was a mortar and pestle – it would have taken forever; you probably could have run a marathon in that time! But as demand increased, so their production methods expanded. From banana flour they have made pasta, corn chips, a savoury loaf that I thought was the best gluten free bread I have ever tried and – yes, of course my friends – there was banana bread, and yes, it was phenomenal!

One of the highlights of the trip was visiting Lady Elliot Island, the most southerly point of the Great Barrier Reef. Eight years ago HQ stayed there for a week as part of his university degree. As we approached it in the plane, I thought we were just passing over a tiny island surrounded by gorgeous crystal clear water, and then Hayden informed me it was our destination! I couldn't imagine where we were going to land until I realised that our landing strip comprised of the entire length of the island. The pilot nailed it; we were all good!

A fun fact regarding this part of the adventure is that, apparently, one of the favourite surf breaks of former world champion surfer Joel Parkinson is just off the island – but it's a secret, so don't let too many people know about it.

Lady Elliot Island is heavily involved in marine research, particularly relating to manta rays. The environment provides their perfect habitat and you can spot them swimming about daily. So there was no time for surfing as we were too captivated by these amazing creatures. It was mesmerising to snorkel with them. They swam in straight lines and everything happened at half-speed. We could even hear whales singing in the distance under the water, while the rays circled their awesome frames like they were dancing. It was seriously magical. If you ever get the chance to hang out with a manta ray, grab a pair of flippers and jump in!

What an awesome spot Bundaberg is. Oh, and if you're like me and have ever wondered if the Bundaberg locals would nominate rum as their number one drink of choice … Well, most of them said no! Now, isn't that another fun fact?

DC

Banana flowers are ridiculous!

The Jowett family

'RUM AND COKE' WINGS

In homage to every true blue Aussie's fave rum, here's the ultimate food for sticky fingers! Frank's Hot Sauce is an American buffalo wing hot sauce. You can find it in large supermarkets, or use your own preferred hot sauce. And don't worry about the rum in this – the alcohol burns off during cooking.

1kg chicken wings, wing tips removed

2 tablespoons smoked paprika

1½ tsp chilli powder

GLAZE

½ cup dark rum

¾ cup Coke

2 tablespoons honey

¼ Frank's Red Hot Sauce

75g butter, chopped

DIP

½ cup sour cream

1 garlic clove, crushed

2 teaspoons Dijon mustard

2 teaspoons chopped chives

1. Preheat the oven to 180°C (160°C fan-forced) and line a large baking tray with baking paper. Put the wings into a large bowl and sprinkle with the paprika and chilli powder. Season with salt and toss to coat. Spread out onto the baking tray and bake for 45 minutes until golden brown.

2. To make the glaze, put the rum, Coke, honey and hot sauce in a saucepan. Stir well to combine. Bring to the boil over medium heat, then reduce the heat slightly and cook at a rapid simmer for about 10 minutes or until reduced to a thick consistency that coats the back of a spoon. Whisk in the butter a little at a time until combined. Pour into a large bowl.

3. Cool the wings slightly, then add to the glaze (in batches) and toss to coat. Return to the oven tray and cook for a further 10 minutes, or until they are nice and sticky.

4. For the dip, combine the ingredients together in a small bowl. Serve the wings with the dipping sauce, and a little extra hot sauce for those who want it.

Serves 4

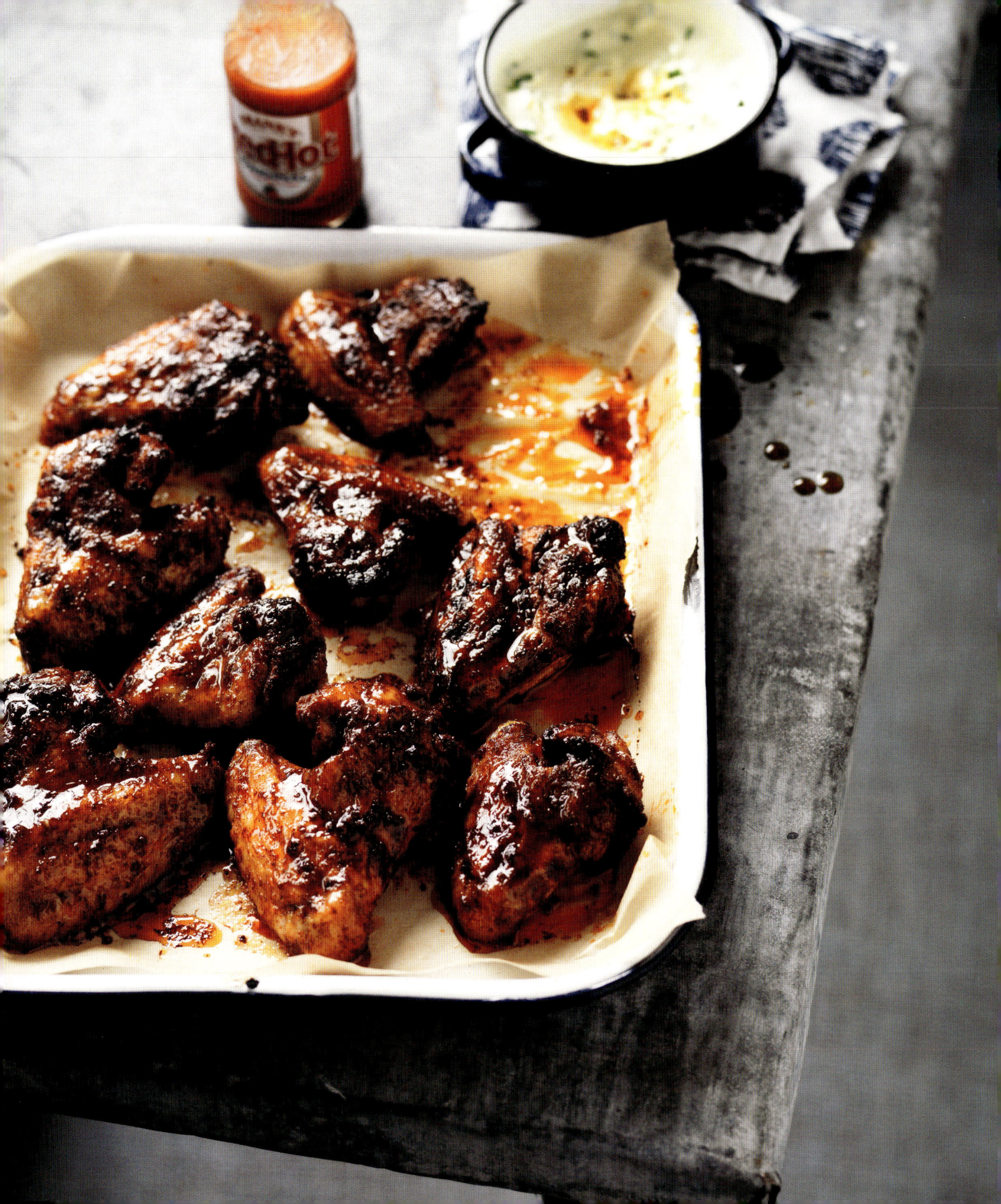

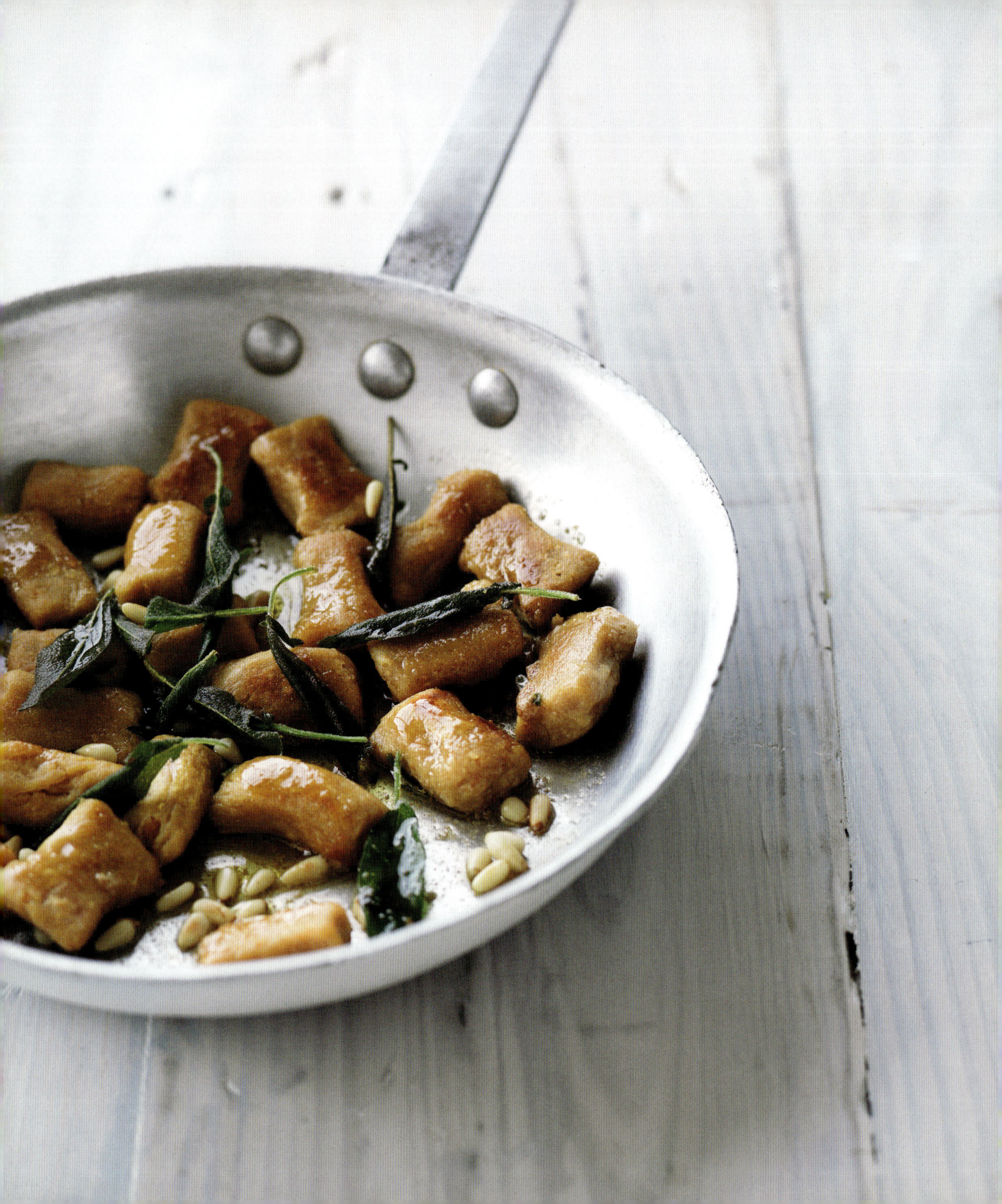

SWEET POTATO GNOCCHI WITH BURNT BUTTER AND SAGE ⓓⓒ

I love poaching this gnocchi and having it available for any sauce I desire. The natural sweetness from the sweet potato is what appeals to me the most. Pairing it with a simple butter sauce is … enough said!

650g sweet potato, peeled and cubed

1 teaspoon salt

1 egg yolk

1½ cups buckwheat flour

80g butter, chopped

¼ cup sage leaves

1 tablespoon pine nuts

3 teaspoons lemon juice

1. Preheat the oven to 180°C (160°C fan-forced) and line a baking tray with baking paper. Bring a large pot of water to the boil and add the sweet potato and salt. Cook over medium heat for 10–12 minutes or until tender when tested with a knife.

2. Drain in a colander and let stand for 5 minutes to release as much moisture as possible. Spread out onto the baking tray and place in the oven to dry out for about 8 minutes, making sure they don't start to brown. Remove from the oven and set aside to cool.

3. Press the sweet potato through a sieve or a ricer, or mash very well. Add the yolk and half the flour and begin to combine the mixture to a dough. Keep adding the rest of the flour until you reach a firm dough consistency. Bring a pot of water to the boil and drop a little portion of the dough in. If it separates, you will need more flour. If it doesn't, you are fine to continue.

4. Divide the dough into quarters. Roll each portion on a lightly floured bench in the shape of a snake to a consistent 1cm thickness. Using a knife, divide the length into 1.5 cm portions. Bring the pot of water back up to the boil, turn the heat to medium and add the gnocchi in batches so you don't overcrowd the pan. Cook for 90 seconds, or until they float to the top, before removing with a slotted spoon to a large plate lined with paper towel. Repeat with remaining gnocchi.

5. Melt the butter in a large frying pan over a medium heat. Once it begins to bubble and lightly brown, add the sage and pine nuts. Continue cooking for a minute or so until the butter browns further, then add the lemon juice. Add the gnocchi and toss through to coat in the butter and lightly colour on both sides. Season with salt and pepper and serve.

Serves 4 as an entree

BUNDABERG BEEF BURGER (HQ)

750g good quality beef mince (not lean mince)

12 slices tasty cheese

12 rashers streaky bacon

6 hamburger buns, halved

60g soft butter

200g bread and butter pickles

potato chips, to serve

SECRET BURGER SAUCE

1 cup sour cream

¼ cup dill leaves, finely chopped

½ small red onion, very finely diced

½ teaspoon chipotle sauce (or other hot chilli sauce)

lemon juice, to taste

drizzle of olive oil

1 To make the secret (well, not so secret now!) burger sauce, mix the sour cream, dill, onion, and chilli sauce in a small bowl. Season with salt, pepper and lemon juice to taste, and drizzle with olive oil. Cover and place into the fridge until ready to use.

2 Divide the beef mince into 6 equal portions and shape into patties. Make them a little bit wider than the buns, as they will shrink up during cooking.

3 Preheat a BBQ flat plate or frying pan over medium-high heat. Season the patties with salt and pepper on both sides. Cook for 2 minutes, then turn over and place 2 slices of cheese on top of each. Cook for another 2–3 minutes for medium rare, or to your liking.

4 Meanwhile, cook the bacon on the BBQ or in another frying pan over medium-high heat until crisp. Toast the buns and spread with butter.

5 Pile the patty, bacon and pickles onto the buns and smother with secret burger sauce. Serve with potato chips.

Serves 6

The sauce will keep for about a week and is great on other sandwiches, or even served with steak or lamb.

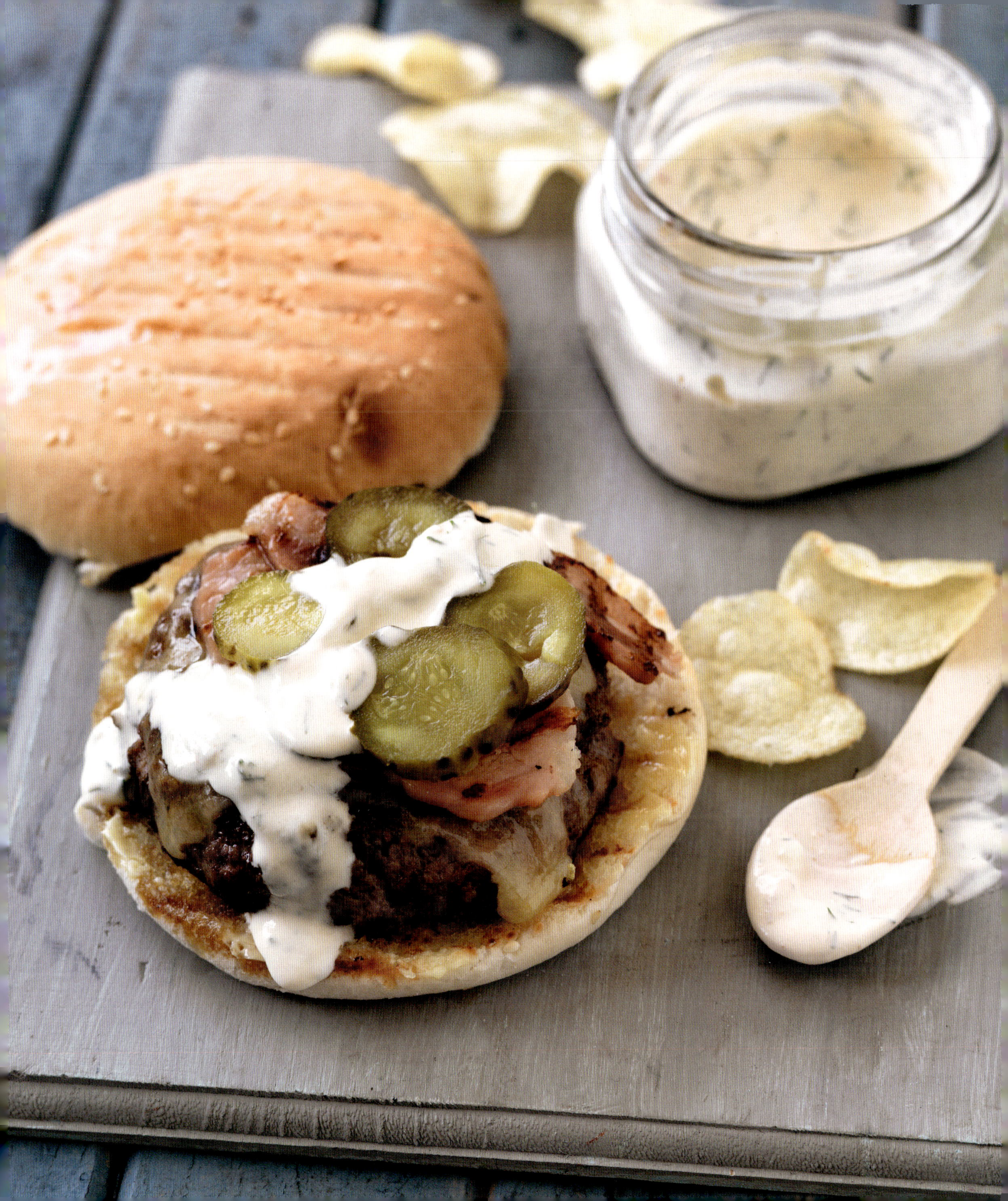

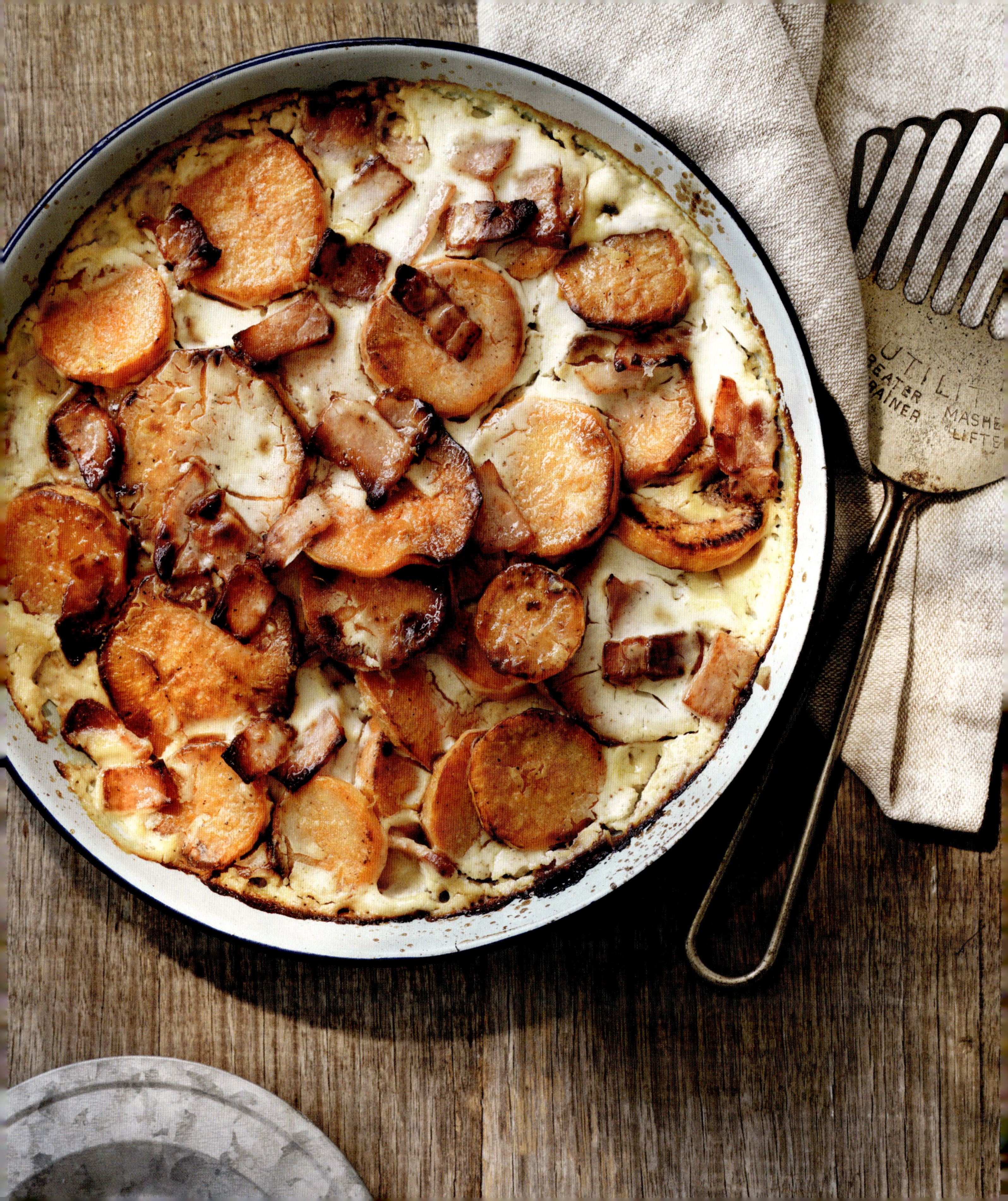

ULTIMATE SWEET POTATO BAKE

I can't tell you how popular this flavoursome dish has become. A few of my mates have claimed it as their own … good on them! It's a healthier version of the traditional potato bake, and seriously amped up in taste and goodness.

2 tablespoons olive or macadamia oil

3 lean rashers bacon, roughly chopped

600g sweet potato, cut into 5mm discs

250g ricotta

1 cup coconut milk

1 teaspoon ground nutmeg

1. Preheat the oven to 200°C (180°C fan-forced) and lightly grease an 8 cup capacity ovenproof dish.
2. Heat the oil in a large frying pan over medium heat and cook the bacon, stirring and turning occasionally, until browned. Remove from the pan. Add the sweet potato slices (in batches) and cook until lightly browned on both sides. Transfer the bacon and sweet potato to the ovenproof dish.
3. Whisk the ricotta, coconut milk and nutmeg until smooth, and season with a pinch of salt. Pour over the sweet potato. Bake for 20–25 minutes, until lightly golden on top.

Serves 4

Use 'smooth' ricotta (which comes in a tub) for this, not the firmer ricotta from the deli.

BANANA CHOC-TELLA MUFFINS (DC)

Now, don't these little beauties look so gorgeous you just want to put the book down and pre-heat the oven? I have tried these with banana flour, taking my inspiration from the farmers of Bundaberg. You could also try coconut flour (1:1) or self-raising flour as we've done here. Regardless, they are a wholesome snack for the kids, your friends … or even yourself!

125g butter, chopped, at room temperature	
½ cup honey	
2 eggs	
3 ripe bananas, mashed	
1½ cups self-raising flour	
½ cup hazelnut spread	

1. Preheat the oven to 170°C (150°C fan-forced) and lightly grease twelve ⅓ cup capacity muffin pans, or line with paper cases. Using electric beaters, beat the butter and honey together until light and fluffy. Add the eggs one at a time, beating well after each addition, then beat in the banana.

2. Sift the flour and a pinch of salt over the banana mixture and fold through until combined. Divide between the muffin pans. Scoop a heaped teaspoon of the hazelnut spread on top. Using a knife, give it a little swirl.

3. Bake for 25–30 minutes or until a skewer comes out clean. Leave in the pans for 5 minutes, then lift out onto a wire rack to cool.

Makes 12

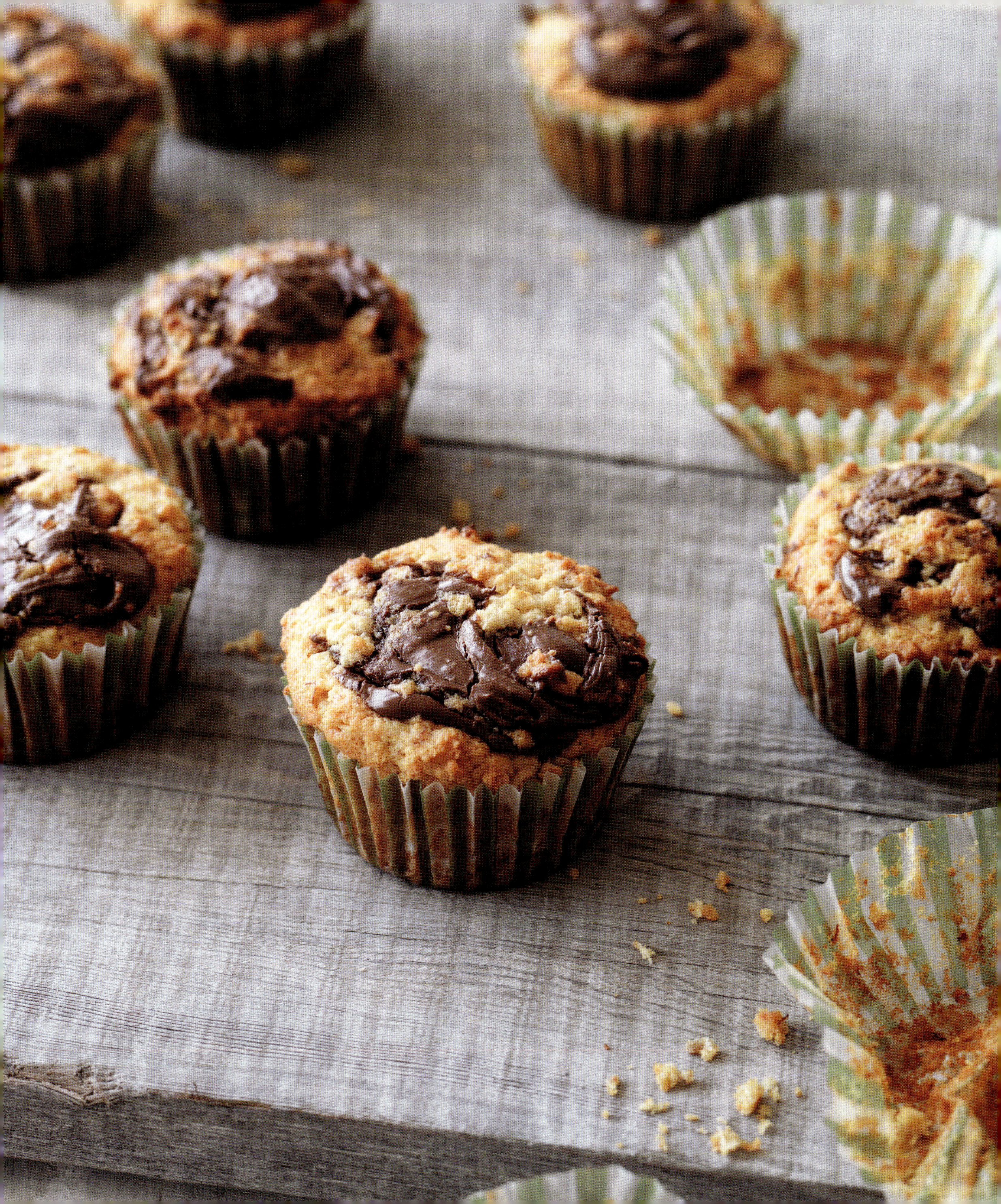

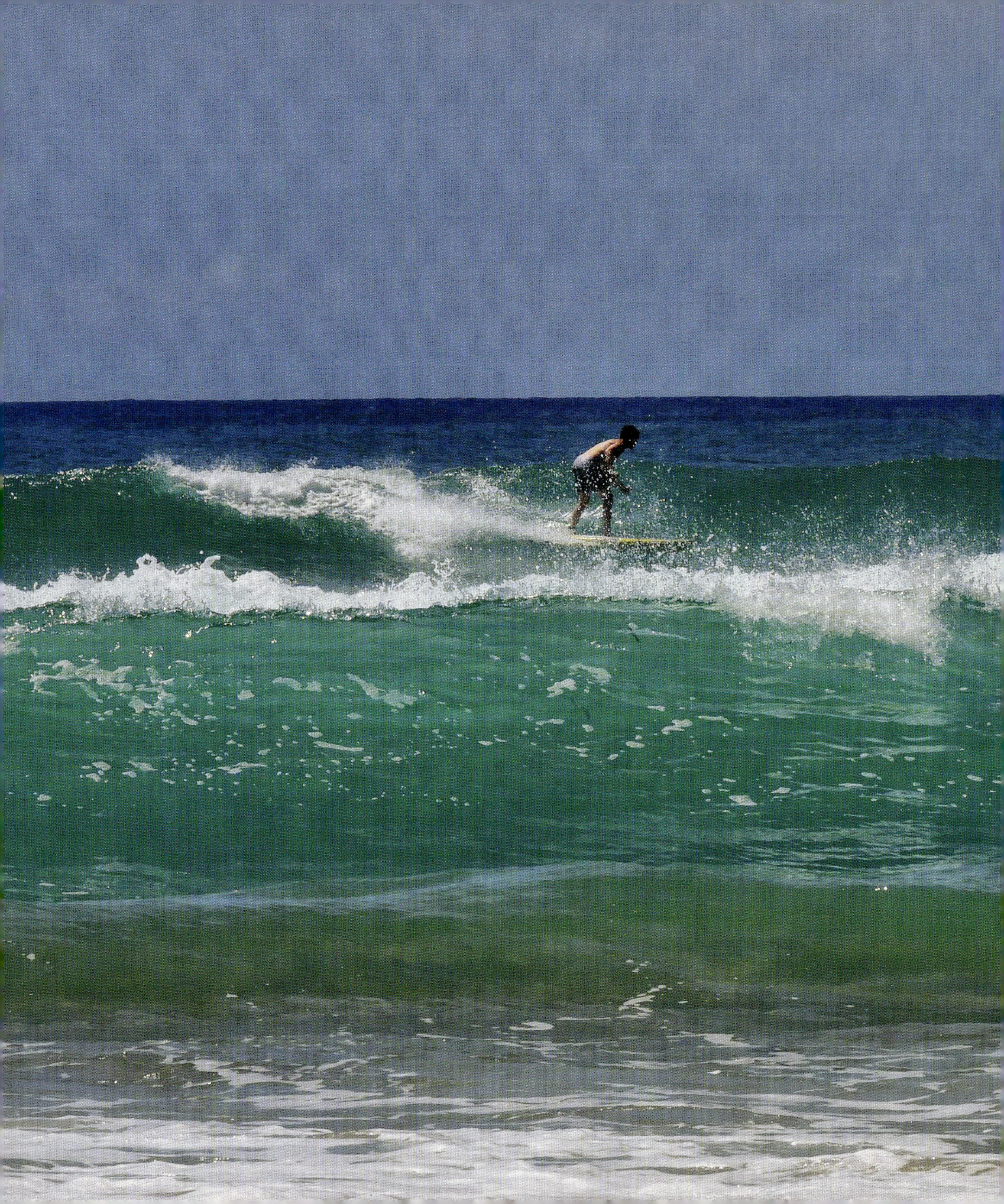

The FAR EAST

And so to Noosa Heads. This cosmopolitan town on the Sunshine Coast is set on a headland and surrounded by golden beaches, national parks and lush hinterland. Best of all, it's home to an excellent surfing beach. Next stop is the garden city of Toowoomba, perched 700 metres above sea level on the edge of the escarpment of the Great Dividing Range. It is the commercial hub for the Darling Downs to the west where rolling farmland is nourished by rich black soils. Last stop is Byron Bay – named not for mad, bad Lord Byron, but John Byron, an esteemed navigator. Cape Byron juts into the Pacific Ocean and is the most easterly point of Australia. There is a sign on the road into Byron that invites you to cheer up, slow down and chill out. The surf breaks are reliable, the coffee is strong and at sunset the dreadlocked drummers meet on Main Beach to celebrate the closing day.

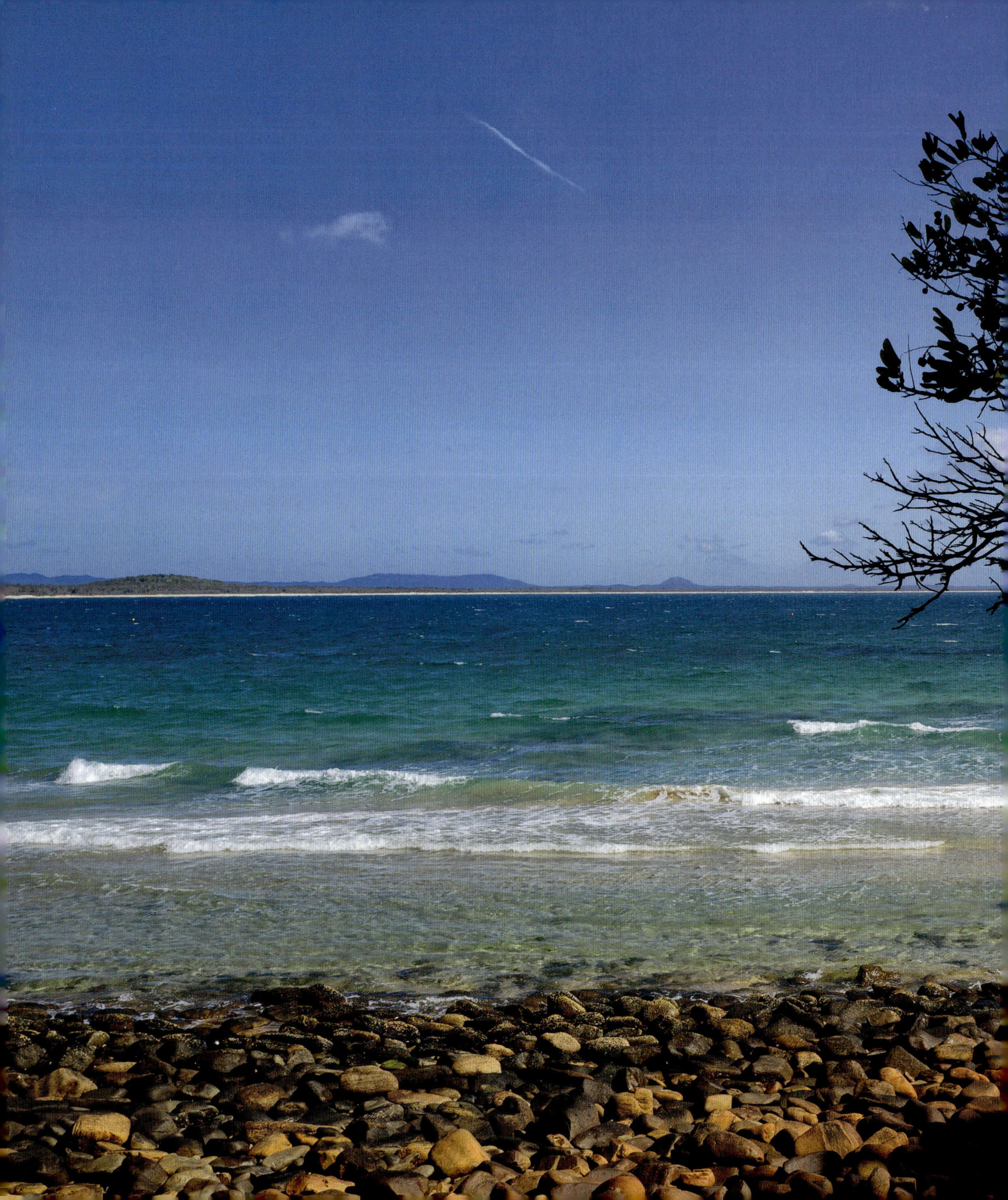

Noosa

Dan and I had both been to Noosa many times before, but generally for work or short trips. This time around, however, we got much more out of our visit than usual. We met amazing people and, as we always like to do, we had a whole heap of fun and cooked, tasted and shared some phenomenal food.

The biggest highlight for me was finally getting some decent waves! The 'surfing' part of *Surfing the Menu* had been conspicuously absent until we got to Noosa. So after checking out the surf by going up in an old-school military sea plane (pretty epic!), we found a spot at Sunshine Beach with a few little lines. It was good to get in the water and catch a couple of fun lefts.

While we were out in the water, Dan ran into two friends, Justin and Michelle Warrick, who have an amazing little café called Little Cove (named after a local surf spot) where they roast their own coffee and have super tasty treats. We popped in there for a post-surf coffee – well, not for me, I'm allergic to caffeine, but Dan is an aficionado of the coffee scene. We also learned the art of roasting coffee beans perfectly. For someone who doesn't drink coffee, I can't go past the smell. It's like all those familiar, comforting aromas we know and love: a wood fire, bread baking, garlic sizzling in a pan, red wine in a glass and, for me, the smell of salt on the air by the beach.

We were lucky to be in Noosa for the weekend as that meant we could visit the Noosa Farmers Market. This is a true farmers market with producers from the local area selling everything from morning-fresh fruit and veg, cured meats, seafood, oils and preserves to ice creams on a stick (my favourite!). DC and I were looking for a couple of specific ingredients, one of which was the kimchi he was going to use for his Korean Pork Pot Roast with Coconut Rice (page 198).

In Noosa we weren't just limited to the short board and stand-up paddle board for a wave, we also had the chance to give kite surfing a go. Now, I'm someone who has grown up his whole life in and around the ocean on all sorts of different surf craft, but never in my life have I tried kite surfing. It was a real thrill, and so different from what I expected. It was tough – not only physically, but mentally as well! There is so much to focus on, and we barely even touched the water. I think we spent most of the time on the sand, just getting the hang of controlling the kite, and when we did make it into the water, we weren't that great! Apparently, we were dealing with some difficult conditions, like limited wind that wasn't coming from the best direction – well, we'll use that excuse anyway! I'm looking forward to giving it another go later and getting the hang of it.

To finish off our time in Noosa, we visited the powerhouse couple Craig Hubbard and Jemma Edwards at Shambhala Farm. Their main focus is producing nutrient-rich leafy greens, such as rocket, spinach, kale, broccoli and medicinal herbs, from a living soil – compost is the lifeblood of the farm, not pesticides. They are devoted to wholesome food that is grown organically and sustainably and connecting people with their food, the environment and the planet. Dan and I got in on the action. Like me, the crew at Shambhala start their day with some yoga to limber up the body and get ready for a day's work. Dan and I were lucky enough to plant our very own row of seedlings in the incredibly rich and moist soils. We then picked some nourishing veg to add to a couple of house-made pizzas.

We topped off our trip to Noosa with a drum session. It was hard for someone like me who has no rhythm, but I was surprised at the end by the beautiful sound we all created together!

HQ

The Warrick family

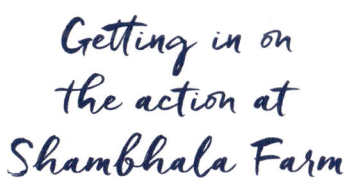

QLD
Cairns
Townsville
Bundaberg
Noosa
Brisbane

Getting in on the action at Shambhala Farm

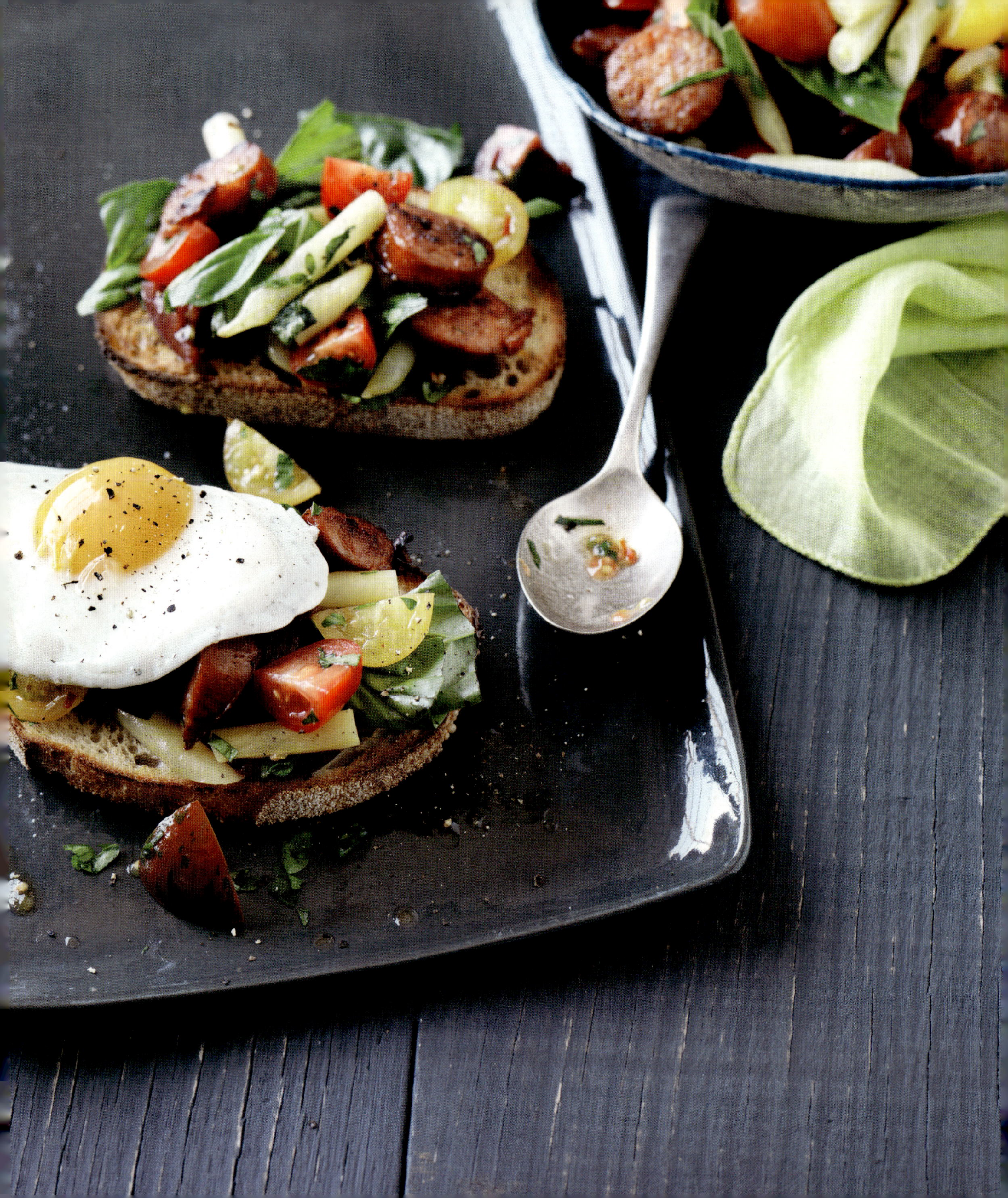

TOMATO BREAKFAST SALAD WITH CHORIZO, HERBS, EGGS AND BREAD

At Noosa Reds, a specialist tomato growing nursery, we met up with Pete who was actually born in a tomato greenhouse! No joke – his mother was working the vines when she went into labour and gave birth to him right there. The incredible variety of juicy tomatoes Pete produces inspired this punchy and satisfying breakfast number.

1 tablespoon olive oil
300g chorizo sausages, randomly chopped ('rustic' is the word!)
1 clove garlic, finely sliced
1 red bird's eye chilli, finely sliced
¼ cup oregano leaves
1 tablespoon red wine vinegar
400g baby heirloom tomatoes, chunkily chopped
100g yellow beans, trimmed and chopped
1 tablespoon extra virgin olive oil
½ cup fresh basil leaves, torn
2 tablespoons roughly chopped flat-leaf parsley
4 thick slices sourdough bread, toasted
4 eggs, fried

1 Heat the oil in a medium heavy-based frying pan over medium heat. Add the chorizo and cook, turning often, to get a nice dark, crisp crust on the outside of each piece.

2 Add the garlic and chilli, and cook, stirring often, for 1 minute. Add the oregano leaves and cook, tossing, until slightly crispy, but take care not to burn the garlic. To stop the cooking, splash in the vinegar. Remove from heat and allow to cool slightly.

3 Toss the tomatoes, beans, olive oil and another splash of vinegar together in a bowl. Add the chorizo mixture (along with pan juices) and toss gently to combine. Fold in the herbs. Serve on crusty sourdough toast, topped with fried eggs.

Serves 4

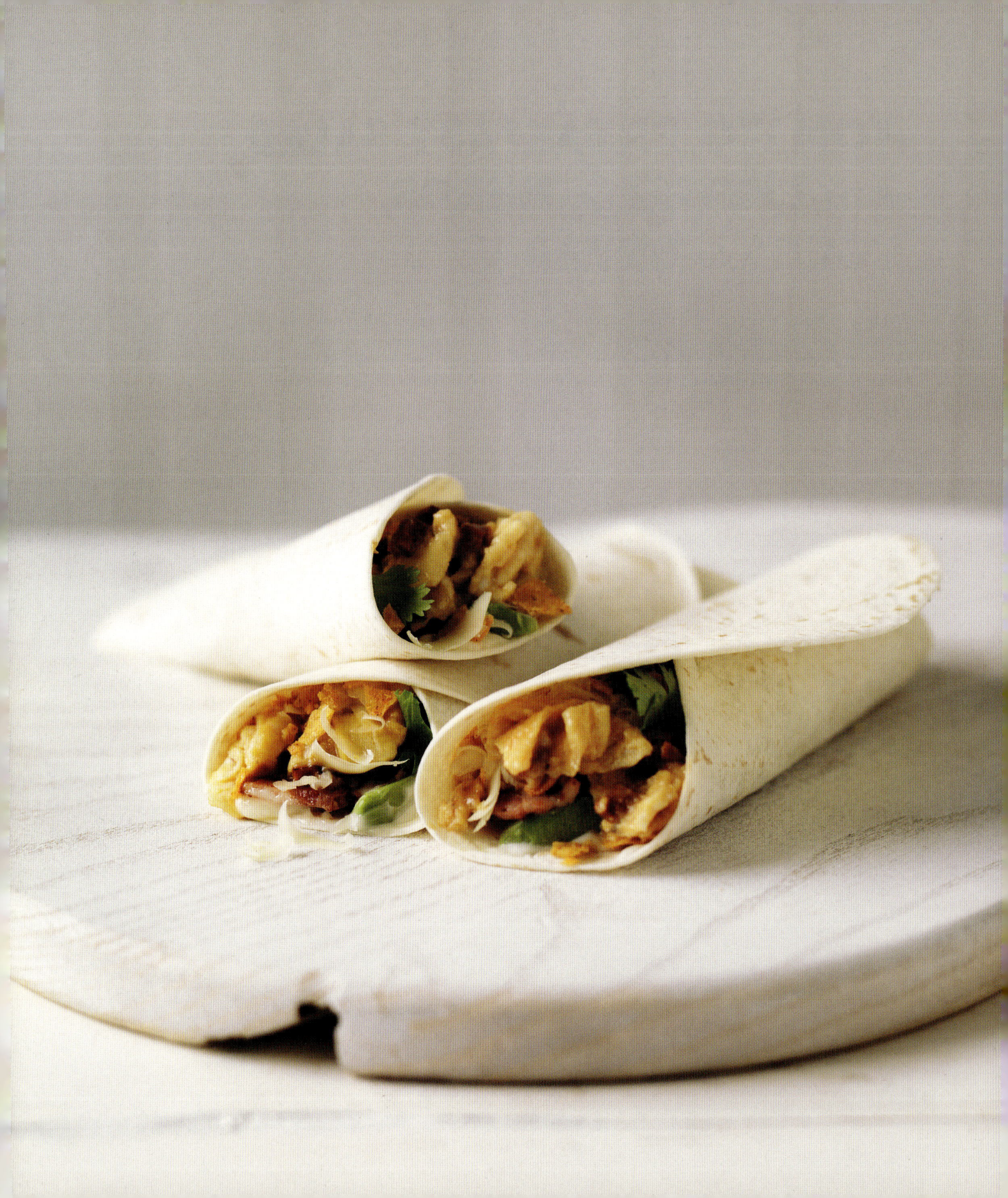

CHORIZO AND BACON BREAKFAST BURRITO (HQ)

It's almost worth going out and having a few drinks the night before just to eat this bad boy! Who would have thought putting smashed-up corn chips inside a burrito would make it so damn good? Well, it does!

6 rashers streaky bacon, cut in half

1 chorizo sausage, finely diced

½ small red onion

5 eggs, lightly beaten

4 flour tortillas (20cm), warmed

1 ripe avocado, sliced

¼ cup whole-egg mayonnaise

chipotle sauce, to taste

½ cup grated cheddar cheese

1 cup nacho cheese-flavoured corn chips, smashed up

¼ cup coriander leaves, roughly chopped

Lime wedges, to serve

1. Preheat the oven to 150°C (130°C fan-forced). Cook the bacon in a large non-stick frying over medium-high heat until crispy. Transfer to an ovenproof dish lined with paper towel and place into the oven to keep warm.

2. Drain any bacon fat from the pan, and cook the chorizo and onion until coloured and crispy. Reduce the heat to medium-low and pour in the eggs. Cook, stirring, until just set.

3. Lay out tortillas on a bench. Divide the avocado, mayo, chipotle sauce, egg mixture, bacon, cheese, corn chips and coriander between them. Roll up to enclose, and serve with wedges of lime.

Serves 4

SHAMBHALA ROAST VEGIE PLATE (DC)

¼ butternut pumpkin, skin removed, deseeded and chopped into 3cm pieces

½ cauliflower, cut into florets

1 head broccoli, cut into florets

1 red onion, quartered

2 tablespoons olive oil

1 tablespoon curry powder

2 teaspoons ground turmeric

40g butter

6 garlic cloves, peeled

3 thyme sprigs

3 oregano sprigs

1 cup natural yoghurt

2 tablespoons tahini

1. Preheat oven to 220°C (200°C fan-forced) and pop a roasting pan into the oven.
2. Combine the vegies, olive oil, curry powder and turmeric in a large bowl. Season with salt and pepper and toss to coat. Remove the roasting pan from the oven and add the butter. When it has melted, add the garlic, thyme and oregano and toss to mix through.
3. Tip the vegies into the roasting tray, and mix with the garlic and herb butter. Pop in the oven for 15 minutes, then reduce the temperature to 200°C (180°C fan-forced) for a final 15 minutes of cooking.
4. Combine the yoghurt and tahini. Serve the vegies on a plate or board, with the yoghurt mixture drizzled over.

Serves 4

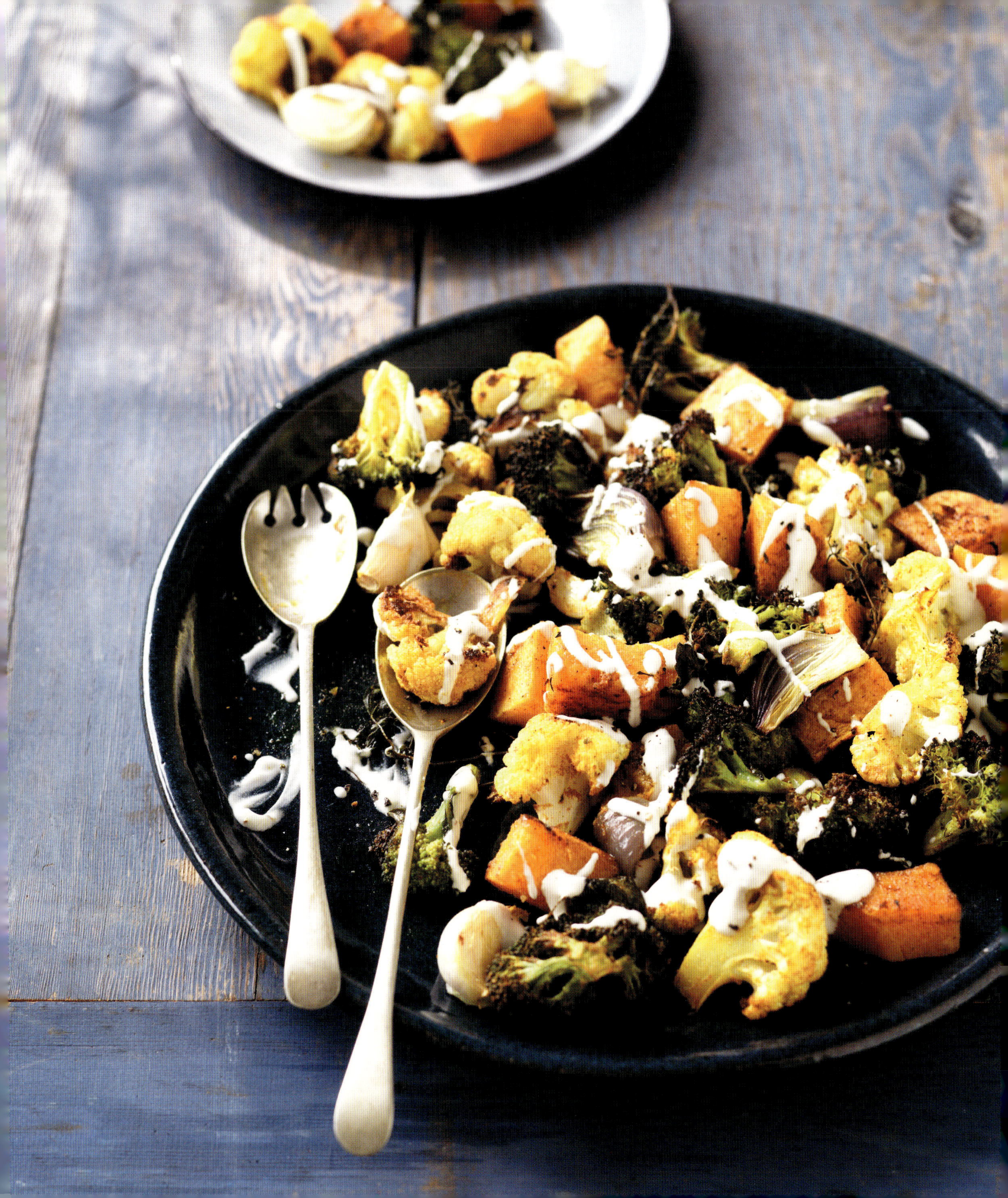

KOREAN PORK POT ROAST WITH COCONUT RICE AND KIMCHI

¼ cup grated palm sugar

½ cup soy sauce

2 tablespoons rice wine vinegar

1 tablespoon sesame oil

2 garlic cloves, finely chopped

1 tablespoon finely grated ginger

1 long red chilli, sliced

1kg pork neck

100g fresh shiitake mushrooms

1 cup basmati rice

1 cup coconut milk

200g bok choy or spinach

2 teaspoons sesame seeds

4 eggs

1 cup kimchi

1. Preheat oven to 150°C (130°C fan-forced). Combine the sugar, soy sauce, rice wine vinegar, 2 teaspoons of sesame oil, garlic, ginger, chilli and 2 cups water in a medium saucepan. Bring to the boil over high heat, then reduce the heat to low and cook until the sugar has dissolved.

2. Place the pork neck into a small ovenproof casserole dish (it should be just big enough fit snugly). Pour the soy mixture over and cover tightly with a lid or foil. Bake for 2–3 hours or until really tender. I like to baste the meat with the marinade every 30 minutes. Remove the lid and add the mushrooms. Cook uncovered for a further 15–20 minutes or until sauce has reduced.

3. Close to serving time, combine the rice, coconut milk and 1 cup water in medium saucepan. Cover and bring to the boil over high heat, then reduce the heat to low and cook, covered, for 12–15 minutes or until all the liquid has been absorbed.

4. Heat 1 teaspoon of sesame oil in a frying pan over medium-high heat. Toss the bok choy in the pan until wilted, transfer to a plate and sprinkle with sesame seeds.

5. Heat the remaining teaspoon of sesame oil in the same pan over medium-high heat and fry the eggs, sunny side up.

6. To serve, divide the rice between serving plates and top with sliced pork. Spoon over the reduced sauce, add some kimchi and sesame bok choy, and top with the fried egg.

Serves 4

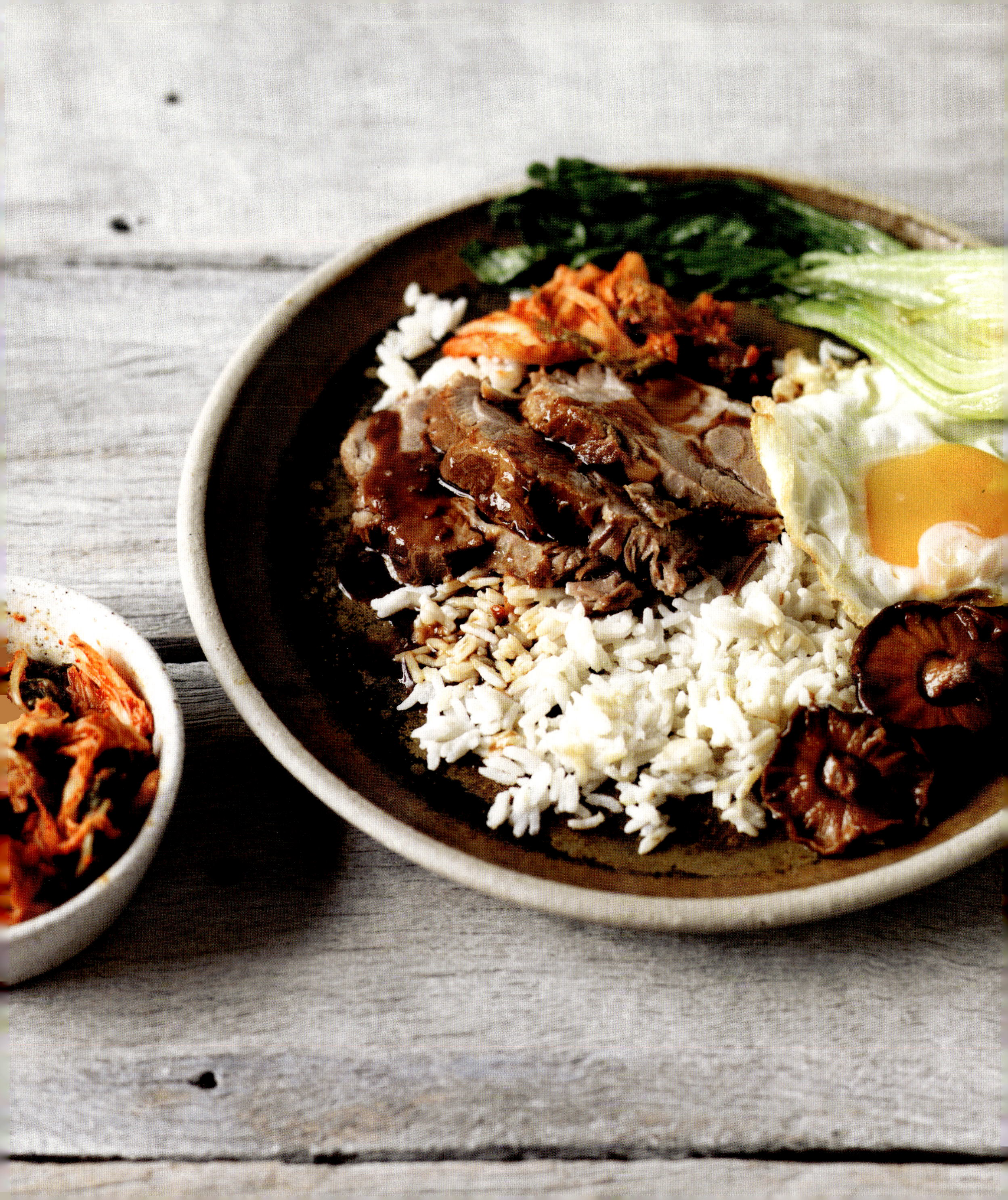

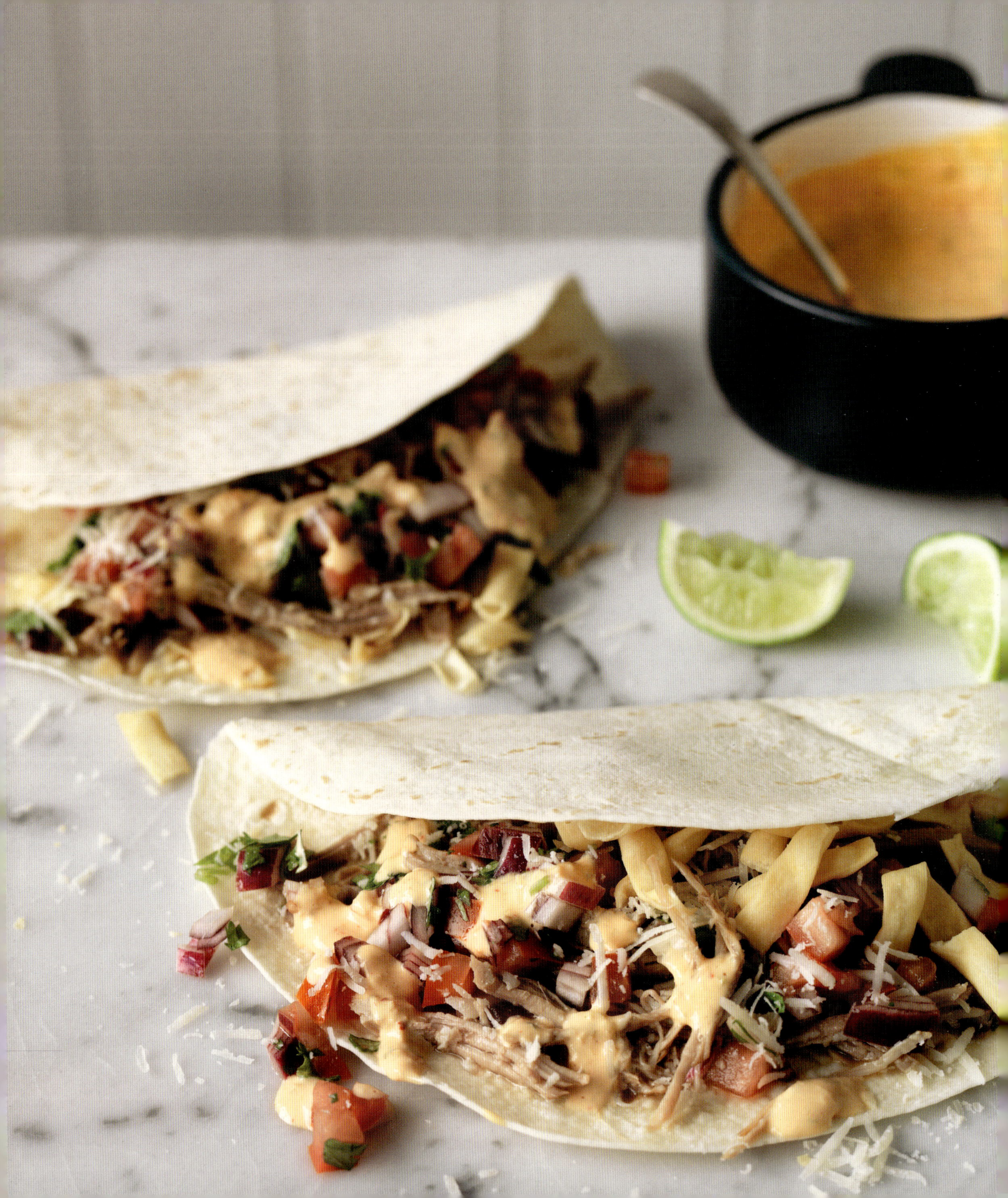

KOREAN PORK TACOS WITH KIMCHI MAYO (HQ)

There is a bit of lead time for these tasty treats and you have to start the day before. Trust me, the wait is definitely worth it. These Asian flavours lend themselves so well to being wrapped up in a tortilla and washed down with a ice-cold beer.

375ml apple cider
¼ cup soy sauce
2 tablespoons hoisin sauce
3 garlic cloves, crushed
2 star anise
1 teaspoon chilli flakes
1kg boneless pork shoulder
8 flour tortillas (20cm), warmed
½ cup crispy Asian noodles, for garnish
½ cup finely grated Parmesan
2 limes, cut in wedges

KIMCHI MAYO

1 cup whole egg mayonnaise
2 tablespoons kimchi

SALSA

½ red onion, finely diced
½ cup coriander leaves, roughly chopped
2 tomatoes, deseeded and diced
2 tablespoons red wine vinegar
2 tablespoons extra virgin olive oil

1. Combine the apple cider, sauces, garlic and spices in a slow cooker. Give them a stir then add the pork. Cover and cook on low for 8 hours.
2. Carefully lift the pork out onto a large board and cool slightly (it should be 'falling apart' tender). Drain the liquid from the slow cooker, keeping most of it in a jug. Use 2 forks to pull the meat into shreds. Return to the slow cooker and stir in enough of the cooking liquid to keep the meat moist. Cover and leave in the slow cooker (on the 'keep warm' function if you have it).
3. For the kimchi mayo, process the mayo and kimchi in a small food processor until well combined.
4. To make the salsa, combine all the ingredients in a serving bowl and season with salt and pepper.
5. Serve the pulled pork in the warm tortillas, topped with kimchi mayo, salsa, crispy noodles and grated Parmesan. Squeeze lime juice over to taste.

Serves 4

You can find kimchi in Asian supermarkets and health food stores.

MUM'S CHOC BEETROOT BIRTHDAY WONDERS

The day my mum surprised me with a mini-muffin birthday chocolate cake, I couldn't wipe the smile off my face. I took one bite and got serious chills! She still makes them better than me ... Maybe it's a mum thing, so ask yours to give them a whirl.

⅔ cup coconut oil, melted

¾ cup coconut sugar

4 eggs, lightly beaten

2 carrots, grated

2 teaspoons vanilla essence

¾ cup raw cacao powder

1 teaspoon maca powder

2 teaspoons baking powder

1 cup almond meal

¼ cup shredded coconut

2 tablespoons beetroot powder

1. Preheat the oven to 180°C (160°C fan-forced) and lightly grease twelve ½ cup capacity muffin pans, or line with paper cases.

2. Combine the coconut oil, sugar, eggs, carrot and vanilla in a large mixing bowl. Sift the cacao, maca, baking powder and a pinch of salt over, and whisk to combine.

3. Fold in the almond meal, coconut and beetroot powder. Spoon the mixture into the pans. Bake for 25–30 minutes or until a knife comes out clean but still slightly moist. Leave in the pans for 5 minutes, then lift out onto a wire rack to cool.

Makes 12

Maca powder and beetroot powder are available at health food stores.

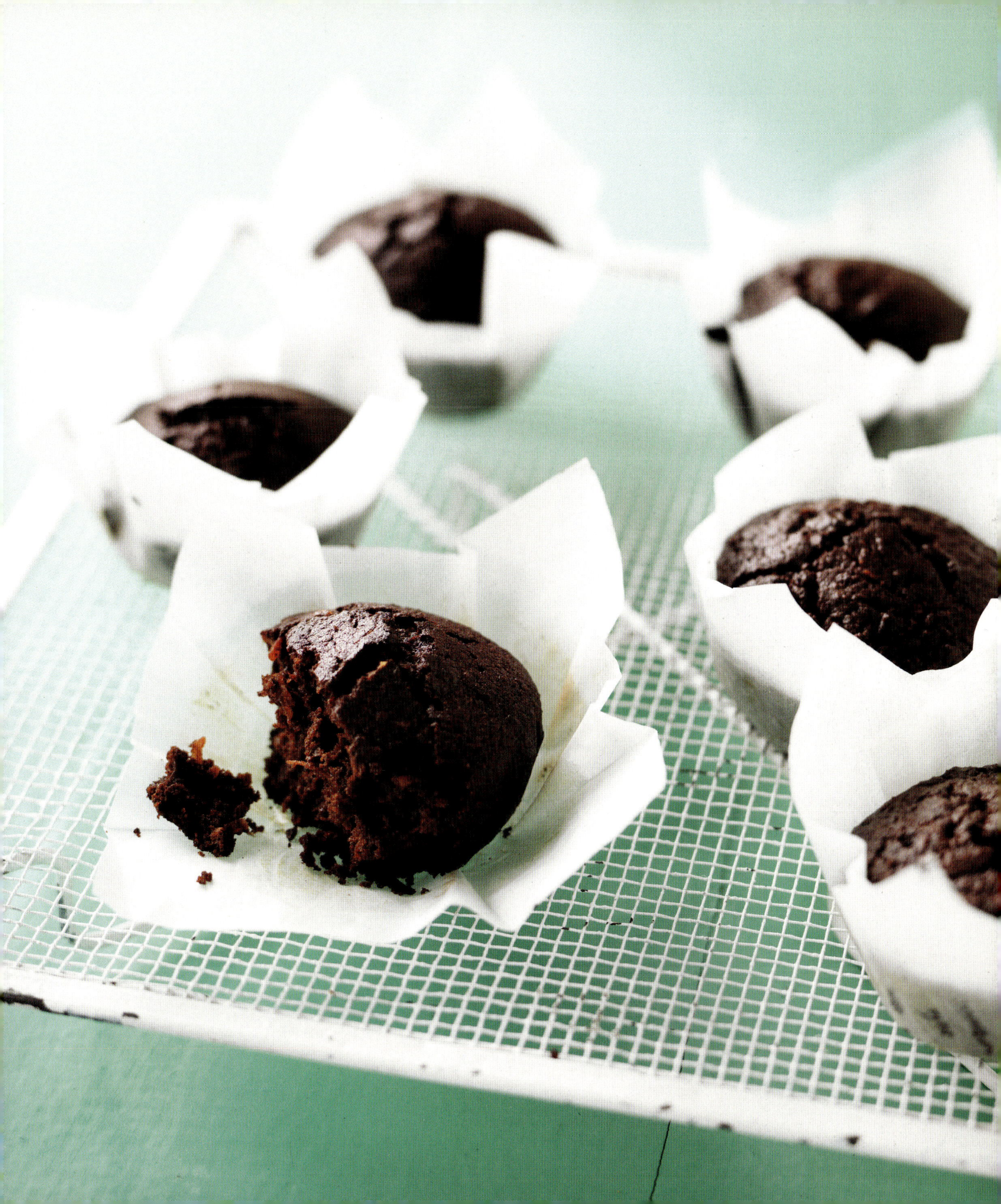

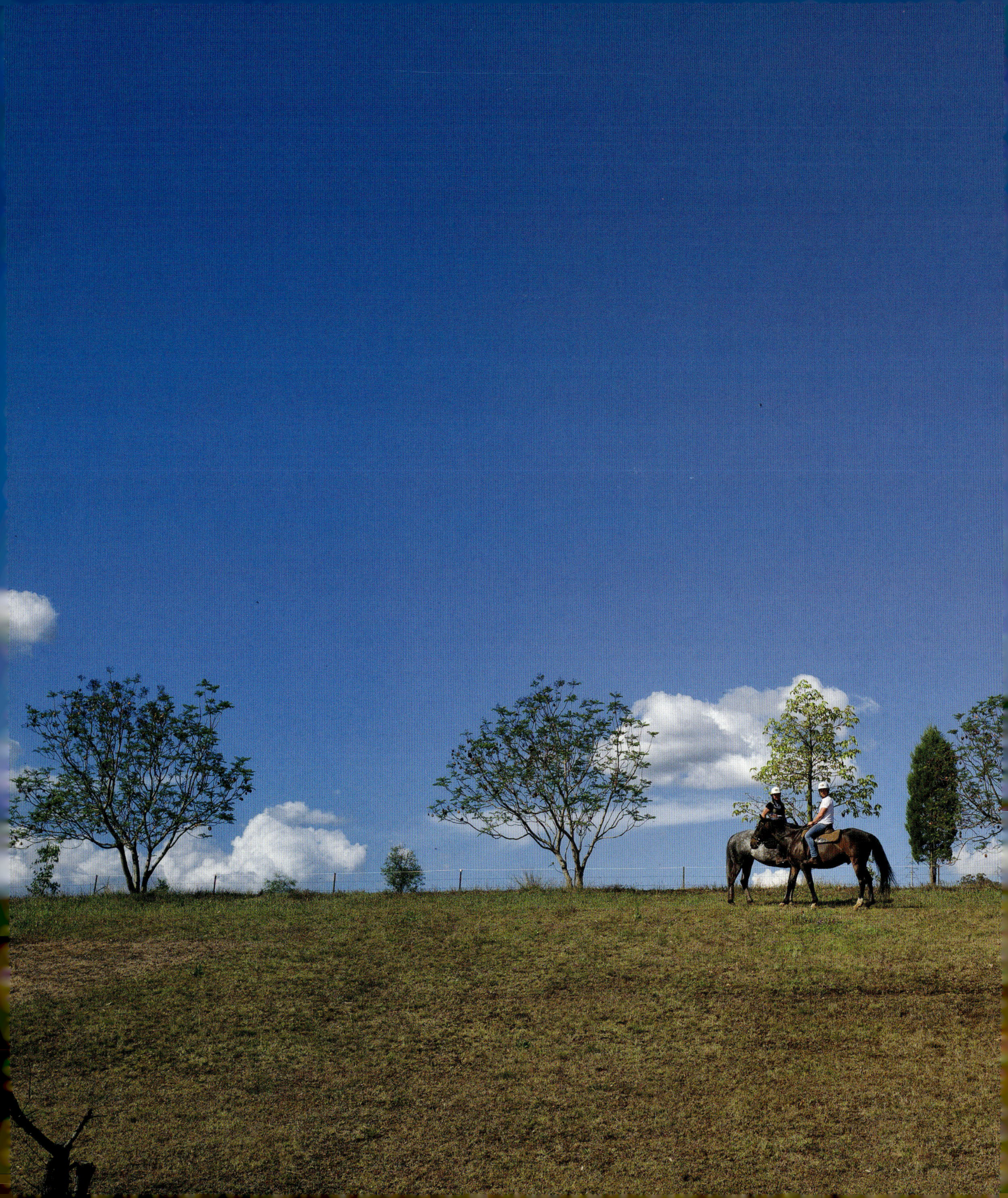

Toowoomba

On this adventure I have seen vivid contrasting colours of red and royal blue, freshwater canals divided by rock crevices, billabongs out in the bush, stunning beaches, and crystal clear waters exposing the Great Barrier Reef. Now I've seen the hills and well-kept, super green pastures of the Darling Downs near the Great Dividing Range. Among the hills are a number of farms, and Hayden and I were fortunate to meet up with the inspiring Fiona May who owns a property and small-scale ethical farm called Paddock to Potager.

What Fiona is doing is so innovative, yet it means stripping life back to an earlier kind of existence. She farms chickens, ducks, pigs, lambs and cows and, yep, she milks those cows by hand. I got to dabble in this myself. I thought I was doing fine before Fiona took a seat and started up. It was if she'd turned on a tap at full blast and I had a leaking problem!

Fiona makes use of all her products in a number of ways, such as feeding the cows' milk to the pigs as well as her family and making butters and creams. But the coolest thing, in my opinion, is the impact she's having on the community. She is creating a natural form of education whereby children, in particular, can learn how to farm and where produce comes from. You can even purchase a pig, or a share in one, and Fiona will look after it for its lifetime. In a world where people are becoming increasingly interested in where their food comes from, she and her young family convey the simplicity behind living ethically. She recently set up the Toowoomba Farmers' Markets and the inaugural event was so popular (with an attendance of 4,600 people) she's had to make it a regular thing. Talk about killing it! My eyes were twinkling with all the cooking ideas running through my head. The duck appealed to me so much that I came up with my Duck Pappardelle recipe (page 210). HQ was all about the butter, grass-fed and in its purest form.

Toowoomba is the archetypal Australian small town where Queensland supporters in the local pub cheer loudly at screens during the Origin series.

When we visited the town, we went to the Cobb + Co Museum as it offers blacksmithing workshops. A volunteer of the museum, Kym, said we could crank up the heat and get a little dirty. I did some metal work at high school, but this was the first time I'd ever worked on an anvil. Now, what would two young blokes want to make when they're given the option of blacksmithing? Marshmallow roasting forks, duh! By following Kym's lead we reproduced a usable roasting fork, but I don't think I'll give up cooking any time soon to become a blacksmith! It was pretty amazing to think we were working like the early settlers in these parts of the country. A blacksmith was well regarded within the community and I can definitely see why.

One thing I had been dying to do all my life was to ride a horse, and this was where I got the chance! We visited a paddock where we met Bella, the horse destined to be my first ride. She was stubborn, but after a few awkward moments (we stuffed up our handshake a few times) I learnt to steer, to sit and stand in the saddle, and to trot and gallop. Horses are smart to the point where they know where you want to go, just by you thinking it. No joke – I felt Bella could read my mind! Riding a horse and watching the sun set with Hayden over these amazing hills and plains was another memorable moment.

DC

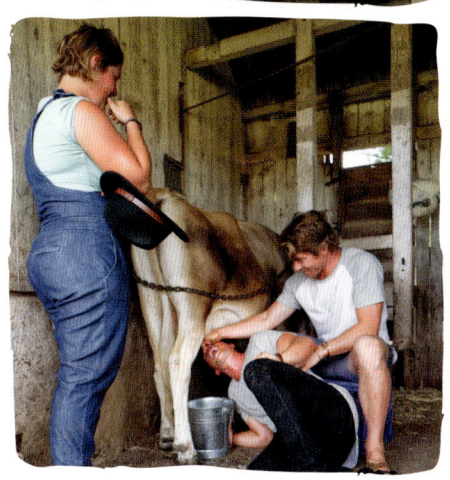

Fiona May, amazing cow-milker!

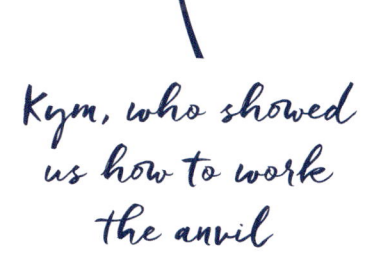

Kym, who showed us how to work the anvil

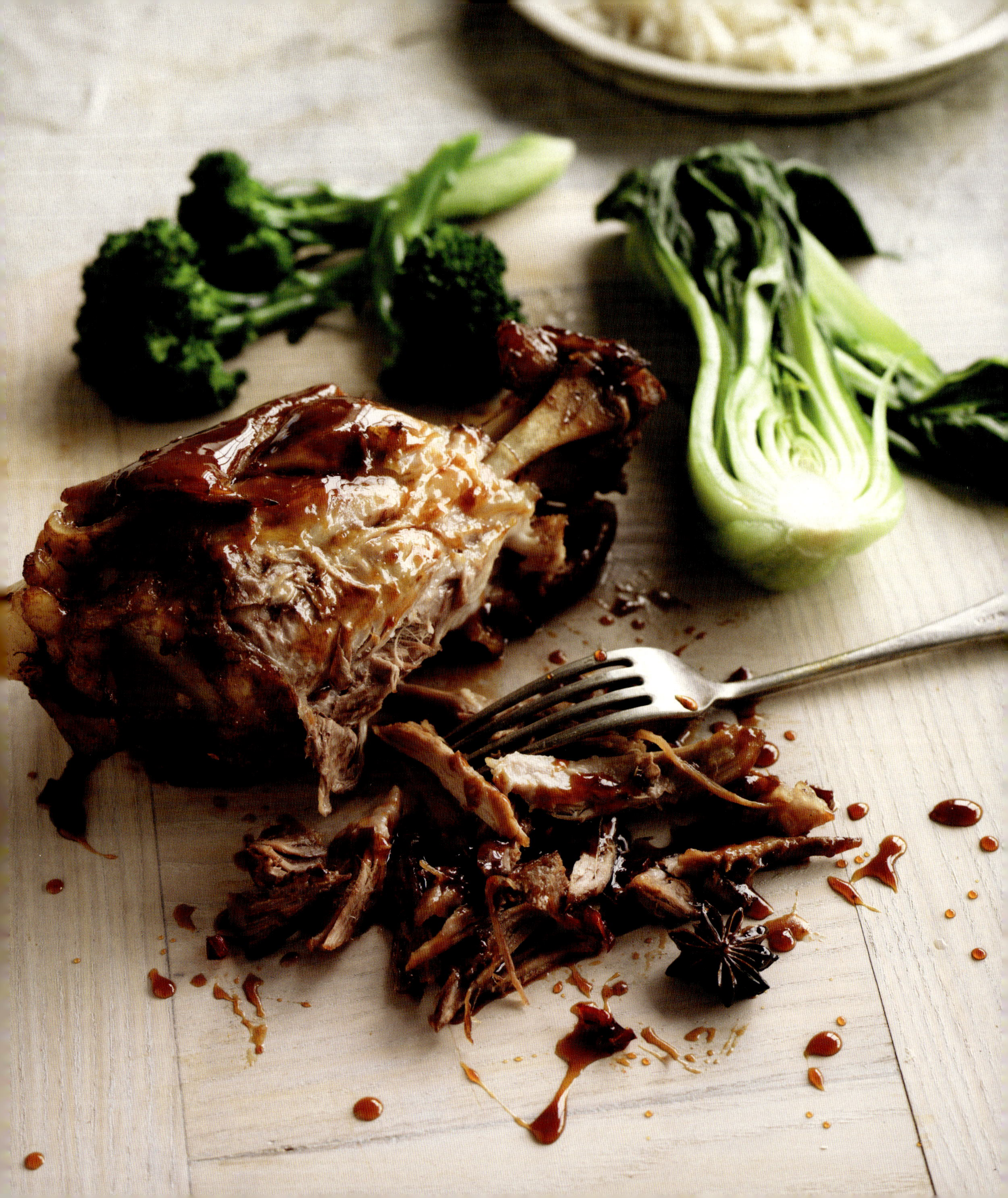

STICKY PORK HOCK WITH SESAME GREENS

This is sticky and naughty, but a serious crowd-pleaser. Take this amazing dish to the table, get your knife in and start pulling apart the tender flesh. Make sure you have someone with a camera ready to catch the jaw-drop reactions from friends and family!

2 pork hocks

3cm knob ginger, finely grated

2 long red chillies, deseeded, finely chopped

4 garlic cloves, bruised

1 star anise

3 litres beef stock

¾ cup honey

¼ cup soy sauce

2 teaspoons sesame oil

1 bunch broccolini, trimmed

1 bunch baby bok choy, halved

steamed rice, to serve

1. Place the hocks in a large pot and cover with cold water. Bring to the boil and cook for 2–3 minutes to allow the impurities to come out. Drain and pat dry, getting rid of any excess scum, and clean the pot. Return the hocks to the pot and add the ginger, chilli, garlic and star anise. Cover with stock and stir in the honey and soy sauce. Bring to the boil on high heat, then reduce heat to very low, cover and simmer for 3½–4 hours.

2. Preheat the oven to 170°C (150°C fan-forced). Remove the hocks from the pot and set aside to cool. Increase the heat to high and reduce the poaching liquid to ⅓ of the volume, or until it starts to become syrupy (if you do this in a wider pan it will reduce more quickly).

3. Place the hocks into a roasting pan. Cover with the reduced liquid and cook for 10 minutes or until they are covered with a super shiny glaze.

4. Meanwhile, heat the sesame oil in a frying pan over high heat. Cook the broccolini, tossing, for 2 minutes, then add the bok choy and cook for a further 2 minutes.

5. Serve the hocks on a plate or board with the greens and rice.

Serves 4

DUCK PAPPARDELLE

1 tablespoon olive oil

4 duck marylands

1 onion, chopped

3 garlic cloves, finely chopped

2 celery sticks, chopped

2 carrots, chopped

1 cup red wine (medium to full body)

800g can diced tomatoes

1 cup chicken stock

1 cinnamon stick

3 bay leaves

3 thyme sprigs

3 oregano sprigs

400g pappardelle pasta

Parmigiano reggiano

1. Heat the oil in a large flameproof casserole dish over medium-high heat. Cook the duck until brown all over (you may need to do this in batches), remove and set aside. Drain off all but 2 tablespoons of the fat in the pan.

2. Add the onion, garlic, celery and carrot and cook for 5 minutes or until the onion starts to turn golden brown. Pour in the red wine to deglaze the pan, scraping all the browned goodness off the bottom. Pop the duck back in. Add the tomatoes, stock, cinnamon stick, bay leaves, thyme and oregano. Season with salt and pepper, bring to the boil, then reduce the heat to very low. Cover and cook for 2½–3 hours, stirring every so often, until the duck is tender.

3. Transfer the duck to a board or plate. Discard the fat and shred the meat off the bone (two forks can come in handy here). Return the meat to the pot, increase the heat to medium and cook uncovered for a further 15–20 minutes or until sauce thickens slightly – you don't want a runny sauce.

4. Bring a large saucepan of water to the boil and add 2 good pinches of salt. Cook the pasta according to packet directions or until al dente. Drain, reserving some of the water, and return to the pan.

5. Add the sauce to the pasta with 1 tablespoon of the reserved water and toss to combine. Divide between serving plates and finish off with a good sprinkle of Parmigiano reggiano.

Serves 4

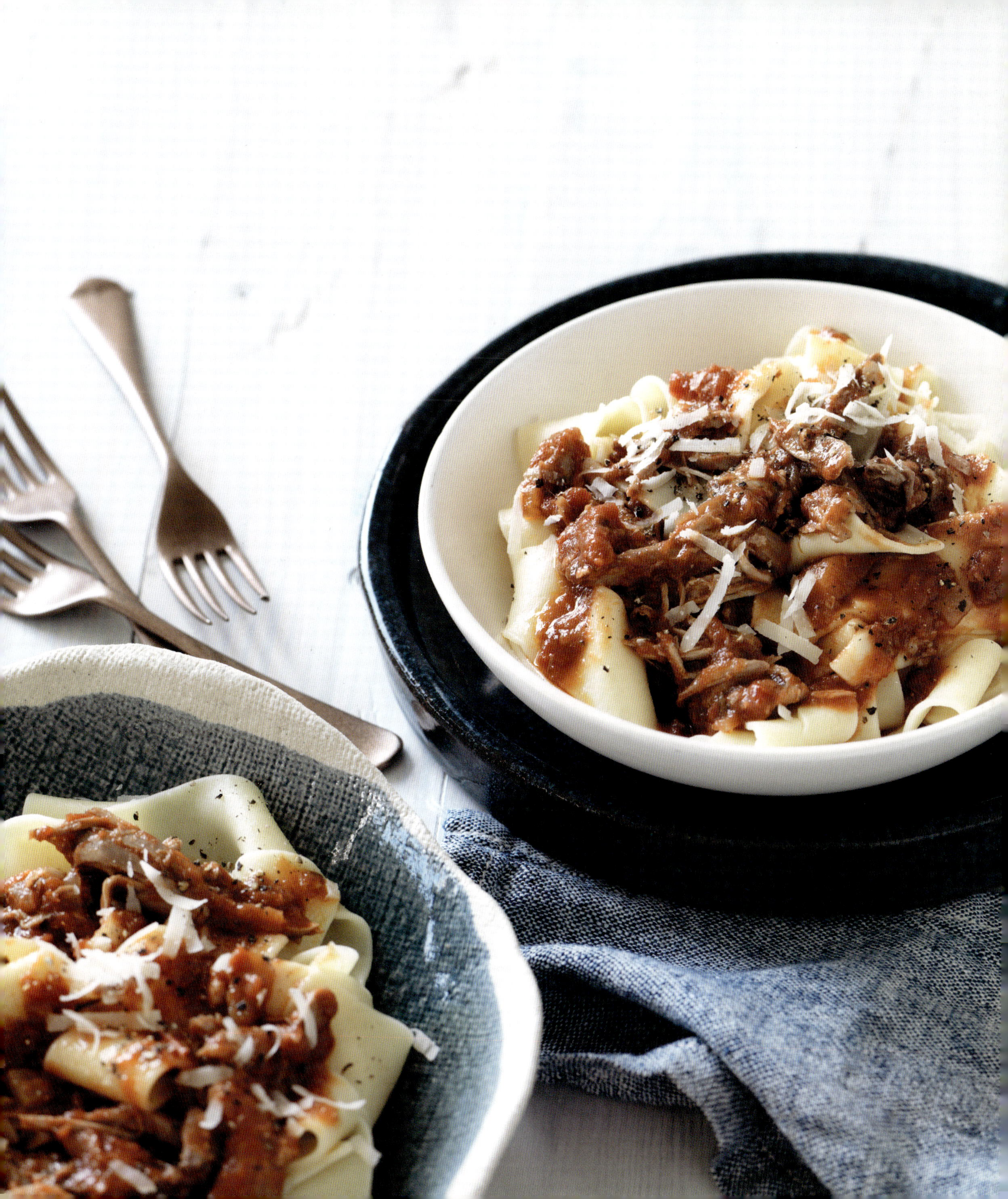

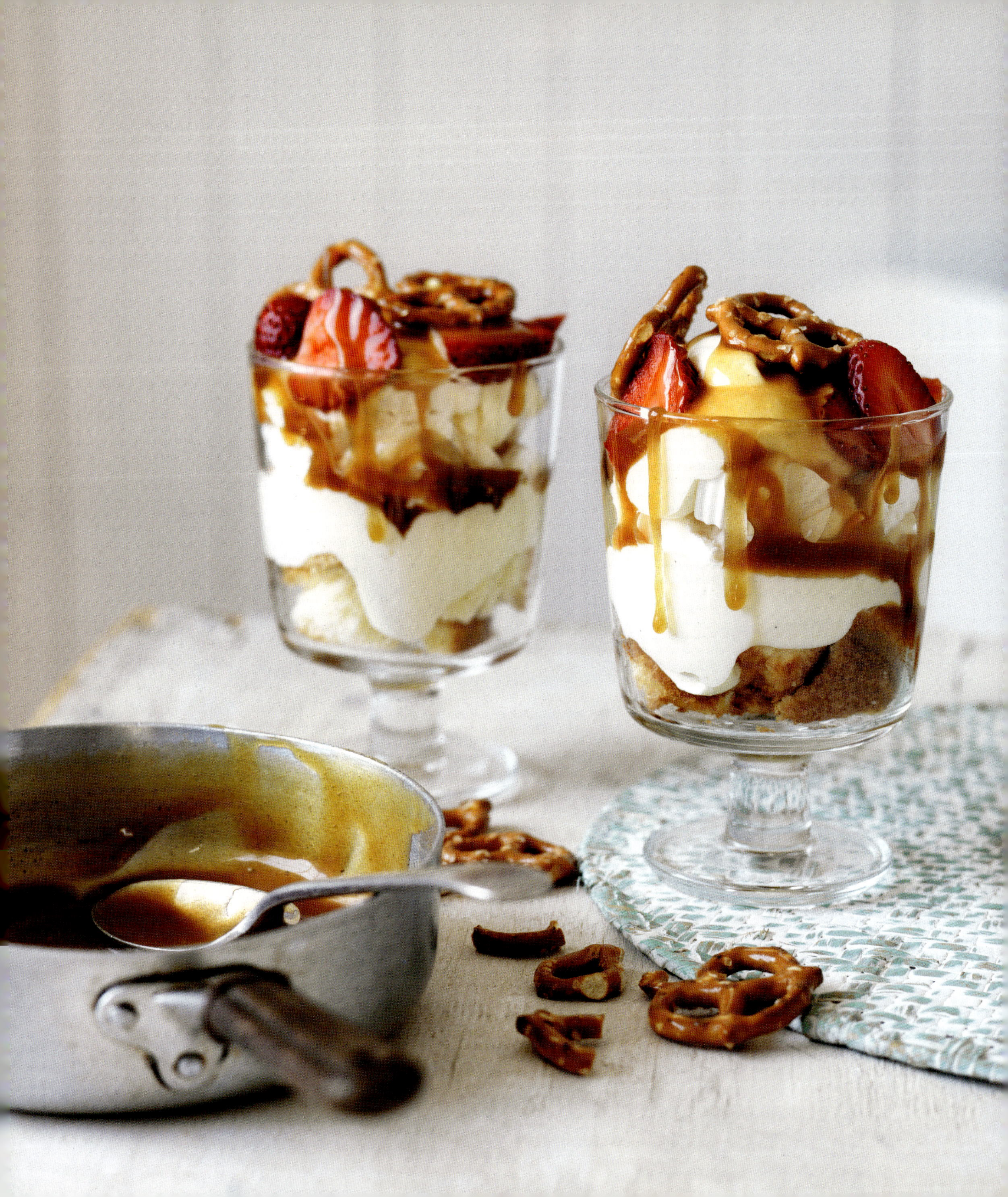

SALTED CARAMEL ETON MESS ⓓⒸ

For this party pleaser, you can purchase the meringues in advance. But in case you're like me and prefer to do everything from scratch, this recipe shows you how to DIY. These desserts look amazing in glasses or jars, and your friends and loved ones will enjoy spooning in for every last bit of caramel.

SPONGE CAKE

225g self-raising flour

1 teaspoon baking powder

225g unsalted butter, chopped, at room temperature

225g caster sugar

4 eggs, lightly beaten

1 teaspoon vanilla essence

MERINGUE

4 egg whites

¾ cup caster sugar

CARAMEL SAUCE

⅔ cup caster sugar

½ cream

whipped cream, sliced strawberries and salted pretzels, to serve

1. To make the cake, preheat the oven to 180°C (160°C fan-forced) and line two 18cm round cake tins with baking paper. Using an electric mixer, beat all the ingredients together with a pinch of salt until combined and airy. Pour into the tins, dividing evenly. Bake for 20–25 minutes or until golden brown and springy to a touch in the centre. Stand in the tins for 5 minutes then turn out onto a wire rack to cool.

2. For the meringues, preheat the oven to 90°C (70°C fan-forced) and line two large baking trays with baking paper. Using an electric mixer, beat the egg whites on high speed until soft peaks begin to form (if you take a spoon out of the mixture, a peak will start to fold over as opposed to staying tall). Add the sugar a little at a time, beating until dissolved between each addition. Continue mixing on high speed until glossy. Rub a bit of mixture between your fingers: if there is a little crystal feeling continue mixing until it is smooth.

3. Using a big spoon, dollop uneven blobs of mixture onto the trays. Bake for 3 hours, until the meringues are crisp and dry. Set aside to cool.

4. For the caramel sauce, put the sugar into a small saucepan and add two tablespoons of water. Place over medium-low heat and allow the sugar to dissolve. Continue to cook for 5–8 minutes or until the sugar starts to turn golden. Take off the heat and stir in the cream until combined and smooth.

5. To serve, break the cake and meringues into large pieces and layer into bowls or glasses with the whipped cream. Pour the caramel sauce over and top with fresh strawberries and salty pretzels.

Serves 4

CHOC BLUEBERRY NO-CHURN ICE CREAM (HQ)

When people think of making ice cream they get a little scared. Don't worry – you don't need an ice cream maker, nor do you need the skills to make custard. All you need is a whisk, some fresh ingredients and the patience to wait until the delectable sweetness is frozen!

125g blueberries, plus extra for garnish

¼ cup caster sugar

1½ teaspoons vanilla bean paste

400ml double cream

1½ tablespoons dark cocoa powder

395g can condensed milk

80g dark chocolate, melted

1. Line a 5 cup capacity loaf tin with plastic wrap or baking paper. Combine the blueberries, sugar and ½ teaspoon of the vanilla paste in a small saucepan. Heat over medium heat until the blueberries start to soften and juices run. Stir to dissolve the sugar, then simmer for a few minutes until the berries begin to break down. Remove from heat and cool slightly.

2. Transfer to a small food processor and process until almost smooth. Press through a sieve into a small bowl and set aside to cool completely.

3. Put the cream into a large mixing bowl and sift the cocoa powder over. Using electric beaters, beat until soft peaks form (take care not to overbeat as it whips up quickly). Add the condensed milk and remaining vanilla paste. Gently fold through with a spatula (take care not to lose the volume of the whipped cream).

4. Pour half the cream mixture into the loaf tin. Drizzle with half the melted chocolate and half the blueberry sauce. Use a fork to swirl the sauce and chocolate through the cream mixture. Add the remaining cream mixture, chocolate and sauce, and swirl again. Top with extra blueberries.

5. Cover with plastic wrap and freeze overnight, or until firm. Serve in bowls or cones.

Makes 1.25L

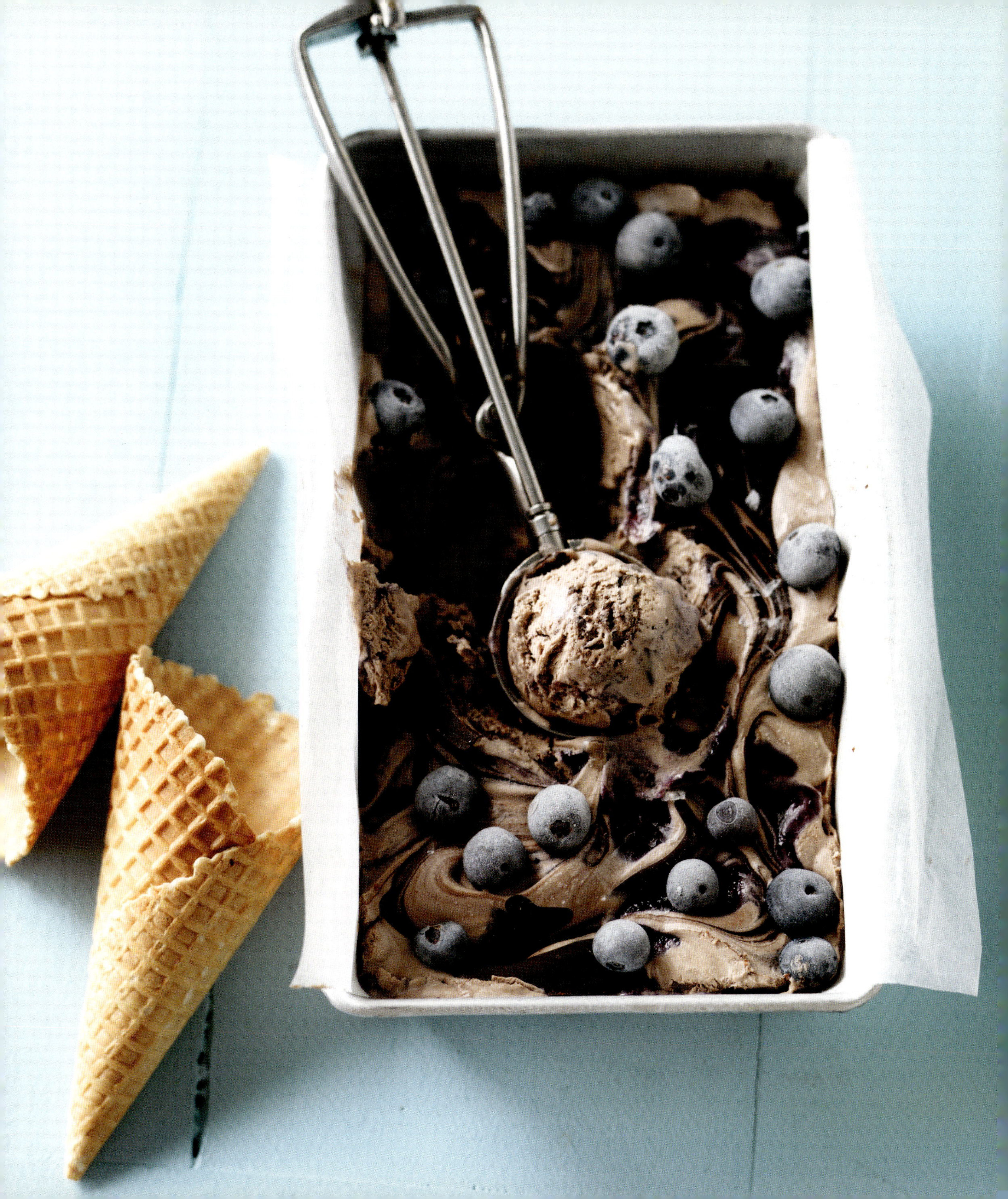

NUTORIOUS GLUTEN FREE CHOC AND RASPBERRY MUFFINS

1 cup coconut flour

3 teaspoons baking powder

2 teaspoons ground cinnamon

¾ teaspoon salt

2 cups almond meal

3 eggs

¾ cup Greek yoghurt

¾ cup macadamia oil

½ cup brown rice malt syrup

1½ teaspoons vanilla essence

1½ cup fresh or frozen raspberries

¾ cup dark chocolate chips

1. Preheat the oven to 170°C (or 150°C fan-forced) and lightly grease twelve ⅔ cup capacity muffin pans, or line with paper cases.

2. Sift the coconut flour, baking powder, cinnamon and salt in a large mixing bowl. Stir in the almond meal and make a well in the centre.

3. Whisk the eggs in a bowl, then add the yoghurt, macadamia oil, rice malt syrup and vanilla essence. Whisk until combined.

4. Add the wet ingredients to the dry and gently fold together until combined. Fold in the raspberries and choc chips (keeping a few of each for the tops). Spoon the mixture into the pans and top with the extra chocolate and raspberries.

5. Bake for 35–40 minutes until golden brown and a skewer comes out clean. Cover loosely with foil if they are starting to become too brown on top before they are cooked. Leave in the pans for 5 minutes, then lift out onto a wire rack to cool.

Makes 12

> Rice malt syrup is available in supermarkets. If you can't find it, use another natural sweetener like honey or maple syrup.

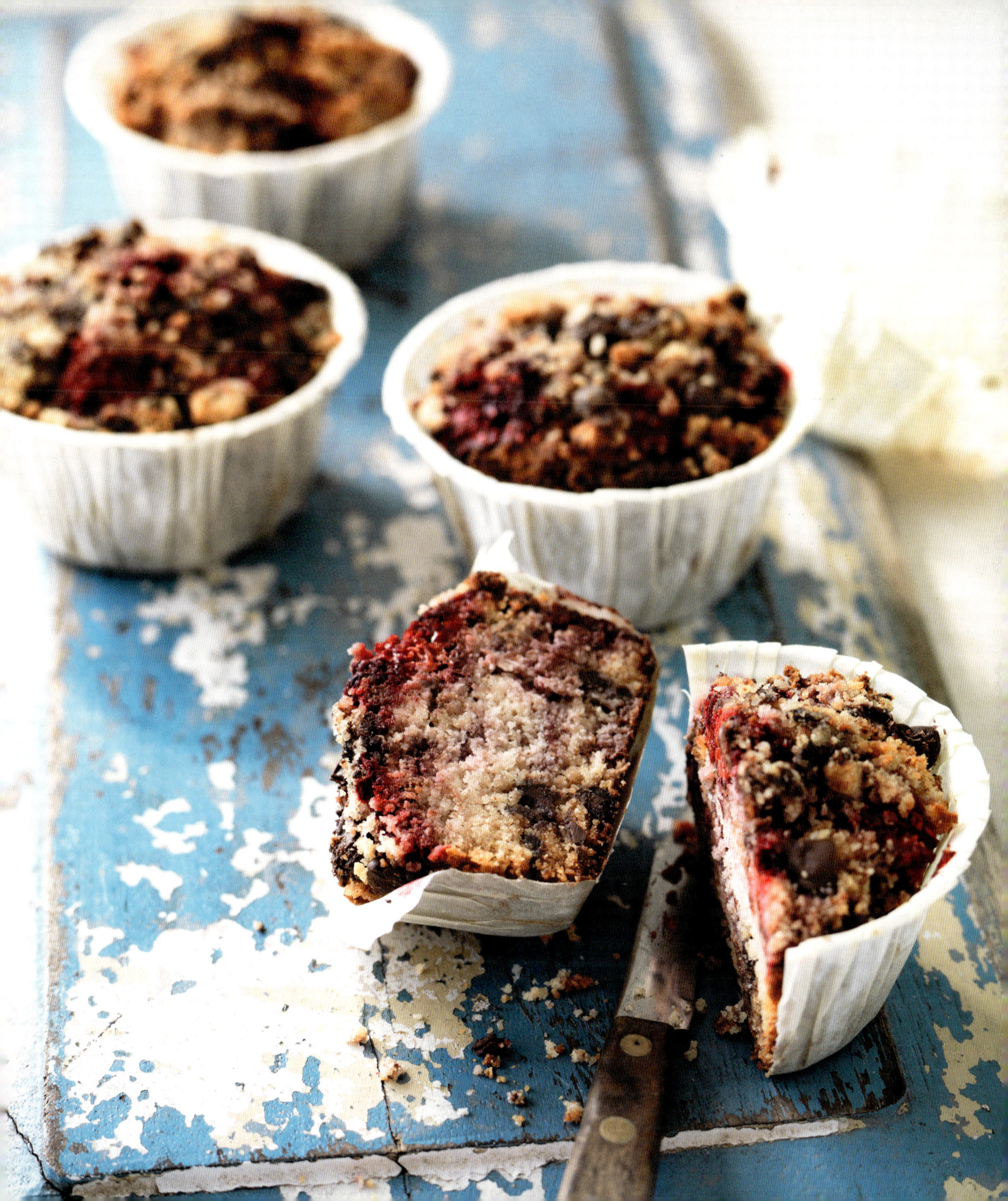

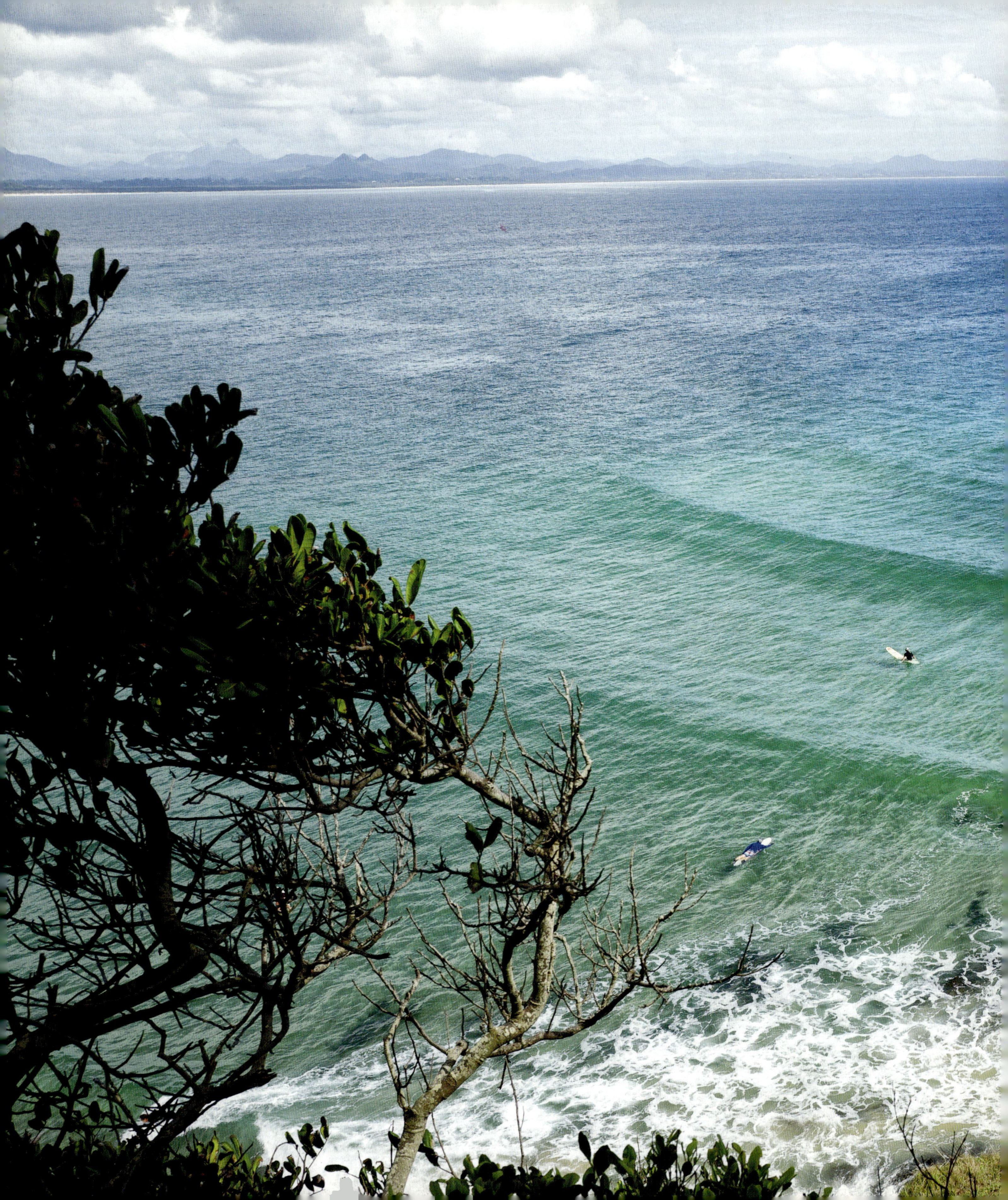

Byron Bay

The day had come. We made our final stop just inside the New South Wales border at Byron Bay, a place world-renowned for its beach lifestyle, beautiful coastline and chilled vibe.

Byron Bay and its surrounding beaches offer plenty of options for waves, from the famous Pass down to Broken Head, but we had to venture further south to Ballina to have a wave on the north wall. It was fun and probably the biggest swell we encountered on the whole trip. But it was super windy and the tricky conditions were not the best for Dan out on the stand-up paddle board.

Out in the water we met Richard Tuohy who was not only a great surfer but also a chocolatier with a thriving business called Byron Bay Cacao. I was pretty pumped because I may have a slight chocolate addiction! He invited us back to his cool set-up, where he taught Churchy and me the art of hand-making chocolates, the importance of getting the best ingredients and how he sources his cocao from all over the world.

Then we went to circus school! But we weren't interested in practising our juggling or clowning around. We went straight up to the top of the pops, the trapeze! No joke, we had a quick run-through for safety and then it was 3-2-1 – go! Neither of us is great with heights and I was a little nervous on the top platform. DC was the first to take the leap of faith and, after a quick swing, he was upside down and hurtling back to our catcher. And he made it! Going second made me even more nervous. The hardest part for me was flipping upside down and getting my legs through the bar as my flexibility isn't that great, but on the count of my catcher I was flying through the air, and the next minute he had me in his hands and we were swinging together. Super exciting, and one of those things you just want to have another go at!

Later we discovered another epic way to check the surf: via a gyrocopter. Imagine a cross between a helicopter and a tiny little plane with no wings or cabin – that's what you get. The take-off was like nothing I have ever experienced before, a bit like a plane, a bit like a helicopter. It was exhilarating being out in the open air. After the initial new-flight jitters, the only thing left to do was to enjoy the view, look out for whales and check the surf!

Then it was time to leave the coast for the hinterland and a visit to Nimbin Valley Dairy, a goat and dairy farm that produces some of the finest small-batch goat's cheeses and milk in the country. The owners, Kerry and Paul, are the real deal, committed to treating their animals well – the goats even have their own nutritionist – and creating a beautiful product. The view from the hills above Nimbin where they are located is spectacular. Maybe that's why the cheese is so good! While we were there, we made sure to grab some goat's cheese to use in our recipes in this chapter, Dan's luscious Goat's Cheese Chocolate Tart (page 232) and tasty Roast Pumpkin, Goat's Cheese and Cauliflower Flatbread (page 228), my Roast Eggplant with Onion, Pistachio and Goat's Cheese (page 231) and my brightly coloured Root Vegetable and Goat's Cheese Tart (page 223).

Now this had to be my favourite part: visiting the Stone and Wood Brewery. I don't mind a beer, but not just any old beer. It has to be made with passion from the best ingredients, or it has to have a story that goes with it. And the beers coming out of this brewery sure ticked those boxes. Not only are they packed with goodness and flavour but we were also fascinated to learn how head brewer, Caolan Vaughan, made his limited release Stone Beer. He adds wood-fired stones to the kettle to intensify the malt flavours with a technique that pays homage to the way brewers used to brew beer. The brewery released the beer to celebrate their annual 'Festival of the Stone' in early autumn 2015. I sampled several more of their specialities and, even though he's not much of a drinker, I got Dan trying a few sips!

HQ

Paul and the well-nourished goats at Nimbin Valley Dairy

NSW — Byron Bay, Coffs Harbour, Sydney

About to take off in the gyrocopter!

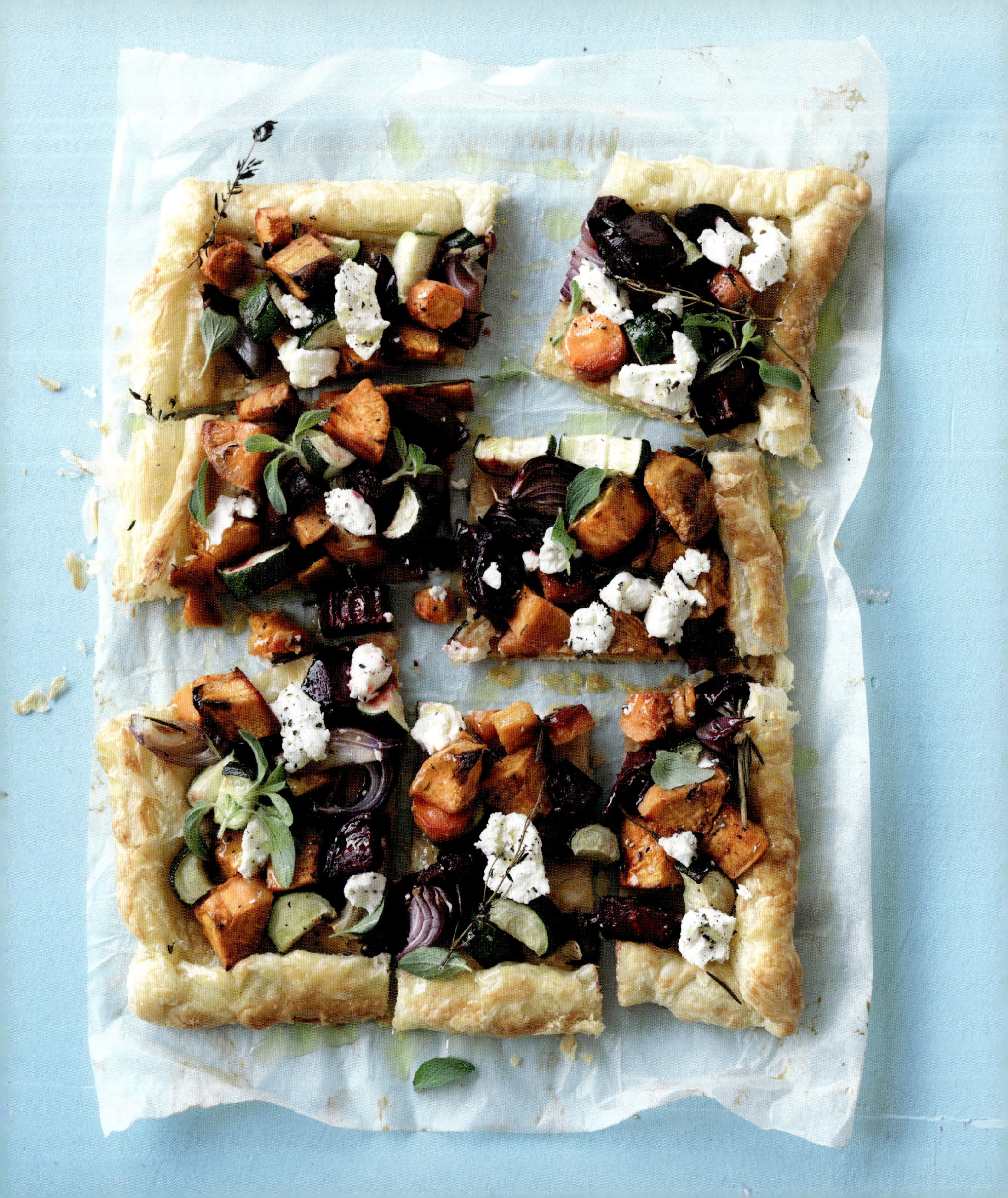

ROOT VEGETABLE AND GOAT'S CHEESE TART (HQ)

The fiery colours from the roasted beetroot and red onion look glorious in contrast with the creamy-white goat's cheese in this super simple tart. Carème frozen puff pastry can be bought at specialist delis and supermarkets – the size and shape works well for this recipe. You can use regular frozen puff pastry, but you may need to join 2 sheets together.

2 medium carrots

2 medium beetroot (250g)

1 small sweet potato (250g)

¼ butternut pumpkin (400g), deseeded

1 head of garlic, cut in half

3 tablespoons olive oil

1½ tablespoons rosemary leaves, chopped

1½ tablespoons thyme leaves

2 zucchini

1 medium red onion

1 sheet Carème frozen puff pastry, thawed

1 egg, lightly beaten

100g goat's cheese, crumbled into chunks

extra virgin olive oil and balsamic vinegar, to drizzle

1 tablespoon oregano leaves

1. Preheat the oven to 180°C (160°C fan-forced) and line 2 baking trays with baking paper. Peel the carrots, beetroot, sweet potato and pumpkin and cut into 2.5cm cubes (the carrots into 2.5cm thick slices). Place into a large bowl and add the garlic, 2 tablespoons of the oil, rosemary and thyme. Season with salt and pepper and toss to combine. Arrange onto the trays and roast for 25 minutes.

2. Cut the zucchini into 2.5cm slices and the onion into thick wedges. Toss with the remaining oil and add to the trays. Cook for a further 20 minutes or until the vegetables are caramelised and soft. Set aside to cool.

3. Increase the oven temperature to 200°C (180°C fan-forced) and place a heavy-based baking tray into the oven to preheat. Roll the pastry between two sheets of baking paper to a 30cm x 45cm rectangle. Remove the top layer of baking paper and brush the edges of the pastry with the egg. Fold 3cm of pastry over on all sides, pushing down firmly to seal, to create a rim. Using a fork, prick the base of the tart. Bake for 20 minutes or until the pastry is golden. Cool.

4. Fill the pastry shell with the roasted vegetables and goat's cheese. Drizzle with olive oil and balsamic vinegar, and scatter with oregano leaves. Cut to slices and serve.

Serves 6

BEER BRAISED BEEF SHORT RIBS WITH SWEET POTATO MASH

Dark beer is best for this recipe. I grabbed a couple of bottles from the Stone & Wood Brewery in Byron Bay – a beautiful craft beer with a spicy bitterness. Add your own favourite and enjoy a full-bodied, earthy taste adventure!

8 beef short ribs (about 300g each)

1 tablespoon rice bran oil

1 onion, cut into rough chunks

2 carrots, cut into rough chunks

2 sticks celery, cut into rough chunks

3 garlic cloves, crushed

1 tablespoon Dijon mustard

1 bottle dark beer (such as stout or porter)

1 litre beef stock

1 large sweet potato (about 500g), peeled and cut into 2.5cm chunks

2 tablespoons butter

¼ cup finely grated Parmesan

chopped parsley, to serve

1. Preheat the oven to 160°C (140°C fan-forced). Take the ribs from the fridge to come to room temperature about 30 minutes before cooking.

2. Season the ribs well with salt and pepper. Heat a large heavy-based ovenproof casserole dish over high heat. Add half the oil and cook the ribs in batches until golden brown all over. Transfer to a large bowl and set aside.

3. Reduce the heat to medium and heat the remaining oil in the pan. Cook the onion, carrot and celery, stirring occasionally, until golden. Stir in the garlic and mustard and cook for a few seconds. Pour in the beer and stock, stirring to kick up any little bits off the bottom of the pot. Return the ribs to the casserole and bring to the boil.

4. Cover with a lid and transfer to the oven. Cook for 2 hours, then uncover and cook for a further 30 minutes.

5. While the ribs are finishing, steam the sweet potato in a steamer until soft. Transfer to a large bowl and add the butter and Parmesan. Mash well, then season with salt and pepper.

6. Serve the ribs on a bed of sweet potato mash, sprinkled with parsley.

Serves 4

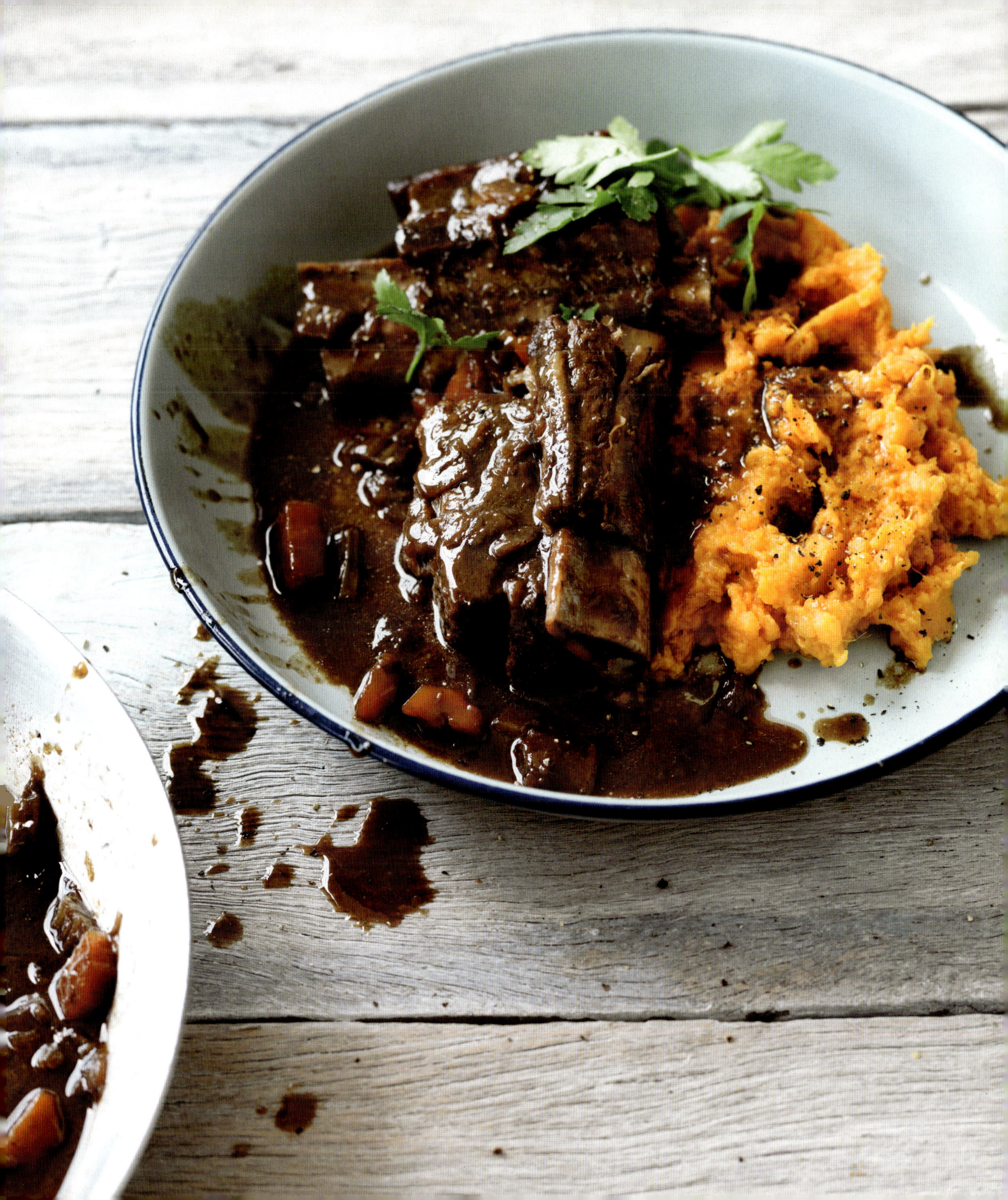

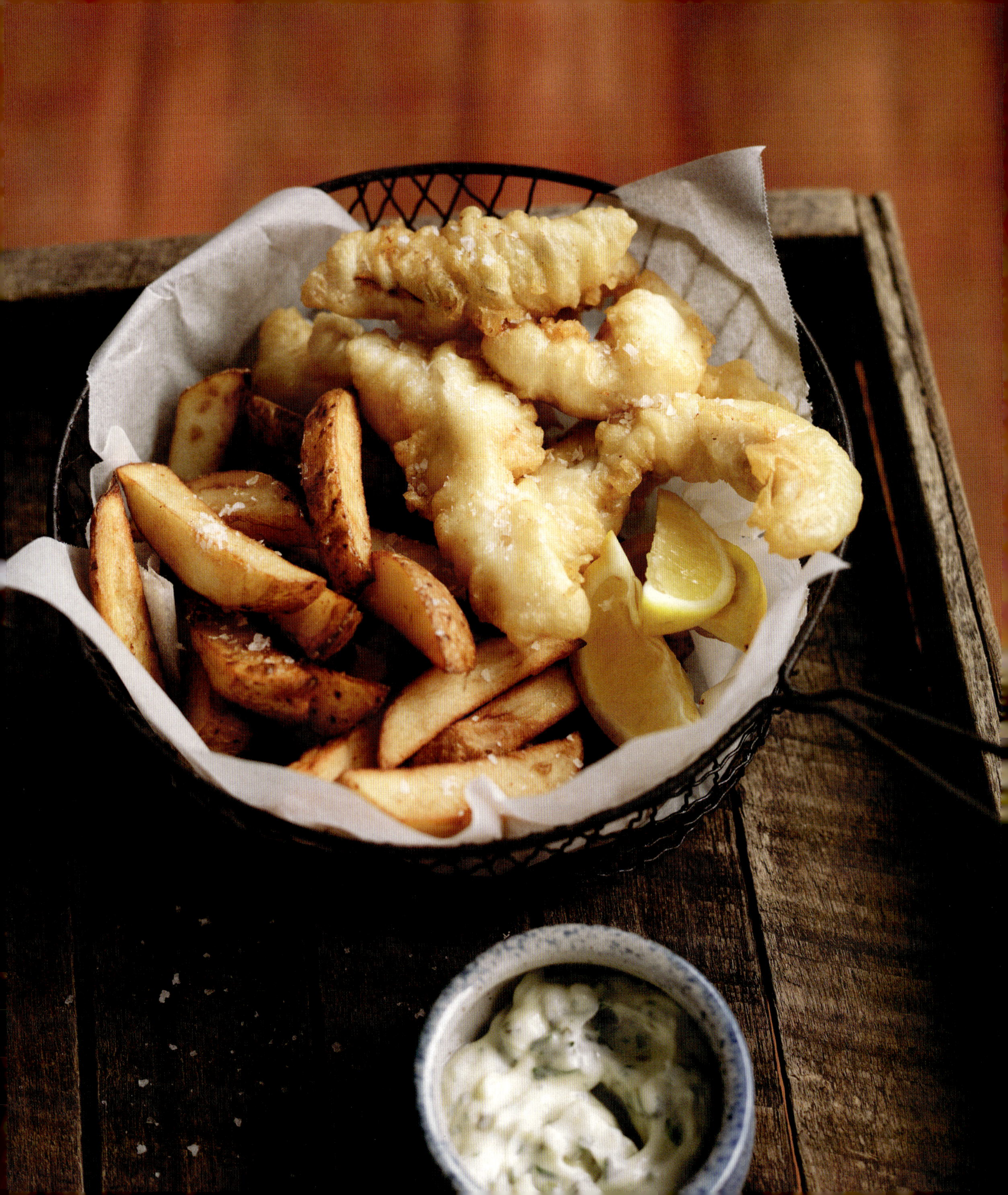

DAD'S BEER BATTERED FISH AND CHIPS (HQ)

This is my Dad's go-to meal whenever we go out to eat. He orders it everywhere – in pubs, restaurants, cafés … So, this one's for you, Dad!

1.5 litres vegetable oil
1kg Sebago potatoes, scrubbed and cut into rough chips, skin on
1 cup plain flour
1 cup beer, ice cold
2 egg whites, whipped to soft peaks
3 cups ice cubes
1 teaspoon salt
12 large flathead fillets (be sure to check for bones)
lemon wedges and tartare sauce, to serve

1. Preheat the oven to 160°C (140°C fan-forced). Heat the oil in a large saucepan (it should only be half-full) over medium-high heat, until a crust of bread sizzles as soon as it hits the oil. Cook chips in small batches (so that the oil temperature doesn't drop too dramatically) for 3–5 minutes or until they just begin to colour. Lift out with a slotted spoon or tongs and transfer to a wire rack over a tray to drain off any excess oil.

2. Repeat this process, this time cooking until the chips are golden brown and crisp. Place into the oven to keep warm while you cook the fish.

3. Put the flour into a large bowl and season with salt and pepper, then whisk in the beer. Fold in the egg whites and the ice.

4. Reheat the oil. Working 2 at a time, dip fillets into the batter to coat completely, and drain off excess. Deep-fry for 4–5 minutes so that the fish is cooked and the batter is golden and crispy. Drain on paper towels and continue with the remaining fish.

5. Season the fish and chips with salt and serve with lemon wedges and tartare sauce.

Serves 6

ROAST PUMPKIN, GOAT'S CHEESE AND CAULIFLOWER FLATBREAD (DC)

For those of you out there who love pizzas but can't stomach gluten, welcome to a new age of epic flavour! The taste of this 'flatbread' seriously breaks all the rules. I make a batch in advance and store it in the freezer. Then all I have to do is roast them in the oven, top them with colourful vegies and we're off!

¼ butternut pumpkin, peeled, deseeded and cut into thin wedges
2 tablespoons olive oil
750g cauliflower
2 tablespoons cottage cheese
1 teaspoon garlic flakes
1 teaspoon onion flakes
1 teaspoon oregano leaves, dried
2 eggs, lightly beaten
2 tablespoons pesto
125g grape tomatoes, halved
50g goat's cheese, crumbled
rocket and balsamic vinegar, to serve

1. Preheat the oven to 200°C (180°C fan-forced) and line a baking tray with baking paper. Toss the pumpkin with the oil and spread onto the tray. Bake for 20 minutes or until golden. Set aside to cool. Reduce oven to 100°C (80°C fan-forced).

2. Trim the cauliflower and finely chop, or process to a crumb texture. Bring a medium saucepan of water to the boil, add the cauliflower and cook for 2 minutes or until soft. Transfer to a sieve lined with muslin cloth to drain. Leave until cool enough to handle.

3. Squeeze as much moisture from the cauliflower as you can. Spread out onto a baking tray lined with baking paper, and place into the oven for 10 minutes to dry out further. Transfer to a bowl. Return the oven to 200°C (180°C fan-forced).

4. Add the cottage cheese, garlic and onion flakes, oregano and egg to the cauliflower and season with salt and pepper. Mix until evenly combined. Transfer to a baking tray lined with baking paper and spread out to a round or oval shape, about 5mm thick. Bake for 10 minutes.

5. Cool the base slightly, then spread with pesto and top with pumpkin, tomatoes and goat's cheese. Season with salt and pepper, and pop back into the oven for about 5 minutes to heat through. Serve topped with rocket and a drizzle of balsamic vinegar.

Serves 4 as a snack

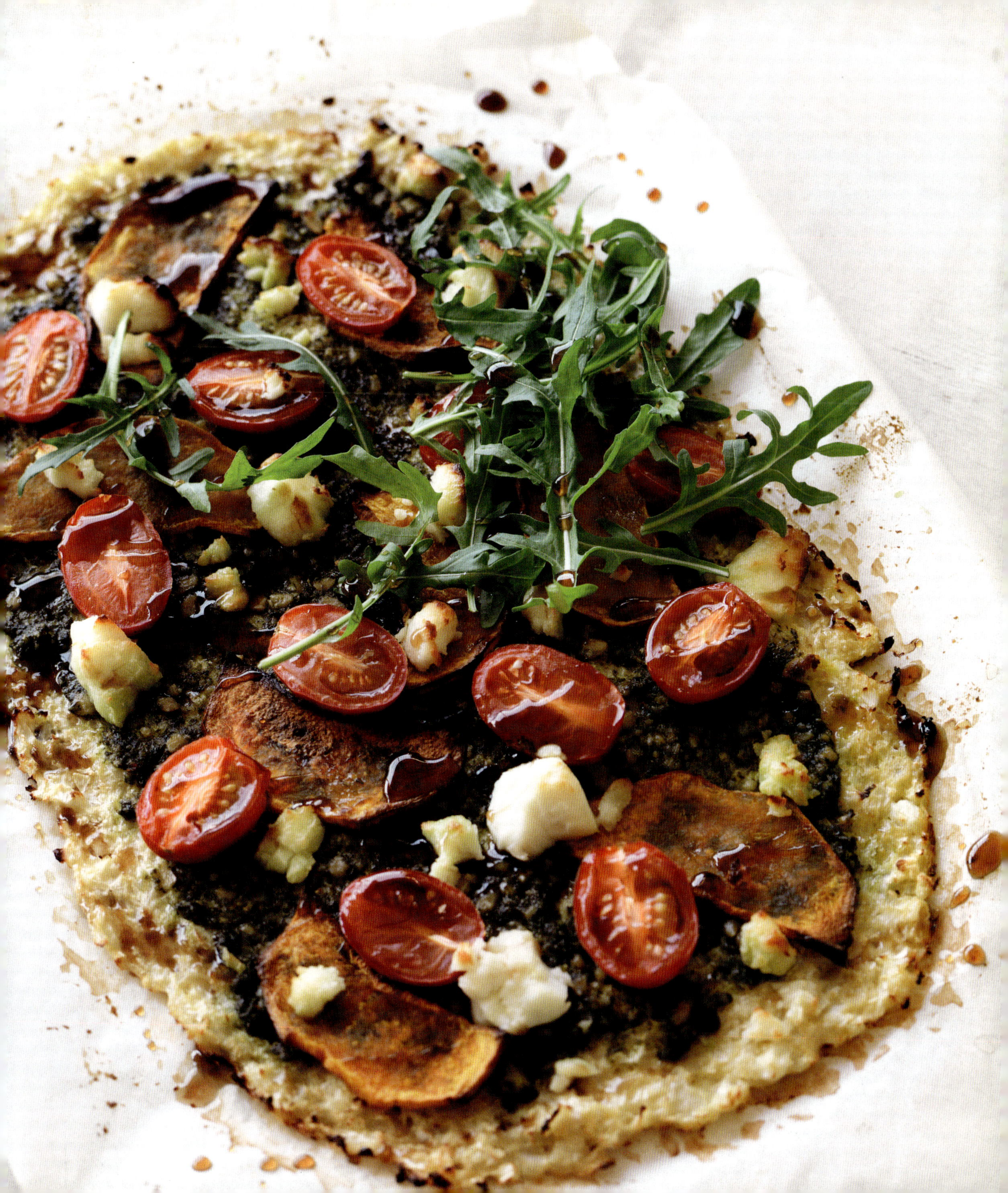

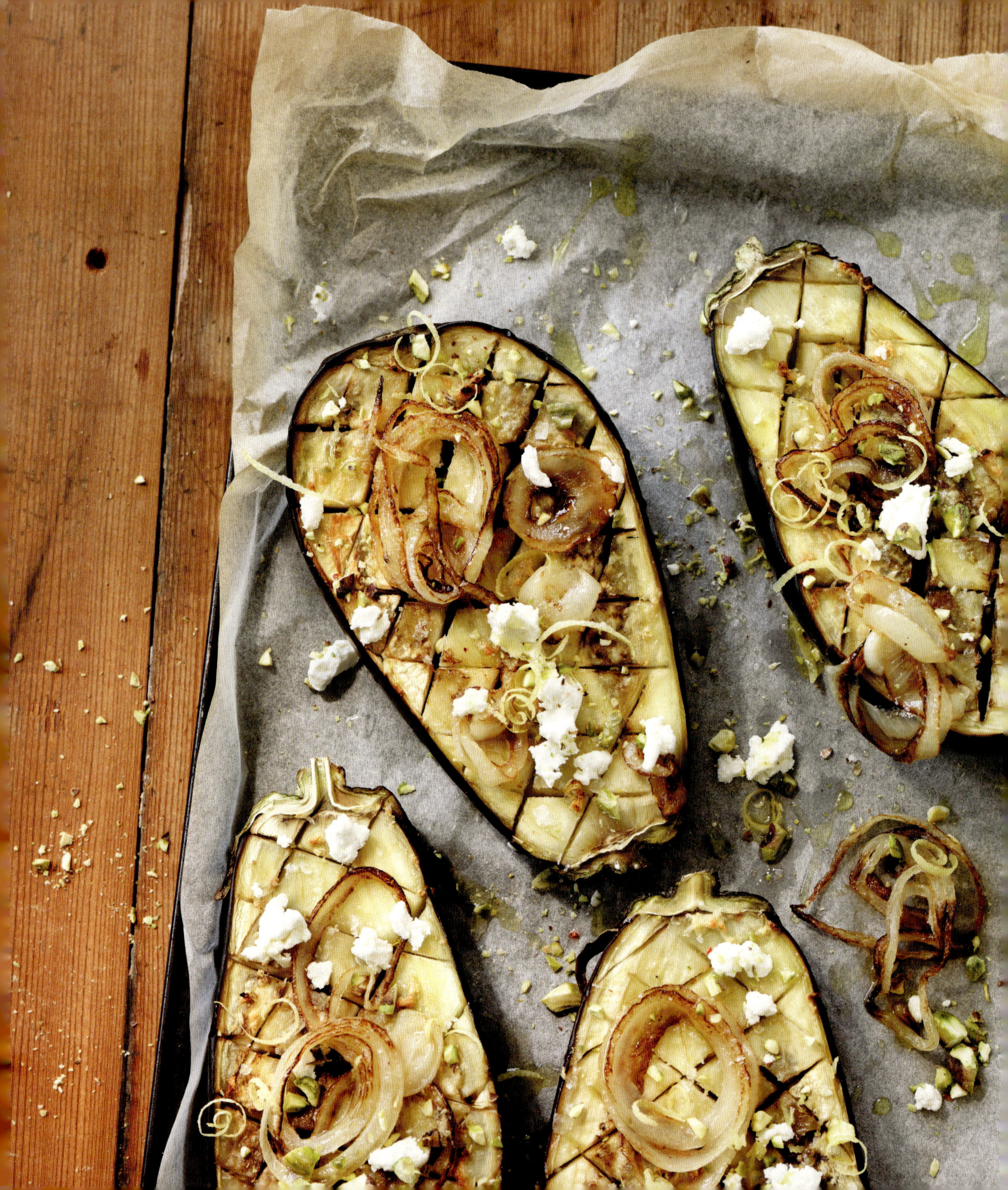

ROAST EGGPLANT WITH ONION, PISTACHIO AND GOAT'S CHEESE

2 eggplants, halved lengthways

2 garlic cloves, crushed

¼ cup olive oil

1 onion, sliced

60g goat's cheese, crumbled

¼ cup pistachios, crushed

finely grated zest and juice of ½ lemon

1. Preheat oven to 220°C (200°C fan-forced) and line a baking tray with baking paper. Deeply score the eggplant flesh in a criss-cross pattern. Rub the garlic in between the cuts and around the flesh.

2. Place the eggplant, cut side up, onto the tray. Drizzle with half the olive oil and season with salt and pepper. Roast for 20–25 minutes or until soft.

3. Heat the remaining oil in a frying pan over medium-high heat. Cook the onion for 5 minutes or until golden brown. Set aside.

4. To serve, spoon the caramelised onion on top of the eggplant. Sprinkle with the goat's cheese, pistachios and zest, and drizzle with the juice.

Serves 4

GOAT'S CHEESE CHOCOLATE TART

After Quinny and I visited a legend of a chocolatier called Rich and then picked up some fresh-as-fresh-can-be soft goat's curd, I had the devilish idea to combine them. This special treat has an no-bake nutty base and the rich filling is curbed by the slight acidity in the goat's cheese. It's simple to make, just allow some time to let each stage set. If the filling splits, remix with a hand blender or add a little extra melted butter.

CHOC

⅓ cup coconut oil, plus extra to grease

2 tablespoons honey

1 cup pecans

1 cup hazelnuts

50g fresh dates, pitted

FILLING

300g dark chocolate, chopped

60g butter, chopped

75g goat's cheese, crumbled

1 tablespoon honey

½ teaspoon ground cinnamon

TOPPING

2 figs, cut into wedges

2 tablespoons honey

sea salt flakes, to sprinkle

1. To make the crust, combine the coconut oil and honey in a small saucepan, and stir over low heat until melted and combined. Place the pecans, hazelnuts, dates and a pinch of salt into a food processor. Add the coconut oil and honey, and process until the nuts are coarsely ground and the ingredients are evenly combined.

2. Grease six 8cm (base measurement) loose-based fluted tart pans with coconut oil. Divide the crust mixture evenly between the tins, and use your fingers to press over the base and sides. Place in the fridge to set for 30 minutes.

3. For the filling, place the chocolate, butter and goat's cheese into a heatproof bowl and stand over a saucepan of simmering water. Make sure the base of the bowl doesn't touch the water. Stir occasionally, until melted and smooth. Remove from the heat and stir in the honey, cinnamon and a pinch of salt. Divide filling between the tarts crusts, and refrigerate for 30 minutes or until set.

4. Just before serving, preheat a grill to high heat. Line a baking tray with lightly oiled foil and spread out the fig pieces. Drizzle with honey and sprinkle with salt. Grill for 3–5 minutes or until caramelised. Arrange figs onto tarts to serve.

Makes 6

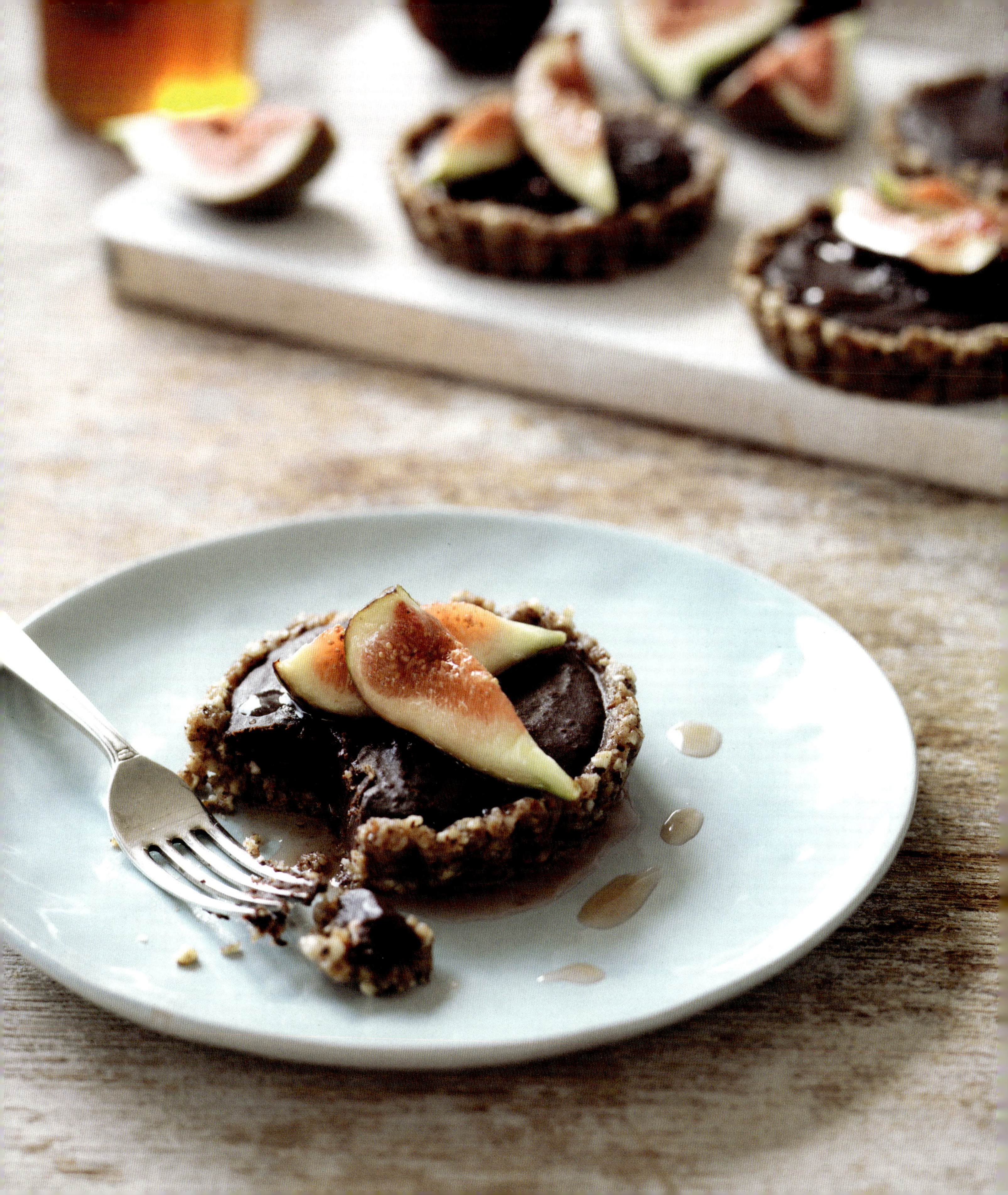

Thanks!

What an epic adventure! I can't believe the places and people HQ and I came across, and the beauty of our cookbook, and these big projects are not possible without teams putting them together. My thanks may overlap with Quinny's, but they all come from my heart.

Marian & Alun – you devised an outstanding concept when you came up with *Surfing the Menu*, and it's a credit to your foresight that it has been commissioned again. Thank you for the opportunity to travel this amazing country.

Jim Fraiter – I can't tell you how stoked I am to have met you. I learnt so much from you. Mick De Montignie – man, you have an eye for a story! Along with a new presenting style, you taught me to breathe, step back and admire. Dan Schist – your persistence and dedication to the shot is inspiring. Noah Norton – you are a seriously awesome editor. Thanks for taking the time to answer my questions. Gaz Goldsmith – you brought so much laughter to the crew, and when you're in each other's pockets for several months that is super important. Chris McCallum, I appreciated your diligence for the little things. Marty Fay, thanks for taking the time to get me extra content and for being so thoughtful. Christian Horgan, you made sure we got to our locations on time and still kept smiling. Miley Tunnecliffe, you know how to have a laugh and make a serious logistics phone call at the same time. A rare quality! Mac Nugent, you were a pleasure to work with and I predict you will go far in the industry.

Jill Brown, our project manager, what would Hayden and I have done without you? Your ability to put our voices on this journey into words without losing authenticity is remarkable. Sorry for my poor grammar!

And we're grateful to the talented team you brought together. We both want to thank Kate Murdoch, Theressa Klein and Grace Campbell for recipe testing and for food prep on the shoot, and Tracy Rutherford for her eagle-eyed food editing and thoughtful food styling. Rob Palmer, our photographer, you did our recipes proud with a series of magnificent shots. And that late afternoon on Belongil Beach when we took the cover shot was a treasured moment. Thanks, Rob, for also making us look like surfing legends! We love the way you entered into the spirit of the adventure.

The book looks gorgeous thanks to designer Kirby Armstrong. And our other brilliant designer, Ingo Voss, kept us on track with an insane schedule. Thanks, guys!

Dan Ruffino, MD at Simon & Schuster – you show your support for me through words and actions. You have supported me from the first day we met … thank you! When this opportunity came about you weren't going to let it slip. You truly get the message.

Mum, Dad, Andrew and Brendan – thank you for always, and I mean always, being there for me.

Lance – what can I say to show how grateful I am to have you in my life? It was your intuition that got this happening. You are my number one supporter, and always encourage me to aim high …You are what I call a legend!

Quinny, my man – how much fun was that?! Travelling around Australia would always be awesome, and now I have a good mate to remember the experience with for the rest of my life. You are a serious talent, mate, and I look forward to working together again.

Thanks to everyone involved! I truly had one of the best times of my life, and with so much of our great country still to see, there is so much more to do!

Dan

I guess this book is a little different to most because not only do we have our amazing team at Simon & Schuster to thank for this book, but also the massive team of people who made *Surfing the Menu – Next Generation*, the TV show.

So let's start there. The first person to thank is Lance Reynolds who had the foresight to bring Dan and me together in the remake of Alun and Marian Bartsch's successful cooking show, *Surfing the Menu*.

On my side of the fence, there are three people who support and guide me in all my projects – Rob Smith and Erin White, who look after all the 'business' side of things; and Dom Smith, who is my right-hand man when it comes to all things food.

On the road we had an incredible crew of people making Dan, me and the food look good – Mick De Montignie (director), Christian Horgan (line producer) Jim Fraiter (DOP), Dan Schist (camera), Chris McCallum (sound), Marty Fay (sound), Noah Norton (editor), Miley Tunnecliffe (researcher/writer) and, of course, Rob 'Gaz' Goldsmith (driver/director of logistics). Back in Sydney, production coordinator Vashti Pontaks was super efficient and always cheerful. Plus, we can't forget all the amazing chefs who assisted us along the way. In particular, I was lucky enough to work with an old mate of mine for the first time in Byron Bay, Chris Lougher.

Doing a trip means a long time away from friends and family, and that is generally tough on the people who miss you. As always I couldn't do anything that I do without the faith, belief, positivity and support from all my family at home – Mum, Dad, Madi, Erin, Blake and the two little ones, Harlem and Hudson. Also, my business partners at The Cube Gym, Lewis and Sam – thank you for supporting me in all my pursuits and allowing me to take leave.

While we were away having fun, the talented team at Simon & Schuster were making the book under the leadership of our publisher, Larissa Edwards. We are grateful for the efforts everyone at S&S, and we owe special thanks to Roberta Ivers, Managing Editor, and Anabel Pandiella, Marketing and Publicity Director. Our amazing project manager, Jill Brown, kept Dan and I on track when we needed it (imagine trying to organise anything with Dan and I!). Jill also wrangled the verbal torrents that we type out into something readable. Thank you. And to the team who created the images for the recipes – Rob Palmer (photographer), Tracy Rutherford (food editor and stylist), and Kate Murdoch and Theressa Klein (home economists), thank you for making our recipes come to life with such style.

If it wasn't for the confidence Simon & Schuster had in *Surfing the Menu* and in Dan and me, you wouldn't be reading such a beautiful publication. Thank you.

And how could I forget the great man himself – Dan! We grew our friendship on this trip and experienced things most people will never have the chance to do. We are both super grateful and lucky to do what we do. I am stoked to do it with you! Bring on season two and our next book together!

Finally, thank you to all you wonderful people out there who have either picked up the book or watched the *Surfing the Menu* series. We love nothing more than sharing our adventures with you and taking you along for the ride.

Until next time, enjoy and remember to live life, eat well and travel far!

Hayden

Index

A
achacha fruit
    Achacha bowl 169
    Achacha sangria 170
Agrodolce 59
avocados
    Stockman's skirt steak with avo salsa and chimichurri 51

B
bacon
    Chorizo and bacon breakfast burrito 195
bananas
    Banana cake with native honey ricotta 136
    Banana choc-tella muffins 184
barramundi
    Barramundi family coconut curry 131
    Family miso barra with soba noodles 117
    Moroccan barra skewers with couscous 115
basil *see* herbs and spices
BBQ whole fish with ginger, coriander and chilli 83
beef
    Beer braised beef short ribs with sweet potato mash 224
    Bundaberg beef burger 180
    Bushman's steak with outback sauce 40
    Smoked buffalo ribs 120
    Stockman's skirt steak with avo salsa and chimichurri 51
beer
    Beer braised beef short ribs with sweet potato mash 224
    Dad's beer battered fish and chips 227
beetroot
    Mum's choc beetroot birthday wonders 202
berries
    Blueberry raw cheesecake with sandalwood crust 120
    Choc blueberry no-churn ice cream 214
    Nutorious gluten free choc and raspberry muffins 216
Blue swimmer crab nachos 32
Blue swimmer crab omelette 34
blueberries *see* berries
bream *see* fish
Broome chicken biryani 99
buffalo *see* beef
Bugs with creole sauce 163
Bundaberg beef burger 180
burgers *see* sandwiches, burgers and wraps
burritos *see* sandwiches, burgers and wraps
Bushman's steak with outback sauce 40
Butterflied crumbed prawns with green aioli 84
Butterflied saltbush chook with charred veg 45

C
cabbage
    Campfire lamb shoulder with simple slaw 48
    Korean pork pot roast with coconut rice and kimchi 198
    Korean pork tacos with kimchi mayo 201
cakes and muffins
    Banana cake with native honey ricotta 136
    Banana choc-tella muffins 184
    Mum's choc beetroot birthday wonders 202
    Nutorious gluten free choc and raspberry muffins 216
Campfire lamb shoulder with simple slaw 48
capsicums
    Chicken and cheese jaffles with spicy capsicum sauce 165
caramel
    Caramelised one-pan chicken of awesomeness! 135
    Salted caramel eton mess 213
carrots
    Spiced carrots and chickpeas on honey yoghurt 145
cauliflower
    Roast pumpkin, goat's cheese and cauliflower flatbread 228
Charred peach, samphire and ricotta salad 25
cheese *see also* goat's cheese
    Banana cake with native honey ricotta 136
    Charred peach, samphire and ricotta salad 25
    Chicken and cheese jaffles with spicy capsicum sauce 165
cherries
    Watermelon, cherry and mint ice pops 86
chia seeds
    Coconut chia pudding 118
    Mango chia lassi 112
    Sandalwood nut chia muesli with yoghurt and seasonal fruit 111
chicken
    Broome chicken biryani 99
    Butterflied saltbush chook with charred veg 45
    Caramelised one-pan chicken of awesomeness! 135
    Chicken and cheese jaffles with spicy capsicum sauce 165
    Honey sriracha roast chook 128
    'Rum and Coke' wings 176
chickpeas
    Spiced carrots and chickpeas on honey yoghurt 145
chilled desserts
    Blueberry raw cheesecake with sandalwood crust 120
    Choc blueberry no-churn ice cream 214
    Coconut chia pudding 118
    Watermelon, cherry and mint ice pops 86
chillies
    BBQ whole fish with ginger, coriander and chilli 83
    Chicken and cheese jaffles with spicy capsicum sauce 165
    Chilli chocolate tart 103
    Honey sriracha roast chook 128
    Jalapeño ponzu pearl meat ceviche 96

Next level chilli crab 74
'Swaghetti' Chilli Prawn Pasta 81
Choc blueberry no-churn ice cream 214
chocolate
  Banana choc-tella muffins 184
  Chilli chocolate tart 103
  Choc blueberry no-churn ice cream 214
  Goat's cheese chocolate tart 232
  Mum's choc beetroot birthday wonders 202
  Nutorious gluten free choc and raspberry muffins 216
chorizo
  Chorizo and bacon breakfast burrito 195
  Tomato breakfast salad with chorizo, herbs, eggs and bread 193
clams *see* seafood
coconut
  Barramundi family coconut curry 131
  Coconut chia pudding 118
  Korean pork pot roast with coconut rice and kimchi 198
condiments *see* sauces, dips, dressings and condiments
coriander *see* herbs and spices
corn chips
  Blue swimmer crab nachos 32
couscous
  Moroccan barra skewers with couscous 115
crab
  Blue swimmer crab nachos 32
  Blue swimmer crab omelette 34
  Green mango mud crab salad 95
  Next level chilli crab 74
Creamy garlic mushroom linguine 150
curries
  Barramundi family coconut curry 131
  Broome chicken biryani 99
  Durban style prawn curry 154
  Goat chop curry with flatbreads 43

D

Dad's beer battered fish and chips 227
dairy products *see also* cheese; yoghurt
  Creamy garlic mushroom linguine 150
  Harissa bream with flatbread and homemade labneh 166
dark chocolate *see* chocolate
dips *see* sauces, dips, dressings and condiments

drinks
  Achacha sangria 170
  Mango chia lassi 112
  Wild wicked watercress juice 68
duck *see* poultry and game
Durban style prawn curry 154

E

eggplant
  Roast eggplant with onion, pistachio and goat's cheese 231
eggs
  Blue swimmer crab omelette 34
  Salted caramel eton mess 213
  Tomato breakfast salad with chorizo, herbs, eggs and bread 193

F

Family miso barra with soba noodles 117
Field of mushrooms on sourdough 148
fish *see also* barramundi
  BBQ whole fish with ginger, coriander and chilli 83
  Dad's beer battered fish and chips 227
  Fish burgers 31
  Fish pie 56
  Harissa bream with flatbread and homemade labneh 166
  Salt baked fish with samphire salad 27
  Savoury pancakes with smoked fish and tomato chutney 63
  Sicilian honey fish with macadamias 132
  Smoked fish healthy hash 59
  Smoked fish paté 67
  Super clean mahi mahi tacos 78
  Watercress pesto orecchiette with smoked fish 60
flatbread
  Goat chop curry with flatbreads 43
  Harissa bream with flatbread and homemade labneh 166
  Roast pumpkin, goat's cheese and cauliflower flatbread 228
fruit *see also* names of fruits
  Sandalwood nut chia muesli with yoghurt and seasonal fruit 111

G

garlic
  Creamy garlic mushroom linguine 150
ginger *see* herbs and spices
gnocchi
  Sweet potato gnocchi with burnt butter and sage 179
goat meat *see* poultry and game
goat's cheese
  Goat's cheese chocolate tart 232
  Pea, mint and white bean salad with goat's cheese 147
  Roast eggplant with onion, pistachio and goat's cheese 231
  Roast pumpkin, goat's cheese and cauliflower flatbread 228
  Root vegetable and goat's cheese tart 223
Green mango gado gado 99
Green mango mud crab salad 95
Grilled seafood platter 77

H

Harissa bream with flatbread and homemade labneh 166
herbs and spices *see also* salt
  BBQ whole fish with ginger, coriander and chilli 83
  Butterflied saltbush chook with charred veg 45
  Harissa bream with flatbread and homemade labneh 166
  Pea, mint and white bean salad with goat's cheese 147
  Pearl meat sashimi with yuzu ginger dressing 92
  Spiced carrots and chickpeas on honey yoghurt 145
  Spiced yoghurt 77
  Stockman's skirt steak with avo salsa and chimichurri 51
  Sweet potato gnocchi with burnt butter and sage 179
  Tomato breakfast salad with chorizo, herbs, eggs and bread 193
  WA clambake 22
  Watercress pesto orecchiette with smoked fish 60
  Watermelon, cherry and mint ice pops 86

INDEX | 237

honey
   Banana cake with native honey ricotta 136
   Honey sriracha roast chook 128
   Sicilian honey fish with macadamias 132
   Spiced carrots and chickpeas on honey yoghurt 145

J
Jalapeño ponzu pearl meat ceviche 96

K
Korean pork pot roast with coconut rice and kimchi 198
Korean pork tacos with kimchi mayo 201

L
labneh *see* dairy products
lamb
   Campfire lamb shoulder with simple slaw 48
   Outback lamb ribs with sticky sweet and sour sauce 46

M
macadamia nuts *see* nuts and seeds
mahi mahi *see* fish
mangoes
   Green mango gado gado 99
   Green mango mud crab salad 95
   Mango chia lassi 112
mint *see* herbs and spices
Moreton bay bugs *see* seafood
Moroccan barra skewers with couscous 112
muffins *see* cakes and muffins
Mum's choc beetroot birthday wonders 202
mushrooms
   Creamy garlic mushroom linguine 150
   Field of mushrooms on sourdough 148

N
#NextLevel chilli crab 74
Nutorious gluten free choc and raspberry muffins 216

nuts and seeds *see also* chia seeds
   Banana choc-tella muffins 184
   Blueberry raw cheesecake with sandalwood crust 120
   Nutorious gluten free choc and raspberry muffins 216
   Roast eggplant with onion, pistachio and goat's cheese 231
   Sandalwood nut chia muesli with yoghurt and seasonal fruit 111
   Sicilian honey fish with macadamias 132
   Watercress, orange and pine nut salad 64
   Watercress pesto orecchiette with smoked fish 60

O
onions
   Roast eggplant with onion, pistachio and goat's cheese 231
oranges
   Watercress, orange and pine nut salad 64
Outback lamb ribs with sticky sweet and sour sauce 46
oysters *see* seafood

P
pancakes
   Savoury pancakes with smoked fish and tomato chutney 63
pasta
   Creamy garlic mushroom linguine 150
   Duck pappardelle 210
   Watercress pesto orecchiette with smoked fish 60
   Pea, mint and white bean salad with goat's cheese 147
peaches
   Charred peach, samphire and ricotta salad 25
pearl meat *see* seafood
pies and pastries
   Fish pie 56
pine nuts *see* nuts and seeds
pistachio nuts *see* nuts and seeds
pork
   Korean pork pot roast with coconut rice and kimchi 198
   Korean pork tacos with kimchi mayo 201
   Sticky pork hock with sesame greens 209

potatoes
   Dad's beer battered fish and chips 227
poultry and game *see also* chicken
   Duck pappardelle 210
   Goat chop curry with flatbreads 43
   Salt and pepper roo tail 28
   Smoked buffalo ribs 120
prawns
   Butterflied crumbed prawns with green aioli 84
   Durban style prawn curry 154
   Prawn fried quinoa 153
   'Swaghetti' Chilli Prawn Pasta 81
pumpkin
   Roast pumpkin, goat's cheese and cauliflower flatbread 228

Q
quinoa
   Prawn fried quinoa 153

R
raspberries *see* berries
rice
   Korean pork pot roast with coconut rice and kimchi 198
ricotta *see* cheese
Roast eggplant with onion, pistachio and goat's cheese 231
Roast pumpkin, goat's cheese and cauliflower flatbread 228
Root vegetable and goat's cheese tart 223
'Rum and Coke' wings 176

S
salads
   Campfire lamb shoulder with simple slaw 48
   Charred peach, samphire and ricotta salad 25
   Green mango gado gado 99
   Green mango mud crab salad 95
   Pea, mint and white bean salad with goat's cheese 147
   Salt baked fish with samphire salad 27
   Tomato breakfast salad with chorizo, herbs, eggs and bread 193
   Watercress, orange and pine nut salad 64

salt
- Salt and pepper roo tail 28
- Salt baked fish with samphire salad 27
- Salted caramel eton mess 213

samphire
- Charred peach, samphire and ricotta salad 25
- Salt baked fish with samphire salad 27

sandalwood nuts *see* nuts and seeds

sandwiches, burgers and wraps
- Bundaberg beef burger 180
- Chicken and cheese jaffles with spicy capsicum sauce 165
- Chorizo and bacon breakfast burrito 195
- Field of mushrooms on sourdough 148
- Fish burgers 31
- Moreton bay bug rolls 160
- Tomato breakfast salad with chorizo, herbs, eggs and bread 193

sauces, dips, dressings and condiments
- Agrodolce 59
- Bugs with creole sauce 163
- Bushman's steak with outback sauce 40
- Butterflied crumbed prawns with green aioli 84
- Caramel sauce 213
- Chicken and cheese jaffles with spicy capsicum sauce 165
- Green mango gado gado 99
- Harissa bream with flatbread and homemade labneh 166
- Korean pork pot roast with coconut rice and kimchi 198
- Korean pork tacos with kimchi mayo 201
- Moreton bay bug rolls 160
- Outback lamb ribs with sticky sweet and sour sauce 46
- Pearl meat sashimi with yuzu ginger dressing 92
- Ponzu sauce 96
- 'Rum and Coke' wings 176
- Savoury pancakes with smoked fish and tomato chutney 63
- Secret burger sauce 180
- Smoked fish paté 67
- Spiced carrots and chickpeas on honey yoghurt 145
- Spiced yoghurt 77
- Stockman's skirt steak with avo salsa and chimichurri 51

Sweet potato gnocchi with burnt butter and sage 179
Yuzu ginger dressing 92
Savoury pancakes with smoked fish and tomato chutney 63

seafood *see also* crab; prawns
- Bugs with creole sauce 163
- Grilled seafood platter 77
- Jalapeño ponzu pearl meat ceviche 96
- Moreton bay bug rolls 160
- Pearl meat sashimi with yuzu ginger dressing 92
- WA clambake 22

Shambhala roast vegie plate 196
Sicilian honey fish with macadamias 132

slaw
- Campfire lamb shoulder with simple slaw 48

Smoked buffalo ribs 127
Smoked fish healthy hash 59
Smoked fish paté 67

soba noodles
- Family miso barra with soba noodles 117

soy products
- Family miso barra with soba noodles 117

Spiced carrots and chickpeas on honey yoghurt 145
Sticky pork hock with sesame greens 209
Stockman's skirt steak with avo salsa and chimichurri 51
Super clean mahi mahi tacos 78
'Swaghetti' Chilli Prawn Pasta 81

sweet potatoes
- Beer braised beef short ribs with sweet potato mash 224
- 'Swaghetti' Chilli Prawn Pasta 81
- Sweet potato gnocchi with burnt butter and sage 179
- Ultimate sweet potato bake 183

T

tacos and burritos
- Korean pork tacos with kimchi mayo 201
- Super clean mahi mahi tacos 78

tarts
- Chilli chocolate tart 103
- Goat's cheese chocolate tart 232
- Root vegetable and goat's cheese tart 223

tomatoes
- Savoury pancakes with smoked fish and tomato chutney 63
- Tomato breakfast salad with chorizo, herbs, eggs and bread 193

U

Ultimate sweet potato bake 183

V

vegetables *see also* salads
- Butterflied saltbush chook with charred veg 45
- Root vegetable and goat's cheese tart 223
- Shambhala roast vegie plate 196
- Sticky pork hock with sesame greens 209

W

WA clambake 22

watercress
- Watercress, orange and pine nut salad 64
- Watercress pesto orecchiette with smoked fish 60
- Wild wicked watercress juice 68

watermelons
- Watermelon, cherry and mint ice pops 86

white beans
- Pea, mint and white bean salad with goat's cheese 147

Wild wicked watercress juice 68

Y

yoghurt
- Sandalwood nut chia muesli with yoghurt and seasonal fruit 111
- Spiced carrots and chickpeas on honey yoghurt 145
- Spiced yoghurt 77

yuzu
- Pearl meat sashimi with yuzu ginger dressing 92

SURFING THE MENU – NEXT GENERATION
First published in Australia in 2016 by
Simon & Schuster (Australia) Pty Limited
Suite 19A, Level 1, 450 Miller Street, Cammeray, NSW 2062

10 9 8 7 6 5 4 3 2 1

A CBS Company
Sydney New York London Toronto New Delhi
Visit our website at www.simonandschuster.com.au

© NOMAfilms PTY LTD 2016

All rights reserved. No part of this publication may be reproduced, stored in a retrieval system, or transmitted in any form or by any means, electronic, mechanical, photocopying, recording or otherwise, without prior permission of the publisher.

National Library of Australia Cataloguing-in-Publication entry
Author: Churchill, Dan, author.
Title: Surfing the menu/Dan Churchill and Hayden Quinn.
ISBN: 9781925368345 (hardback)
                      9781925368352 (ebook)
Subjects: Cooking, Australian.
Other Authors/Contributors: Quinn, Hayden, author.
Dewey Number: 641.5994

Cover and internal design by Kirby Armstrong
Front cover and food photography by Rob Palmer
Location photography by Alun Bartsch
Food styling and recipe editing by Tracey Rutherford
Recipe testing and food prep by Kate Murdoch, Grace Campbell and Theressa Klein
Project management by Jill Brown
Project coordination by Vashti Pontaks
Typesetting by Ingo Voss
Maps by Ice Cold Publishing
Printed by Leo Paper Group, in China

The paper used to produce this book is a natural, recyclable product made from wood grown in sustainable plantation forests. The manufacturing processes conform to the environmental regulations in the country of origin.

Series producers Marian Bartsch and W Lance Reynolds

The ABC 'Wave' device is a trademark of the Australian Broadcasting Corporation and is used under license by Simon & Schuster.

Surfing the Menu soundtrack available on Universal Music